Communities Surviving Migration

Out-migration might decrease the pressure of population on the environment, but what happens to the communities that manage the local environment when they are weakened by the absence of their members? In an era where community-based natural resource management has emerged as a key hope for sustainable development, this is a crucial question.

Building on over a decade of empirical work conducted in Oaxaca, Mexico, *Communities Surviving Migration* identifies how out-migration can impact rural communities in strongholds of biocultural diversity. It reflects on the possibilities of community self-governance and survival in the likely future of limited additional migration and steady – but low – rural populations, and what different scenarios imply for environmental governance and biodiversity conservation. In this way, the book adds a critical cultural component to the understanding of migration–environment linkages, specifically with respect to environmental change in migrant-sending regions.

Responding to the call for more detailed analyses and reporting on migration and environmental change, especially in contexts where rural communities, livelihoods and biodiversity are interconnected, this volume will be of interest to students and scholars of environmental migration, development studies, population geography, and Latin American studies.

James P. Robson is Assistant Professor (Human Dimensions of Sustainability) at the University of Saskatchewan, Canada.

Dan Klooster is Professor of Environmental Studies at the University of Redlands, USA.

Jorge Hernández-Díaz is Research Professor at the Universidad Autónoma Benito Juárez de Oaxaca (UABJO), Mexico.

Routledge Studies in Environmental Migration, Displacement and Resettlement

For more information about this series, please visit: www.routledge.com/ Routledge-Studies-in-Environmental-Migration-Displacement-and-Resettlement/ book-series/RSEMDR

Communities Surviving Migration

Village Governance, Environment, and Cultural Survival in Indigenous Mexico

Edited by James P. Robson, Dan Klooster and Jorge Hernández-Díaz

Routledge
Taylor & Francis Group

LONDON AND NEW YORK

from Routledge

First published 2019
by Routledge
2 Park Square, Milton Park, Abingdon, Oxon OX14 4RN

and by Routledge
52 Vanderbilt Avenue, New York, NY 10017

Routledge is an imprint of the Taylor & Francis Group, an informa business

© 2019 selection and editorial matter, James P. Robson, Dan Klooster and Jorge Hernández-Díaz; individual chapters, the contributors

British Library Cataloguing-in-Publication Data
A catalogue record for this book is available from the British Library

Library of Congress Cataloging-in-Publication Data
A catalog record has been requested for this book

ISBN: 978-1-138-74002-0 (hbk)
ISBN: 978-1-315-18384-8 (ebk)

Typeset in Goudy
by Wearset Ltd, Boldon, Tyne and Wear

Contents

Figures

Tables

Contributors

James P. Robson, *Assistant Professor in Human Dimensions of Sustainability (University of Saskatchewan), UNESCO Co-Chair in Biocultural Diversity, Sustainability, Reconciliation, and Renewal.* PhD in Natural Resources and Environmental Management from the University of Manitoba, Canada. He conducts interdisciplinary and applied environmental research, with special emphasis on the drivers and impacts of demographic, social, and environmental change as they affect remote and rural communities. Current work focuses on community innovations, especially those targeted at or directly involving youth, to adapt customary systems of governance and resource use. His work on migration and change in Mexico has been supported by a Government of Canada Banting Postdoctoral Fellowship, a University of Manitoba Graduate Fellowship, and an Aboriginal Issues Press Scholarship. He has an MA in Environment, Development, and Policy (University of Sussex, UK), and a BSc in Geography (University of Liverpool, UK).

Dan Klooster, *Professor, Department of Environmental Studies (University of Redlands).* PhD in Geography from the University of California-Los Angeles. His research examines sustainable community development strategies in Mexico, including community forestry, forest certification, payment for environmental services, and environmental dimensions of commodity chains involving certified community forests and direct marketing of cacao for chocolate. His teaching interests encompass conflicts between environment and development, environmental services and the socio-natural systems that produce and distribute food. He has been awarded university-wide teaching awards at Florida State University and the University of Redlands. His work on the ways that migration affects rural sustainable development in Mexico has been supported by the National Science Foundation (No. 1127534), a Fulbright-Garcia Robles Scholarship, the Center for US–Mexican Studies, University of California-San Diego, UC-Mexus, University of California-Riverside, and the University of Redlands.

Jorge Hernández-Díaz, *Professor-Researcher, Instituto de Investigaciones Sociológicas (Universidad Autónoma Benito Juárez de Oaxaca).* PhD in Anthropology from the University of Connecticut, USA. Masters in Anthropology from the University of Brasilia, Brazil. His research focuses on the ways by which government recognition manifests and impacts Indigenous government and governance structures in Mexico and Latin America. He has authored and coordinated multiple books, including: *Las Imágenes del Indio en Oaxaca* (Instituto Oaxaqueño de las Culturas-Fondo Nacional para la Cultura y las Artes-Universidad Autónoma Benito Juárez de Oaxaca, 1998); *Reclamos de la identidad: La formación de las organizaciones indígenas en Oaxaca* (Miguel A. Porrúa, 2000); *Grupos indígenas en Oaxaca* (Plaza y Valdés, 2006); *Ciudadanías diferenciadas en un estado multicultural: los usos y costumbres en Oaxaca* (Siglo XXI, 2007); *Dilemas de la institución municipal; una incursión en la experiencia oaxaqueña* (Miguel Ángel Porrúa, 2007); and *Comunidad, Migración y Ciudadanía: Avatares de la organización indígena comunitaria* (Miguel Ángel Porrúa, 2011).

Mario Fernando Ramos Morales, *Research Professor, Universidad de la Sierra Juárez, Ixtlán de Juárez, Ixtlan de Juarez, Oaxaca*. Mario Fernando Ramos Morales is Indigenous Zapotec, and a citizen of the community of Santa María Yavesía, located in the Sierra Norte region of Oaxaca. He holds a Masters in Rural Development from the Universidad Autónoma Metropolitana-Unidad Xochimilco, and a degree in Political Science from the Universidad Autónoma Metropolitana-Unidad Iztapalapa. His research and teaching, at a regional university in Oaxaca's northern highlands, focuses on critical issues shaping and impacting life for local Indigenous communities. These include: changes in communitarian governance structures; water management; cultural development; myth, knowledge, and environment; migration and change; and youth and their ties to community life and institutions.

Fermín Sosa Pérez, *Director, Indayu A.C.* Fermín Sosa Pérez is Indigenous Zapotec, and a citizen and comunero (commoner) of the community of San Juan Evangelista Analco, located in the Sierra Norte region of Oaxaca. At 15, he left his community to further his studies – graduating in 2001 with a degree in agronomy from Oaxaca's Technological Agricultural Institute (ITAO) and a Masters in Water Sciences from the University of Guanajuato in 2006. He returned to Oaxaca in 2007, working for the National Forestry Commission (CONAFOR) and INCA Rural AC, where he provided training to technicians working in and with Oaxaca's rural Indigenous communities. Since 2009, he has been a founding partner of Indayu AC, a local/regional NGO that supports Oaxacan rural communities with territorial and resource management and planning. In his community of Analco, he has been actively supporting several initiatives, including community-based ecotourism, land use zoning, and forestry.

Acknowledgements

We express our sincere thanks to the authorities and members of Santa María Tindú, Santa María Yavesía, Santiago Comaltepec, Santa Cruz Tepetotutla, San Miguel Maninaltepec, San Juan Evangelista Analco, as well as those from the Zoogocho micro-region (San Baltazar Yatzachi el Bajo, San Andrés Solaga, Santa María Tavehua, Santo Domingo Yojovi, Yatzachi el Alto, San Jerónimo Zoochina, Santa María Yohueche, Santa María Xochixtepec, San Bartolomé Zoogocho, San Juan Tabaá, Santa María Yalina, Santiago Zoochila, and Santiago Laxopa) for opening their doors to us and participating in the research that we report on in this book. A special note of appreciation goes to the migrant families from these communities who invited us into their homes and places of work in Oaxaca City, Mexico City, Los Angeles, Madera, Las Vegas, and Chicago.

This book is also a product of conversations with colleagues from academia, civil society, and government. Our thanks to the individuals who gave up their time to talk to us about issues (big and small) related to this book, and/or to review or comment on earlier drafts of work featured: Yolanda Lara (ERA, AC); Israel Hernández López (ERA, AC), Filemón Manzano (Consultor de Proyectos Forestales-Oaxaca), David Kaimowitz (Ford Foundation), David Bray (Florida International University), Tad Mutersbaugh (University of Kentucky), Holly Worthen (Universidad Autónoma Benito Juárez de Oaxaca), Froylán Martinez Rojas (CONANP-Oaxaca), Norberto López Hernández (formerly with CONAFOR-Oaxaca), Marco Antonio González (GAIA, A.C.), Leticia Merino Pérez (IIS-UNAM), Fikret Berkes (University of Manitoba), Fernando Mondragon (Geoconservación, AC), and Felícito García Juárez (CONAFOR-Oaxaca).

Our appreciation to Lisa Benvenuti at the Center for Spatial Studies, University of Redlands, for producing the maps, and to Maria Celeste Nunez, University of Saskatchewan, for helping with the graphs and other figures.

The research that underpins this book was made possible by the following financial and institutional support: Government of Canada Banting Postdoctoral Fellowship, University of Manitoba Graduate Fellowship, National Science Foundation Grant (No. 1127534), Fulbright-Garcia Robles Fellowship, Visiting Scholarship from UC-Mexus (University of California-Riverside),

Center for US–Mexican Studies (University of California-San Diego), University of Redlands, School of Environment and Sustainability (University of Saskatchewan), and Consejo Nacional de Ciencia y Tecnología (CONACYT, Mexico).

Lastly, we thank Annabelle Harris and Matthew Shobbrook at Routledge and Pete Waterhouse for their assistance during the editing and production process.

Glossary of Spanish and local (Oaxacan) terms

adobe   sun-dried mud brick
agencia municipal   a political unit below the level of municipality or county
albañil   construction labourer
alcalde   municipal magistrate
ama de casa   housewife
Analqueño   native of San Juan Evangelista Analco; member of the translocal community of San Juan Evangelista Analco
anciano   elder in Indigenous communities in Oaxaca
artesanía   handicraft
asamblea   assembly of municipal citizens or common property owners
atole   thick, non-alcoholic drink, usually maize-based
ayuntamiento   local community council
barrio   district or neighbourhood of a village
bienes comunales   communal land or property
cabildo   council; municipal executive committee
cacique   hereditary ruler or chief; now often translates as local boss
caciquismo   dominant, abusive influence of cacique in political and social life of village/community
campo   open countryside; often used to refer to areas under cultivation
campesino   rural dweller; peasant
cargo   village governance post or obligation
cerro   hill or peak
ciudadano   village citizen, with voting rights in municipal assemblies
colonia   informal settlement or neighbourhood
comal   hot plate for cooking tortilla over firewood stove; also used in this book as shorthand for the community of Santiago Comaltepec
Comaltepecano   native of Santiago Comaltepec; member of the translocal community of Santiago Comaltepec
comisariado de bienes comunales   common property commissioner; comunal executive committee
comunal   communal
comunalidad   concept developed to help explain Indigenous communal life in Oaxaca (and Mesoamerica more broadly)

comunero   common property rights holder, with voting rights in communal assemblies; commoner

comunidad agraria   agrarian (Indigenous) community with traditional collective property rights recognized by the Mexican government

consejo de vigilancia   oversight or surveillance committee

cooperación   a quota expected from villagers and sometimes migrants to support collective activities

coyote   people smuggler

distrito   administrative district

ejido   land reform unit (instituted post-revolution as a collective land grant)

el Norte   in reference to the US as migrant destination

estatuto   written laws codifying village rules

fiesta   religious festival (usually a saint's day)

guelaguetza   reciprocal work or exchange

yunta   pair of oxen, used to plough fields ahead of planting

leña   firewood

localidad   locality

maguey   agave plant from which mezcal is distilled

mayordomo   community members given the responsibility to finance/organize a particular village fiesta

mercado   market

mesa directiva   management board (of active migrants)

mestizo   person of mixed European and Indian origin

mezcal   distilled spirit made from the maguey (agave) plant

milpa   traditional MesoAmerican cropping system; often used to refer to corn plant or field of corn

monte   upland area; often used to refer to forested areas not under cultivation; bush

municipio   municipality or county

ordenamiento territorial comunitario   land use zoning and planning

palacio municipal   municipal offices or town hall

paisano   name used to refer to somebody from the same community; or sometimes from the same region

parcela   plot or parcel of land

patrón   boss or employer

policía   village policeman

presidente municipal   municipal president

pueblo   village or people

rancho   ranch, small landed property

regidor/a   councilman or councilwoman

riego   irrigation system; or irrigated land

roza, tumba y quema   slash and burn (or long fallow) cultivation system

serrano   highlander; used here to denote a person native to a particular highland region of Oaxaca (e.g. Sierra Norte de Oaxaca)

sierra   highlands or mountain range

sindico   *syndic*; municipal government representative charged with enforcing municipal decrees

solar   yard or compound adjacent or close to family home; home garden

suplente   alternate (for an office or post of municipal or communal government)

temporada   season of year

temporal   seasonal; often used to refer to rain-fed agriculture or agricultural fields

tequio   an obligatory labour day levied by village authorities

terreno   piece of land belonging to a community member

tesorero   treasurer

tierra caliente   warm (dry or humid) lowland

tierra o terreno communal   communal land

tierra templada   temperate zone that falls between *tierra caliente* and *tierra fría*

tierra fría   cold upland

Tindureño   native of Santa María Tindú; member of the translocal community of Santa María Tindú

topil   messenger boy

tortilla   flat maize bread

usos y costumbres   traditional system of governance used by Indigenous communities in Oaxaca

Yavesian   native of Santa María Yavesía; member of the translocal community of Santa María Yavesía

Part I
Setting the scene

1 Communities *surviving* migration?

The migration–community–environment nexus

James P. Robson, Dan Klooster, and Jorge Hernández-Díaz

Introduction

In this opening chapter, we introduce the main topic and focus for our book –
Indigenous communities affected by out-migration – mostly from the perspective of village governance and land management. We make the case that in
areas with significant out-migration, the migration–environment nexus involves
not only demographic change and the de-territorialization of rural livelihood,
but also changes in resource use, and – crucially – change and continuity in
village governance. We argue that community is an essential component of
migration-environment linkages. After outlining the broad trends of demographic change and changing rural livelihoods that our study area shares with
much of Latin America and much of the rural Global South, we briefly introduce Oaxaca, southern Mexico. We end with an explanation of the book's
structure and provide brief chapter synopses.

Demographic transitions and a changing rurality

Two general trends transform the rural landscapes that migration also affects.
The first is the decline of traditional agriculture and the diversification of off-
farm activities. Rural areas in the developing world are changing as globalization and neoliberalism combine to construct complex linkages between these
areas and global markets, and provoke a major restructuring and realignment of
local economies and societies (Berdegué, Bebbington, and Rosada 2014;
Fairbairn et al. 2014; Kay 2015). This is manifest in a diversification of rural
activities, the importance of non-agricultural employment and non-agricultural
incomes for rural livelihoods, changing patterns of female participation in rural
work, growing rural–urban interactions, and the rising importance of migration
and migrant remittances (Haggblade, Hazell, and Reardon 2007; Kay 2008).
The second is that many rural areas are also undergoing far-reaching demographic changes as fertility levels fall, life expectancy rises (Anríquez and Stloukal 2008; United Nations 2017), and resident populations decline and age. Even
in places where populations have increased, this likely reflects population
momentum – inertial growth from former high fertility, with declines expected

in the medium- to long-term (Keats and Wiggins 2016). Simply put, rural families are not as large as they used to be.

In Latin America, such changes are driving what some have called a 'new rurality' of smaller, but persistent rural settlements where people cobble together livelihoods in which farming is only one part of a diverse portfolio of activities (Burkham 2012; Kay 2008). The region currently accounts for around 9 per cent of the world's population (646 million) (FAO 2014), with population growth rates projected to decline to the level of Europe and North America by 2030 (Lanza and Valeggia 2014). The region saw fertility rates drop by 60 per cent between 1970 and 2011 (*The Economist* 2013), with some notable exceptions in tropical lowland areas (McSweeney and Arps 2005). The demographic transition evident across Latin America has taken place in tandem with increased urbanization – where rates have been as high as 70 to 90 per cent in some countries – and much of that growth accounted for by a relatively small number of cities (i.e. Mexico City, Guatemala City, Tegucigalpa, Laz Paz, Lima, Bogota) (Anríquez and Stloukal 2008). By 2050, it is anticipated that 90 per cent of people living in Latin America will be in urban centres (UN-Habitat 2012).

However, while the region is becoming less rural as a proportion of total population (Keats and Wiggins 2016), rural populations and rural livelihoods remain significant. Almost half the world's population continue to live in rural areas (United Nations 2017). In Latin America, while many rural regions have seen significant population losses, the number of rural localities remains high (IFAD 2016). In several countries, agriculture accounts for between one-third and two-fifths of the national workforce (Anríquez and Stloukal 2008). Over half of the region's food production comes from approximately 14 million small-holder farmers (Berdegué and Fuentealba 2014). Migration often supports this new rurality; in Latin America and globally, over 40 per cent of migrant remittances are sent to rural areas (Keats and Wiggins 2016; IFAD 2016).

The long-term effects of demographic and livelihood changes on rural life remain uncertain (Berdegué, Bebbington, and Rosada 2014). While the study of rural and agrarian change has long constituted an important topic for scholarly inquiry (Borras Jr 2009; Harriss 1992; Woods 2007), there is debate as to whether rural life is persisting while diversifying under processes of change (see Fairbairn *et al.* 2014) or undergoing a deep-seated transformation (Béné *et al.* 2014; Vertovec 2004) characterized by fundamental change in social and political regimes (Berdegué, Bebbington, and Rosada 2014; Wiltshire 2001).

This uncertainty is reflected in divergent forecasts for remote and rural communities globally (Kay 2015). The widespread disappearance of rural production systems was once expected under processes of structural adjustment and market liberalization (Bryceson, Kay, and Mooji 2000), with migration and the shift to off-land activities sounding a 'death knell for the peasantry' in places such as Mexico (Otero 1999). More recently, it has been posited that the responses of rural areas to the policies and projects of neoliberal capitalism is producing a hybridization in rural livelihoods (see Hecht 2014), which can create opportunities for rural landscapes and economies to be reinvented, reimagined, and possibly strengthened (Van der Ploeg 2012; Davidson-Hunt *et al.* 2016). Indeed, local demographic transitions may aid such a scenario, as changes in age structure create situations conducive for local development as smaller families are better able to save and invest in economic growth (Saad 2010), and fewer pregnancies work in tandem with improved schooling to enhance female empowerment through improved opportunities to work, earn, and gain status and autonomy (Acharya *et al.* 2010; Colfer *et al.* 2017).

Migration and environment in Indigenous commons

Migration, as a key social process and phenomenon of this new rurality, intersects with demographic change and rural livelihood diversification. Like others across the globe, rural Latin Americans have long taken part in migration streams to cities and other countries – and these movements have become a defining characteristic of the region (Boillat *et al.* 2017; Cohen and Sirkeci 2011; McSweeney and Jokisch 2007). Migration has the potential to reshape rural communities and livelihoods by exacerbating demographic change, introducing new flows of capital, and forging novel rural–urban linkages (Greiner and Sakdapolrak 2013; Kay 2008; Woods 2007), which can then trigger social and economic reorganization (Bebbington and Batterbury 2001; McMichael 1997).

Migration is also a well-known driver of land use change (Lambin *et al.* 2001; Zimmerer 2010). However, the full scope of migration–environment linkages in migrant-sending regions remain under-reported and poorly understood (Hecht *et al.* 2015). While work on the migration–environment nexus has moved beyond linear environmental 'push' theories, toward a greater integration of context (Hunter, Luna and Norton 2015), studies remain heavily focused on migration as a response strategy to environmental change (Black *et al.* 2011; López-Carr 2012; Massey, Axinn, and Ghimire 2010; McLeman and Smit 2006; Neumann and Hilderink 2015; Piguet 2013). Although migration drives specific land use changes in migrant-sending regions (e.g. Gray and Bilsborrow 2014; Hecht *et al.* 2012; Moran-Taylor and Taylor 2010; Radel and Schmook 2008; Zimmerer 1991), there are few comprehensive and integrative analyses of socio-ecological change following the abandonment or deterritorialization of rural livelihoods (Hecht *et al.* 2015; Hunter, Luna and Norton 2015). In places such as Latin America, this becomes particularly pertinent in light of widespread agricultural abandonment and forest recovery (Aide *et al.* 2013; Hecht *et al.* 2012).

Many of these lands are managed as resource commons – broadly defined as lands that rural communities use collectively in accordance with community-derived norms (Alden Wily 2011). Frequently, the communities managing these commons are effective at maintaining diverse land-cover, conserving biodiversity, and maintaining their ecological functioning over time. Indeed, the conservation practices of community actors can be more effective at maintaining biodiversity than government-decreed protected areas (Charnley and Poe 2007; Porter-Bolland *et al.* 2012).

Commons, however, exist in a world undergoing accelerated processes of change (Berkes 2009), and out-migration is a driver of change with the potential to reshape, even undermine, communities and commons management. On the one hand, through remittances and circular migration, migration gives small rural communities access to a broader world with important livelihood opportunities and additional resources. Furthermore, out-migration removes people from rural areas, ostensibly reducing the pressure of population on the environment. On the other hand, migration removes the hearts and minds and backs and hands of commoners, presumably weakening the institutions and organizational structures expected to manage rural resource commons. In this way, the temporary or permanent movement of people away from their places of origin can present a dilemma for the sustainability of local land management systems, which typically rest on collective decision-making, and the labour of those who access these resources (Gavin *et al.* 2015; Klooster 2013). Although out-migration should reduce the pressure of population on land, forest, water, and other environmental goods and services, what happens when land-managing communities can no longer count on the physical presence of so many of their members?

While the rural development literatures emphasize the role of migration as a household-level adaptation strategy to help diversify livelihoods and generate resources at times of need (Adger *et al.* 2002; Ellis 1998; Wood 1981), much less is known about the impact of migration on the community-level institutions and structures essential for self-governance, cultural reproduction, and territorial use and management (Robson *et al.* 2018; VanWey *et al.* 2005). While demographic change, cultural change, and new economic opportunities related to migration can alter the bounded rationality and politics of institutional choice in the commons (Ostrom 2005; Ribot, Chhatre, and Lankina 2008), community responses to such change remain understudied by theorists (Agrawal 2005; Agrawal and Ribot 2014; Nayak and Berkes 2011). We know little about how commons institutions and organizational structures react following shifts in the livelihood strategies, identities, and voice of community members (Baker 2005; McCay 2002; Robson *et al.* 2018). Change following migration may create potential for new commons configurations to emerge (Klooster 2013; Robson 2010).

These migration–environment questions are particularly important in Indigenous areas. Indigenous Peoples number as many as 370 million globally, are distributed across 70–90 countries, and represent as many as 5000 ethnic groups (United Nations 2009). An estimated 42 million Indigenous people were living in Latin America in 2010, or close to 8 per cent of the region's total population. Mexico, Guatemala, Peru, and Bolivia together account for over 80 per cent (or 34 million) of the regional total (Freire *et al.* 2015). This cultural diversity overlaps with globally-significant biological diversity (Boillat *et al.* 2017; Gorenflo *et al.* 2012). While Indigenous and other traditional peoples may account for just 5 per cent of the world's population, their customary territories account for as much as one-fifth of the planet's land mass and as much as four-fifths of the planet's terrestrial biodiversity (RRI 2015). The use and management of these customary territories depends on communities that are often affected by out-migration; nearly half of Latin America's Indigenous people currently live in urban areas (Freire *et al.* 2015). Indigenous commons, therefore, give us an important opportunity to better understand the role of a vital component of migration–environment processes – the community.

Oaxaca, Mexico as case study

Mexico is a useful case for understanding such processes. Within Latin America, it is the country furthest along a demographic transition that other countries in the region are expected to follow (Saad 2010). Mexico is characterized by a growing, urbanizing, and rapidly aging population, with the number of people aged 65 and over expected to triple by 2050 (Pew Research Centre 2014). This includes rural areas, which have experienced significant rural change following an extended period of internal and international migration (Robson *et al.* 2018). Limited livelihood opportunities in communities of origin or the lure of work in regional and national urban centres, northern agricultural zones, and in recent decades the US, has encouraged millions of rural Mexicans to leave their homes (Bada and Feldmann 2016; Durand and Massey 2004). While wage labour migration, and US-bound migration in particular, has fallen sharply over the past decade (Durand 2013; Jardón Hernández 2016; Passel, Cohn, and Gonzalez-Barrera 2012), Mexico's main migrant-sending regions remain burdened by reduced village populations – as first-generation migrants remain mostly absent (Bada and Feldmann 2016; Massey, Durand, and Pren 2015), fertility rates drop to historical lows (CONAPO 2014; INEGI 2015), and youth leave in large numbers to pursue education and other opportunities (Aquino-Moreschi and Contreras-Pastrana 2016; Lynn Lopez 2015, personal communication).

For Indigenous rural livelihoods and territorial governance, such changes hold profound implications. More than one-third of Mexico's land base and approximately two thirds of its forests are found on community lands (Sarukhan and Jiménez 2016), managed under common property regimes (Torres-Rojo, Moreno-Sánchez, and Mendoza-Briseño 2016). Each of these commons consists of a physical territory, a membership who hold a full 'bundle' (after Ribot and Peluso 2003) of legal rights to local lands and resources, and institutions through which both people and resources are governed (Klooster, 2013). These regimes are both extensive and very important from environmental and rural development perspectives. They shelter globally-important biodiversity and carbon, regionally-important ecosystem services, and resources vital for local livelihoods (Boege 2008; Sarukhán and Jiménez 2016).

Within this country context, the southern state of Oaxaca (Figure 1.1) is an especially rich area in which to explore migration–environment relationships, within a globally-relevant context of transformations in rural livelihoods and demographics.

Figure 1.1 Location of the State of Oaxaca in southern Mexico.

Source: map produced by Lisa Benvenuti, Center for Spatial Studies – University of Redlands.

Approximately two-thirds of the state's 3.9 million inhabitants self-identify as Indigenous. As many as one third speak an Indigenous language (INEGI 2010). At 94,000 km², Oaxaca is about the size of the US State of Indiana and a bit larger than Portugal. Four-fifths of Oaxaca is owned by thousands of communities in legally-recognized commons (INEGI 2016). Migration affects these communities. The flow of people leaving Oaxaca had reached such levels by the mid-2000s that close to half of the state's population were believed to be semi-permanent or permanent residents of the Mexico City metropolitan area, the northern states of Mexico, or the US (Bezaury 2007; Cohen and Ramirez Rios 2016).

In addition to individually and family-organized activities of agriculture, agroforestry, animal husbandry, and the harvest of wood and non-timber forest products, many of Oaxaca's Indigenous communities are involved in centrally-organized land management activities such as land use zoning and planning (*ordenamiento territorial comunitario*), cooperative coffee production, commercial forestry, ecotourism, payment for environmental services, and other forest conservation activities (Klooster 2003; Robson 2007; Van Vleet, Bray, and Duran 2016). They participate disproportionately in the country's commercial forestry sector, with many involved with logging and/or timber processing activities nationwide (Herrera Guerra 2015). Community forest management in Mexico has been shown to better integrate forest use, rural development, and biological conservation than the large forest concessions it replaced (Bray, Merino-Pérez, and Barry 2005), and in Oaxaca communities often do a better job of conserving biodiversity than government-decreed protected areas (Duran *et al.* 2012; Martin *et al.* 2011).

Migration, environment, and community in Indigenous Oaxaca

Migration is a potential problem for community survival and commons management in Oaxaca. Together with demographic change and the transformation of rural livelihoods, migration transforms the value and meaning of local commons resources. As more people move away and take up off-farm livelihood activities, communal territories may be used and perceived differently. Do the economic opportunities of migration diminish the propensity of Oaxacan commoners to invest in their commons? Against a general backdrop of partial agricultural abandonment and forest recovery, how might communities look to develop alternative land-based livelihoods?

Of arguably greater concern is the way that migration draws people away from villages and communal territories, reducing the resources available for community development, including the collective resident labour and ideas that underpin customary forms of civic and communal governance (Kearney and Besserer 2004; Klooster 2013; Mutersbaugh 2002; Robson and Berkes 2011). Put more bluntly, migration robs communities of the people needed for collective action. Over a decade ago, Kearney and Besserer (2004: 453), writing in the context of Indigenous Mexico, noted their concern about the 'vitality of [these] communities to staff offices and deliver basic services, maintain and improve infrastructure, maintain law and order, and preserve communal ceremonial and religious life and identities.'

We know that migration stresses community-level institutions and structures essential for self-governance, cultural reproduction, and common property management (Curiel 2015; Hernández-Díaz 2013; Klooster 2013; Robson 2010; Robson *et al.* 2018; VanWey *et al.* 2005). In fact, by removing commoners, migration should diminish the ability of communities to reproduce themselves and their commons management institutions. Yet, at the same time, migration alters the social boundaries that define these systems, opening them up to encompass translocal organizations and institutional links (Fox 2007; Stiffler

2007) and, with them, new forms of commoner profile, membership and voice (Robson 2010; Stephen 2007). Although the populations of many Mexican rural communities are declining, the total number of commoners may be growing when non-residents are considered (Klooster 2013). 'Ethno-geographic' migrant organizations in Mexico and US destination centres have emerged to reconnect migrants with their territories of origin, to reintegrate migrants with their 'home' village (Camacho Robles 2004; Mines *et al.* 2010), and to potentially facilitate new forms of commons governance (Robson 2010; Klooster 2013). For development practitioners, there is hope in the establishment and strengthening of such translocal[1] institutions and connections (Fox and Bada 2008; Fox and Rivera-Salgado 2004). This has encouraged analysts to shift focus from the individual migrant to the so-called 'collective migrant' (Moctezuma 2000) – groups of active migrants who organize to support their communities of origin (Fitzgerald 2008; Orozco and Rouse 2007). Do such translocal communities mitigate the negative community effects of migration to reinvigorate communities and commons management?

Structure of the book

In this book we make the case that communities are central actors in migration-environment outcomes, based on three general themes. First, we show how migration can tear communities apart, making it difficult for them to govern themselves and manage their territories. Second, we shed light on how communities try to mitigate the impacts of migration for community self-governance and survival. Third, we clarify the impacts of migration on conservation and territorial management and discuss what decades of intense out-migration imply for local commons of global environmental value. Building on this work, the book applies lessons learned from Oaxaca to discuss how out-migration might be expected to impact rural Indigenous communities in Mexico and beyond, to reflect on the possibilities of community self-governance and survival in the likely future of limited additional migration and steady – but low – rural populations, and what different scenarios imply for environmental governance and biodiversity conservation. In this way, we add the cultural component of 'community' to our understanding of the migration–environment nexus in migrant-sending regions. This responds directly to calls by Hecht *et al.* (2015) and Hunter, Luna, and Norton (2015) for more detailed analysis and reporting on migration and environmental change, especially in contexts where rural communities, livelihoods, and biodiversity are interconnected.

The empirical insights that inform our work and findings come from ethnographic, multi-sited research on Zapotec, Chinantec, and Mixtec Indigenous communities located in Oaxaca's Sierra Norte and Mixteca regions (Figures 1.2 and 1.3). This research encapsulated work in both the communities of origin in Oaxaca and their translocal migrant communities in Mexican and US destination centres.

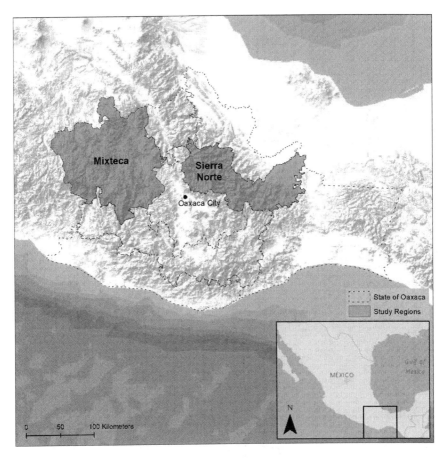

Figure 1.2 Location of Sierra Norte and Mixteca, as study regions in Oaxaca.

Source: map produced by Lisa Benvenuti, Center for Spatial Studies – University of Redlands.

The case studies and longer discussion chapters that follow are based on the presentation and interpretation of findings from this empirical work, which is used to assess and reflect upon the cumulative impact of migration on the identity, territory, landscapes, and institutions of participating communities. These chapters consider how Indigenous communal life affects the decision to migrate, how migration impacts the self-governance ability of Indigenous communities, how migration changes land use that presents challenges and opportunities for Indigenous environmental governance, and how Indigenous migrant organizations can maintain their commitments to local, collective projects of autonomy.

We have divided the book into three main parts. For the final section of this introductory chapter, we describe the purpose of each of these parts, including brief synopses of the chapters they contain.

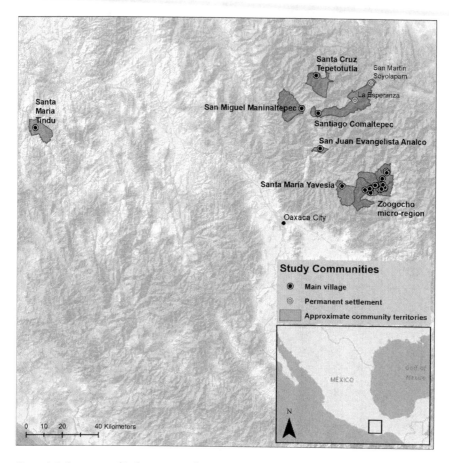

Santa Cruz
Tepetotutla

San Martin
Soyolapam

La Esperanza

Santa
Maria
Tindu

San Miguel Maninaltepec

Santiago Comaltepec

San Juan Evangelista Analco

Santa María Yavesía

Zoogocho
micro-region

Oaxaca City

Study Communities

◉   Main village

◎   Permanent settlement

▨   Approximate community territories

MÉXICO

Golf of Mexico

N

0   10   20   40 Kilometers

Figure 1.3 Location of Indigenous study communities and territories.

Source: map produced by Lisa Benvenuti, Center for Spatial Studies – University of Redlands.

Part I: Setting the scene

Chapters 1–3 of the book introduce and set the context for the empirical and analytical chapters that follow. The next two chapters provide essential background on contemporary village life and migration dynamics in rural Oaxaca. Chapter 2 describes the state's demographics, economy, land tenure, and village and municipal governance arrangements. Chapter 3 provides migration histories for our two study regions of the Sierra Norte and Mixteca, and introduces the idea of the Trans-Border Corporate Community, where village and community life becomes stretched across state and national borders. Together, these chapters provide the reader with the contextual information that they need to better understand the situations and scenarios described in Parts II and III.

Part II: Empirical case studies

In Chapters 4–9 we present a series of rich community case studies, with each case highlighting particular aspects of change that help illustrate how migration impacts these places and the people who call them 'home'. All cases touch on the theme of *migration and institutional change* to show how demographic and cultural change impinges upon village governance systems; and how institutional adaptations are diverse, unstable, and can be unsatisfactory. They reveal how collectives harness migration's economic and cultural contributions for family and community reproduction, they describe community strategies for coping with the shortage of labour for community governance, and they show how tighter controls at the US border are affecting migration dynamics and translocal community connections. Although Oaxacan culture is durable and reproducible in destination centres, translocal governance can erode over time. Four of the six cases provide additional focus on the theme of *migration and environmental change*, and cover agricultural decline and forest transitions, the new geographies of forest use and conservation emergent in Indigenous Oaxaca, the dilemma of managing territorial commons with fewer commoners, and the role that migrants themselves play in questions of territorial use and governance.

The presentation of empirical data for each case incorporates the 'voice' of the study community or communities in question, through the liberal use of long, direct quotations and photographs. Two of the cases (Chapters 6 and 8) are lead-authored by a member of the Indigenous community that they focus on. All cases provide a summary of the main data collection methods that were used.

Part III: Synthesis and conclusions

Chapters 10 and 11 provide detailed analyses to make sense of the lessons generated by our featured case studies, supplemented by insights from other communities in the Sierra Norte and Mixteca regions where we have worked over the past 12 years.

Chapter 10, 'The changing landscapes of Indigenous Oaxaca', makes the case that there is a significant change of direction for forest- and farm-based livelihoods, and new forms of people–environment interactions in Indigenous Oaxaca. Robson and Klooster argue that agricultural crisis, migration, and the de-territorialization of rural livelihood has led to a new landscape of forest use and conservation as: migration challenges community practices for self-governance of forest resources; declines in agriculture create new spaces for forest recovery and use; and forest conservation policies create economic opportunities around both extractive and non-extractive forest use. However, while forest transitions may allow new opportunities to emerge, we argue that such activities may struggle to replace agriculture's traditional foundational contribution to village life and territory. While communities might have more income than decades prior, this new or emergent rural economy may not provide the kind of livelihood that links people to community and territory, or at least not in the way that long-held conceptualizations posit.

Chapter 11, 'Migrant organizing, village governance, and the ephemeral nature of translocality', provides an important reminder that migration and the migratory experience is dynamic and subject to change, with apparent trends rarely permanent. Hernández-Díaz and Robson argue that previous work on transnationality has failed to grasp its ephemeral quality, rather emphasizing a moment of intense connection across borders. While we see continued cultural reproduction in the US based on Indigenous traditions of organizing around fiestas and dance and music and food, and ethnic tourism back to their communities of origin, we do not see a recreation or a repopulating of translocal or transborder communities. Instead, the migrants with deepest connections to their communities of origin are aging out, affecting continuity and renewal among the transborder or translocal communities that they belong to. This chapter underscores the role of border enforcement and macro-economic policies in limiting the reproduction of translocal communities, and enables speculation as to their future after the US border is closed and net national migration drops to zero. This has important ramifications for communities in Oaxaca whose economies and governance arrangements have been modified to exhibit a level of dependence on the individual and collective investments of non-resident (migrant) members.

The book draws to a close with Chapter 12, 'Communities *shaping* migration: the migration–community–environment nexus', in which we summarize key findings and consider their relevance for migration–community–environment linkages beyond Mexico. We place the question of migration in its broader rural Southern context of demographic transitions (smaller families, better educational opportunities, etc.), and associated rural transformations, including declines in agriculture, greater rural–urban connectivity, and an emphasis on formal conservation. We argue that migration–environment relationships depend on that broader context, and on what happens to the communities buffeted by migration and associated rural change. We revisit our proposal that *community* be added to the migration–environment nexus. Our observations and analysis show how rural cultural capital can adapt to incredibly disruptive global economic and demographic forces. Despite potentially transformative change, we argue that Indigenous territorial communities can remain viable in many cases, maintaining the capacity to take advantage of new environmental management and conservation opportunities.

This constitutes yet one more path that communities have taken as they adapt to a history of pressures, stresses, and possibilities since European contact. Far from being swept away, rural communities are fighting to maintain their place in the world, even as their membership is stretched across borders, and becomes less and less rooted in the agricultural traditions of the past. These are communities that survive a changed social-ecological context and setting to remain crucial actors in ongoing projects of biocultural heritage and conservation.

Note

1 *Translocal* is used throughout this book to reflect the mix of international and internal migration dynamics that have shaped (and continue to shape) sending communities in Oaxaca, and follows Stephen's (2007: 65) definition of: 'movement of place-specific culture, institutions, people, knowledge, and resources within several local sites and across borders – national and otherwise'. The term specifically permits 'broader interpretations of rural people who patch together livelihoods through activities that take place in many different locales in the same country, including periods of work in urban areas or areas of commercial agriculture distant from their rural villages' (Klooster 2005: 340).

References

Acharya, D.R., J.S. Bell, P. Simkhada, E.R. Van Teijlingen, and P.R. Regmi. 2010. Women's autonomy in household decision-making: a demographic study in Nepal. *Reproductive Health*, 7(1): 15.

Adger, W.N., P.M. Kelly, A. Winkels, L.Q. Huy, and C. Locke. 2002. Migration, remittances, livelihood trajectories, and social resilience. *AMBIO: A Journal of the Human Environment*, 31(4): 358–366.

Agrawal, A. 2005. *Environmentality: Technologies of Government and the Making of Subjects*. Durham, NC: Duke University Press.

Agrawal, A. and J. Ribot. 2014. Are Ostrom's design principles sufficient for design? In: Robson, J.P. *et al.* (eds), Remembering Elinor Ostrom: Her Work and its Contribution to the Theory and Practice of Conservation and Sustainable Natural Resource Management. *Policy Matters Issue 19*, April 2014. IUCN Commission on Environmental, Economic and Social Policy.

Aide, T.M., M.L. Clark, H.R. Grau, D. López-Carr, M.A. Levy, D. Redo, M. Bonilla-Moheno, G. Riner, M.J. Andrade-Núñez, and M. Muñiz. 2013. Deforestation and reforestation of Latin America and the Caribbean (2001–2010). *Biotropica*, 45(2): 262–271.

Alden Wily, L. 2011. *The Tragedy of Public Lands: The Fate of the Commons under Global Commercial Pressure*. Contribution to ILC Collaborative Research Project on Commercial Pressures on Land. Rome, Italy: ILC.

Anríquez, G. and L. Stloukal. 2008. Rural population change in developing countries: lessons for policymaking. *European View*, 7(2): 309–317.

Aquino-Moreschi, A. and I. Contreras-Pastrana. 2016. Comunidad, jóvenes y generación: disputando subjetividades en la Sierra Norte de Oaxaca. *Revista LatinoAmericana de Ciencias Sociales, Niñez y Juventud*, 14(1): 463–475.

Bada, X. and A. Feldmann. 2016. New challenges for migration studies in the Western Hemisphere. *Practicing Anthropology*, 38(1): 33–34.

Baker, J.M., 2005. *The Kuhls of Kangra: Community-managed Irrigation in the Western Himalaya*. Seattle, WA: University of Washington Press.

Bebbington, A.J. and S.P.J. Batterbury. 2001. Transnational livelihoods and landscapes: Political ecologies of globalization. *Ecumene*, 8(4): 369–380.

Béné, C., A. Newsham, M. Davies, M. Ulrichs, and R. Godfrey-Wood. 2014. Resilience, poverty, and development. *Journal of International Development*, 26: 598–623.

Berdegué, J.A. and R. Fuentealba. 2014. The state of smallholders in agriculture in Latin America. In: Hazell, P.B.R. and A. Rahman (eds), *New Directions for Smallholder Agriculture*, pp. 115–152, Oxford Scholarship Online, March 2014.

Berdegué, J.A., A.J. Bebbington, and T. Rosada. 2014. The rural transformation. In: B Currie-Alder, R. Kanbur, D.M. Malone, and R. Medhora (eds), *International Development: Ideas, Experience, and Prospects*. Oxford, UK: Oxford University Press.

Berkes, F. 2009. Revising the commons paradigm. *Journal of Natural Resources Policy Research*, 1(3): 261–264.

Bezaury, J.A. 2007. Organized coffee producers: mitigating negative impacts of outmigration in Oaxaca, Mexico. *Mountain Research and Development*, 27(2): 109–113.

Black, R., W.N. Adger, N.W. Arnell, S. Dercon, A. Geddes, and D. Thomas. 2011. The effect of environmental change on human migration. *Global Environmental Change* 21: S3–S11.

Boege, E. 2008. *El patrimonio biocultural de los pueblos indígenas de México: hacia la conservación in situ de la biodiversidad y agro-diversidad en los territorios indígenas*. Mexico City, Mexico: Instituto Nacional de Antropología e Historia, Comisión Nacional para el Desarrollo de los Pueblos Indígenas.

Boillat, S., F.M. Scarpa, J.P. Robson, I. Gasparri, T.M. Aide, A.P. Dutra Aguiar, L.O. Anderson *et al.* 2017. Land system science in Latin America: challenges and perspectives. *Current Opinion in Environmental Sustainability*, 26: 37–46.

Borras Jr, S.M. 2009. Agrarian change and peasant studies: changes, continuities and challenges – an introduction. *The Journal of Peasant Studies*, 36(1): 5–31.

Bray, D.B., L. Merino-Pérez, and D. Barry (eds). 2005. *The Community Forests of Mexico: Managing for Sustainable Landscapes*. Austin, TX: University of Texas Press.

Bryceson, D.F., C. Kay, and J. Mooji (eds), 2000. *Disappearing Peasantries? Rural Labour in Africa, Asia, and Latin America*. London, UK: Intermediate Technology Publications.

Burkham, J.M. 2012. The city will come to us: Development discourse and the new rurality in Atotonilco El Bajo, Mexico. *Journal of Latin American Geography*, (2012): 25–43.

Camacho Robles, S., 2004. Migration and return in the Sierra Juárez. In: Fox, J. and G. Rivera-Salgado (eds), *Indigenous Mexican Migrants in the United States*. San Diego: Center for U.S.–Mexican Studies, UC San Diego.

Charnley, S. and M.R. Poe. 2007. Community forestry in theory and practice: where are we now? *Annual Review of Anthropology*, 36(1): 301.

Cohen, J.H. and B. Ramirez Rios. 2016. Internal migration in Oaxaca: its role and value to rural movers. *International Journal of Sociology*, 46(3): 223–235.

Cohen, J.H. and I. Sirkeci. 2011. *Cultures of Migration: The Global Nature of Contemporary Mobility*. Austin, TX: University of Texas Press.

Colfer, C., M. Elias, B. Basnett, and S. Hummel (eds). 2017. *The Earthscan Reader on Gender and Forests*. London and New York: Routledge.

CONAPO. 2014. *Dinámica demográfica 1990–2010 y proyecciones de población 2010–2030*. Retrieved on November 15, 2016, at: www.conapo.gob.mx/es/CONAPO/Proyecciones_Analisis.

Curiel, C., 2015. La amenaza de 'terminar con la costumbre': Migración y recreación de los sistemas normativos internos en la Mixteca. In: Curiel, C., J. Hernández-Díaz, and H. Worthen (eds), *Los Dilemas de la Política del Reconocimiento en México*. Oaxaca, México: UABJO, Juan Pablos Editor.

Davidson-Hunt, I.J., H. Asselin, F. Berkes, K. Brown, C.J. Idrobo, M.A. Jones, P. McConney, R.M. O'Flaherty, J.P. Robson, and M. Rodriguez. 2016. The use of biodiversity for responding to globalised change: a people in nature approach to support the resilience of rural and remote communities. *People in Nature: Valuing the Diversity of Interrelationships between People and Nature*. Gland, Switzerland: IUCN.

Duran, E., J.P. Robson, M. Briones-Salas, D.B. Bray, and F. Berkes. 2012. Mexico: wildlife conservation on community conserved lands in Oaxaca. *Protected Landscapes and Wild Biodiversity*, 71.

Durand, J., 2013. Nueva fase migratoria. *Papeles de* Población, 19(77): 83–113.

Durand, J. and D.S. Massey (eds). 2004. *Crossing the Border: Research from the Mexican Migration Project*. Russell Sage Foundation.

Economist. 2013. *Autumn of the Patriarchs*. Available online at: www.economist.com/news/americas/21578710-traditional-demographic-patterns-are-changing-astonishingly-fast-autumn-patriarchs.

Ellis, F. 1998. Household strategies and rural livelihood diversification. *The Journal of Development Studies*, 35(1): 1–38.

Fairbairn, M., J. Fox, S.R. Isakson, M. Levien, N. Peluso, S. Razavi, I. Scoones, and K. Sivaramakrishnan. 2014. Introduction: new directions in Agrarian political economy. *The Journal of Peasant Studies*, 41(5): 653–666.

FAO. 2014. *The State of Food and Agriculture. The Next Global Breadbasket: How Latin America Can Feed the World*. IDB/Global Harvest Initiative.

Fitzgerald, D. 2008. Colonies of the little motherland: Membership, space, and time in Mexican migrant hometown associations. *Comparative Studies in Society and History*, 50(1): 145–169.

Fox, J., 2007. *Accountability Politics: Power and Voice in Rural Mexico*. Oxford, UK: Oxford University Press.

Fox, J. and X. Bada, 2008. Migrant organization and hometown impacts in rural Mexico. *Journal of Agrarian Change*, 8(2 and 3): 435–461.

Fox, J. and G. Rivera-Salgado (eds). 2004. *Indigenous Mexican Migrants in the United States*. La Jolla, CA: Center for U.S.–Mexican Studies, UCSD.

Freire, G., O. Schwartz, S. Daniel *et al.* 2015. *Indigenous Latin America in the Twenty-First Century: The First Decade*. Washington, DC: World Bank Group. http://documents.worldbank.org/curated/en/145891467991974540/Indigenous-Latin-America-in-the-twenty-first-century-the-first-decade.

Gavin, M.C., J. McCarter, A. Mead, F. Berkes, J.R. Stepp, D. Peterson, and R. Tang. 2015. Defining biocultural approaches to conservation. *Trends in Ecology & Evolution*, 30(3): 140–145.

Gorenflo, L.J., S. Romaine, R.A. Mittermeier, and K. Walker-Painemilla. 2012. Co-occurrence of linguistic and biological diversity in biodiversity hotspots and high biodiversity wilderness areas. *Proceedings of the National Academy of Sciences*, 109(21): 8032–8037.

Gray, C.L. and R.E. Bilsborrow. 2014. Consequences of out-migration for land use in rural Ecuador. *Land Use Policy*, 36: 182–191.

Greiner, C. and P. Sakdapolrak. 2013. Translocality: Concepts, applications, and emerging research perspectives. *Geography Compass*, 7: 373–384.

Haggblade, S., P.B. Hazell, and T. Reardon (eds). 2009. *Transforming the Rural Nonfarm Economy: Opportunities and Threats in the Developing World*. Washington, DC: International Food Policy Research Institute.

Harriss, J. 1992. *Rural Development: Theories of Peasant Economy and Agrarian Change*. Abingdon, UK: Routledge.

Hecht, S. 2014. Forests lost and found in tropical Latin America: the woodland 'green revolution'. *The Journal of Peasant Studies*, 41(5): 877–909.

Hecht, S., S. Kandel, A. Morales, and S.C. Greenblatt. 2012. *Migration, Rural Livelihoods, and Natural Resource Management*. San Salvador, El Salvador: PRISMA.

Hecht, S.B., A.L. Yang, B.S. Basnett, C. Padoch, and N.L. Peluso. 2015. *People in Motion, Forests in Transition: Trends in Migration, Urbanization, and Remittances and their Effects on Tropical Forests.* Vol. 142. Bogor, Indonesia: Centre for International Forestry Research (CIFOR). Indigenous and Northern Affairs Canada (INAC). 2015.

Hernández-Díaz, J. 2013. *Comunidad, Migración y Ciudadanía: Avatares de la Organización Indígena Comunitaria.* Mexico, D.F.: MA Porrúa.

Herrera Guerra, E. 2015. *Protecting Forests, Improving Livelihoods: Community Forestry in Mexico.* Brussels, Belgium: FERN.

Hunter, L.M., J.K. Luna, and R.M. Norton. 2015. Environmental dimensions of migration. *Annual Review of Sociology*, 41: 377–397.

IFAD. 2016. *Rural Development Report 2016: Fostering Inclusive Rural Transformation.* Rome, Italy: International Fund for Agricultural Development.

INEGI. 2010. *Censo general de población y vivienda, 2010.* Accessed July 11, 2015 at: www3.inegi.org.mx//sistemas/iterm5000/.

INEGI, 2015. *Encuesta Nacional de la Dinámica Demográfica 1992, 1997, 2009, 2014.* Instituto Nacional de Estadística, Geografía e Informática. Retrieved on November 15, 2016, www3.inegi.org.mx/sistemas/temas/default.aspx?s=est&c=17484.

INEGI. 2016. *Actualización del Marco Censal Agropecuario.* Available at: www.inegi.org. mx/est/contenidos/proyectos/agro/default.aspx (accessed October 30, 2017).

Jardón Hernández, A.E. 2016. *International Migration and Crisis: Transition toward a New Migratory Phase.* New York: Springer.

Kay, C., 2008. Reflections on Latin American rural studies in the neoliberal globalization period: A new rurality.' *Development and Change*, 39(6): 915–943.

Kay, C. 2015. The agrarian question and the neoliberal rural transformation in Latin America. *European Review of Latin American and Caribbean Studies*, 100: 73–83.

Kearney, M. and F. Besserer. 2004. Oaxacan municipal governance in transnational context. In: J. Fox and G. Rivera-Salgado (eds), *Indigenous Mexican Migrants in the United States.* La Jolla, CA: Center for U.S.-Mexican Studies, UCSD, pp. 449–466.

Keats, S. and S. Wiggins. 2016. Population change in the rural developing world: Making the transition. Overseas Development Institute (ODI), March 2016, 117 pp.

Klooster, D. 2003. Forest transitions in Mexico: Institutions and forests in a globalized countryside. *The Professional Geographer*, 55(2): 227–237.

Klooster, D. 2005. Producing social nature in the Mexican countryside. *Cultural Geographies*, 12: 321–344.

Klooster, D. 2013. The impact of transnational migration on commons management among Mexican indigenous communities. *Journal of Latin American Geography*, 12(1): 57–86.

Lambin, E.F., B.L. Turner, H.J. Geist, S.B. Agbola, A. Angelsen, J.W. Bruce, O.T. Coomes, R. Dirzo, G. Fischer, C. Folke, and P. George. 2001. The causes of land-use and land-cover change: moving beyond the myths. *Global Environmental Change*, 11(4): 261–269.

Lanza, N. and C. Valeggia. 2014. Cambios demográficos en una población rural de la etnia Toba del norte de Argentina. *Latin American Research Review*, 49(2): 107–128.

López-Carr, D. 2012. Agro-ecological drivers of rural out-migration to the Maya Biosphere Reserve, Guatemala. *Environmental Research Letters*, 7(4): 045603.

Martin, G.J., C.I. Camacho Benavides, C.A. Del Campo García, S. Anta Fonseca, F. Chapela Mendoza, and M.A. González Ortíz. 2011. Indigenous and community conserved areas in Oaxaca, Mexico. *Management of Environmental Quality: An International Journal*, 22(2): 250–266.

Massey, D.S., W.G. Axinn, and D.J. Ghimire. 2010. Environmental change and out-migration: evidence from Nepal. *Population and Environment*, 32(2–3): 109–136.

Massey, D.S., J. Durand, and K.A. Pren. 2015. Border enforcement and return migration by documented and undocumented Mexicans. *Journal of Ethnic and Migration Studies*, 41(7): 1015–1040.

McCay, B.J. 2002. Emergence of institutions for the commons: contexts, situations, and events. In: Ostrom, E., T. Dietz, N. Dolšak, P.C. Stern, S. Stonich, and E.U. Weber (eds), *The Drama of the Commons*. National Research Council. Washington, DC: National Academy Press.

McLeman, R. and B. Smit. 2006. Migration as an adaptation to climate change. *Climatic Change*, 76(1-2): 31–53.

McMichael, P. 1997. Rethinking globalization: the agrarian question revisited. *Review of International Political Economy*, 4(4): 630–662.

McSweeney, K. and S. Arps. 2005. A 'demographic turnaround': the rapid growth of the indigenous populations in Lowland Latin America. *Latin American Research Review*, 40(1): 3–29.

McSweeney, K. and B. Jokisch. 2007. Beyond rainforests: urbanisation and emigration among lowland Indigenous societies in Latin America. *Bulletin of Latin American Research*, 26(2): 159–180.

Mines, R., S. Nichols, and D. Runsten. 2010. *California's Indigenous Farmworkers*. Final Report of the Indigenous Farmworker Study (IFS). California Rural Legal Assistance.

Moctezuma, M. 2000. La organización de migrantes Zacatecanos en Estados Unidos. *Cuadernos Agrarios*, 19–20.

Moran-Taylor, M.J. and M.J. Taylor. 2010. Land and leña: linking transnational migra-tion, natural resources, and the environment in Guatemala. *Population and Environ-ment*, 32(2–3): 198–215.

Mutersbaugh, T., 2002. Migration, common property, and communal labour: cultural politics and agency in a Mexican village. *Political Geography*, 21: 473–494.

Nayak, P.K. and F. Berkes. 2011. Commonisation and decommonisation: under-standing the processes of change in Chilika Lagoon, India. *Conservation & Society*, 9: 132–145.

Neumann, K. and H. Hilderink. 2015. Opportunities and challenges for investigating the environment-migration nexus. *Human Ecology*, 43(2): 309–322.

Orozco, M. and R. Rouse. 2007. *Migrant Hometown Associations and Opportunities for Development: A Global Perspective*. Washington, DC: Migration Information Source.

Ostrom, E., 2005. *Understanding Institutional Diversity*. Princeton, NJ: Princeton Univer-sity Press.

Otero, G. 1999. *Farewell to the Peasantry? Political Class Formation in Rural Mexico*. Boulder, CO: Westview Press.

Passel, J., D. Cohn, and A. Gonzalez-Barrera. 2012. *Net Migration from Mexico Falls to Zero and Perhaps Less*. Washington, DC: Pew Hispanic Center.

Pew Research Centre. 2014. *Attitudes about Aging: A Global Perspective*. Available online at: http://assets.pewresearch.org/wp-content/uploads/sites/2/2014/01/Pew-Research-Center-Global-Aging-Report-FINAL-January-30-20141.pdf.

Piguet, E. 2013. From 'primitive migration' to 'climate refugees': the curious fate of the natural environment in migration studies. *Annals of the Association of American Geo-graphers*, 103(1): 148–162.

Porter-Bolland, L., E.A. Ellis, M.R. Guariguata, I. Ruiz-Mallén, S. Negrete-Yankelevich, and V. Reyes-García. 2012. Community managed forests and forest protected areas: an assessment of their conservation effectiveness across the tropics. *Forest Ecology and Management*, 268: 6–17.

Radel, C. and B. Schmook. 2008. Male transnational migration and its linkages to land-use change in a southern Campeche ejido. *Journal of Latin American Geography*, 7(2): 59–84.

Ribot, J.C. and N.L. Peluso. 2003. A theory of access. *Rural Sociology*, 68(2): 153–181.

Ribot, J.C., A. Chhatre, and T. Lankinad. 2008. Introduction: Institutional choice and recognition in the formation and consolidation of local democracy. *Conservation and Society*, 6(1): 1–11.

Rights and Resources Initiative (RRI). 2015. *Who Owns the World's Land? A global baseline of formally recognized indigenous and community land rights*. Washington DC: Rights and Resources Initiative.

Robson, J.P. 2007. Local approaches to biodiversity conservation: lessons from Oaxaca, southern Mexico. *International Journal of Sustainable Development*, 10(3): 267–286.

Robson, J.P., 2010. *The Impact of Rural to Urban Migration on Forest Commons in Oaxaca, Mexico*. Unpublished PhD Thesis. Winnipeg, Canada: University of Manitoba.

Robson, J.P. and F. Berkes, 2011. How does out-migration affect community institutions? A study of two indigenous municipalities in Oaxaca, Mexico. *Human Ecology*, 39(2): 179–190.

Robson, J.P., D.J. Klooster, H. Worthen, and J. Hernández-Díaz. 2018. Migration and agrarian transformation in Indigenous Mexico. *Journal of Agrarian Change*, 18(2): 299–323.

Saad, P. 2010. Demographic trends in Latin America and the Caribbean. In: Cotlear, D. (ed.), *Population Aging: Is Latin America Ready?* Washington, DC: World Bank, pp. 43–77.

Sarukhán, J. and R. Jiménez. 2016. Generating intelligence for decision making and sustainable use of natural capital in Mexico. *Current Opinion in Environmental Sustainability*, 19: 153–159.

Stephen, L., 2007. *Transborder Lives: Indigenous Oaxacans in Mexico, California, and Oregon*. Durham, NC: Duke University Press.

Stiffler, S. 2007. Neither here nor there: Mexican immigrant workers and the search for home. *American Ethnologist*, 34: 674–688.

Torres-Rojo, J.M., R. Moreno-Sánchez, and M.A. Mendoza-Briseño. 2016. Sustainable forest management in Mexico. *Current Forestry Reports*, 2(2): 93–105.

United Nations. 2009. *The State of the World's Indigenous Peoples*. New York: United Nations, 238 pp.

United Nations. 2017. *World Population Prospects: The 2017 Revision*. Available online at: https://esa.un.org/unpd/wpp/.

UN-Habitat. 2012. *State of Latin America and Caribbean Cities in 2012: Towards a New Urban Transition*. Nairobi, Kenya: United Nations.

Van der Ploeg, J.D. 2012. *The New Peasantries: Struggles for Autonomy and Sustainability in an Era of Empire and Globalization*. Abingdon, UK: Earthscan.

Van Vleet, E., D.B. Bray, and E. Durán. 2016. Knowing but not knowing: Systematic conservation planning and community conservation in the Sierra Norte of Oaxaca, Mexico. *Land Use Policy*, 59: 504–515.

VanWey, L.K., C.M. Tucker, and E.D. McConnell, 2005. Community organization, migration, and remittances in Oaxaca. *Latin American Research Review*, 40(1): 83–107.

Vertovec, S. 2004. Migrant transnationalism and modes of transformation. *International Migration Review*, 38(3): 970–1001.

Wiltshire, K. 2001. Management of social transformations: introduction. *International Political Science Review*, 22(1): 5–11.

Wood, C. 1981. Structural changes and household strategies: a conceptual framework for the study of rural migration. *Human Organization*, 40(4): 338–344.

Woods, M., 2007. Engaging the global countryside: globalization, hybridity, and the reconstitution of rural place. *Progress in Human Geography*, 31(4): 485–507.

World Bank. 2015. *Indigenous Latin America in the Twenty-First Century*. Washington, DC: World Bank. License: Creative Commons Attribution CC BY 3.0 IGO.

Zimmerer, K.S., 1991. Labor shortages and crop diversity in the southern Peruvian sierra. *Geographical Review*, (1991): 414–432.

Zimmerer, K.S. 2010. Biological diversity in agriculture and global change. *Annual Review of Environment and Resources*, (35): 137–166.

2 Population, territory, and governance in rural Oaxaca

Jorge Hernández-Díaz and James P. Robson

Introduction

Oaxaca in southern Mexico, provides the ideal setting for researching the themes of this book, thanks to its biocultural diversity, the extent of state territory that remains under community control, and the role that migration plays in local and regional economies (Boege 2008; Cohen 2004a; Robson 2010). This is the first of two chapters that provide essential context to understanding the people and places of contemporary rural Oaxaca, and a base upon which subsequent analyses are framed. In this chapter, we focus on demographics, socio-economic status, land tenure systems, and village governance arrangements.

Demographics, biocultural diversity, and poverty

Oaxaca is the fifth largest state in Mexico, covering a little over 9.5 million hectares or 4.8 per cent of national territory (INEGI 2017).

It borders the states of Veracruz and Puebla to the north and northeast, Chiapas to the east, and Guerrero to the west. The Pacific Ocean lies to the south. Oaxaca is divided into eight geo-political regions: Cañada, Costa, Istmo, Mixteca, Papaloapan, Sierra Norte, Sierra Sur, and Valles Centrales. These regions are further divided administratively into 30 districts, 570 municipalities, and 12,919 localities (INEGI 2017). The very high number of (predominantly small) municipalities – almost a quarter of the country's total – is a consequence of Oaxaca's abrupt and mountainous terrain, colonial and independent policies and politics, and the divisions that have existed among and between the principal ethnic groups (Bailón Corres 1999).

In 2015, Oaxaca was home to 3,967,889 people, of whom 2.6 million (or 65 per cent) self-identify as Indigenous (INEGI 2015),[1] with an Indigenous language spoken by 40 per cent or more of the inhabitants in 245 of Oaxaca's 570 municipalities (INEGI, 2015). The State is home to 16 language groups, with a much higher number of regional dialects (Frizzi 2000). Zapotec is the most commonly spoken (by 33.6 per cent of Indigenous speakers), followed by Mixtec (22.1 per cent), Mazateco (14.9 per cent); Mixe (9.5 per cent); and Chinanteco (8.9 per cent) (INEGI 2015). Each ethno-linguistic group possesses a set of characteristics that both bind them and set them apart: centuries old histories; common identities; shared and differentiated cultures; communally-held territories; and, structures of self-governance.

In addition to its remarkable cultural-linguistic diversity, Oaxaca is the most biologically diverse state in Mexico (García-Mendez *et al.* 2004; CONABIO-CONANP 2007). Sitting at the confluence of the neo-arctic and the neo-tropical biogeographic regions, Oaxaca marks the point where the Sierra Madre Occidental and the Sierra Madre Oriental mountain chains converge. The result is a uniquely complex physiographic landscape, where peaks that rise above 3000 metres above sea level (m.a.s.l.) punctuate deep canyons and valleys, and a highly varied mix of topographic, geological and climatic conditions provide for a full range of temperate and tropical forest ecosystems (Martin 1993; Robson 2007). Oaxaca is home to 12 vegetation types, 8431 recorded species of vascular plant, and 4500 recorded species of terrestrial vertebrates and invertebrates (SERBO 2010; García-Mendez *et al.* 2004). Of these, 702 plants and 128 vertebrates are endemic to the state (SERBO 2010). Oaxaca is home to over one-third of plant species recorded in Mexico (Ordóñez and Rodríguez 2008).

These biodiverse landscapes continue to be shaped by human presence and practice. Oaxaca has been steadily urbanizing since the mid-twentieth century. Prior to 1950, no locality had a population exceeding 40,000. By 2014, Oaxaca City alone accounted for over 300,000 people, while the city of Tuxtepec had 145,000 residents as far back as 2005. Yet despite the growth of regional urban centres, Oaxaca retains a strong rural characteristic. The very large number of municipalities (570) and localities (12,000+) are evidence of a widely dispersed population. In 2009, more than half the state's population (53%) was living in rural areas, defined as localities with fewer than 2500 inhabitants (INEGI 2010). Farming remains the primary economic occupation in these rural areas (Murat 2017: 124).

From a socio-economic standpoint, Oaxaca is one of most impoverished and marginalized states in Mexico. Over half its population (close to two million inhabitants) live in conditions representing high to very high levels of marginalization (INEGI 2017). Over 60 per cent of Oaxaca's municipalities (360 of 570) fall into this category, while a further 171 municipalities exhibit moderate levels of marginalization, 28 have low levels of marginalization, and only 11 exhibit 'very low' levels of marginalization (CONEVAL 2016). Almost one-fifth of Oaxaca's population live in houses with dirt floors, half of all households suffer from overcrowding, a quarter of the population lack facilitated access to potable water, and 5 per cent remain without electricity (INEGI 2017). Many rural communities experience low agricultural productivity, inequitable market access for agricultural and forest-based products, and below-average incomes (INEGI 2017).

A significant proportion of Oaxaca's population are considered to be 'moderately' or 'extremely' impoverished (Table 2.1), with the situation worsening in recent years. Between 2012 and 2014, the proportion accounted for by one of

Table 2.1 Poverty levels for the State of Oaxaca (2010–2014)

	% of total population			Thousands of people		
	2010	2012	2014	2010	2012	2014
Poverty indicators						
Population in conditions of moderate poverty	37.7	38.6	38.4	1462.8	1518.0	1532.5
Population in conditions of extreme poverty	29.2	23.3	28.3	1133.5	916.6	1130.3
Population classed as socially-vulnerable	22.2	26.1	23.3	859.6	1024.5	927.9
Population classed as economically-vulnerable	1.3	1.7	2.1	50.2	65.1	83.6
Population classed as not poor and not vulnerable	9.5	10.3	7.9	369.7	406.6	314.9

Source: CONEVAL, based on data from MCS-ENIGH (2010, 2012, and 2014).

these two categories rose from 61.9 per cent to 66.8 per cent of the state population. A reported 26.9 per cent of the Oaxaca's population do not receive a wage (INEGI 2010). In 2007, the per capita gross domestic product in Oaxaca was $35,252 Mexican pesos, the second lowest of any state in the country (INEGI 2009). Literacy rates among individuals aged 15 or over stood at 16 per cent in 2010 (CONAPO 2010), with a third of those not having completed primary-level education. The State Development Plan for 2011–2016 (Cué 2011: 295) found that fewer than half of all young people (12–29 years of age) (507,789 individuals) were actively employed.

Poverty and limited employment opportunities are among the main factors cited by people for looking beyond their home village – whether within the state of Oaxaca, or to other parts of Mexico or the US – to meet work, education, and other needs and aspirations.

Territorial use and land tenure

Traditionally, livelihoods in rural Oaxaca have been shaped by access and adaptation to a diversity of ecological zones and environmental conditions (Gonzalez 2001; Robson 2007). The distribution of vegetation types, climates and soils have generally determined where people have settled, farmed, and harvested (Chapela 2005; Martin 1993; Robson 2007). While subsistence production begins in cultivated fields, it can extend deep into local forests where people find plants and animals that enrich their diet, health care and rituals (Martin 1993). This knowledge is codified in classification systems that recognize different soils, climatic zones, successional stages, and seasons (González 2001; Hunn 2008; Martin 1993), guiding decisions about where and when to cut and burn forest cover, how many years to cultivate a specific plot of land, where to gather NTFPs and uncultivated plants, or where to look for game animals. The mix of knowledge systems and productive zones (according to ecological niche) have traditionally helped communities to adapt to variable market conditions (Chapela 2005; Martin 1993; Robson 2007) – oscillating between subsistence and commercial production, and a back-and-forth movement between different climatic zones.

Most land in Oaxaca is held communally; that is, it is 'owned' and managed by local communities.[2] In 2015, the proportion of titled land in Oaxaca under community control stood at a remarkable 87.50 per cent – with 6,248,554.44 hectares (or 69.08 per cent) belonging to *comunidades agrarias* (Indigenous communities) and 1,666,310.69 hectares (18.42 per cent) belonging to *ejidos* (peasant communities of Indigenous or mixed heritage) (INEGI 2016). The highest proportions of communal land tenure are found in the Sierra Norte and Mixteca regions (Table 2.2).

Under these systems, forests, grazing lands and watercourses remain common property resources. Resource rights within 'owner' communities are traditionally granted to resident men (and sometimes women) upon award of *comunero* or commoner status. This provides them with the right to access communal lands, including local forests, harvest resources or products, contribute to their management, and take part in decision-making about how these territories are accessed, used, and managed. In the case of agrarian (Indigenous) communities, communal lands are not subject to purchase by outsiders. However, community members can hold individual usufruct rights to agricultural parcels and urban lots (including *solares* or home gardens), and these can be transferred internally among family members or other community members – as long as those involved have complied with their collective work and communal service obligations. The above rights allocations help to maintain a functional organizational structure, contribute to community cohesion, and provide an incentive to the members of these collectives to invest time, energy, and sometimes financial resources into village and territorial governance.

Table 2.2 Distribution and extent of communal land tenure in Oaxaca

Region	Area (ha)	Area under common property	% of total
Papaloapam	819,165	217,306	26
Sierra Sur	1,409,982	1,138,071	80
Sierra Norte	852,683	743,165	87
Istmo	2,031,199	1,286,720	63
Cañada	406,997	257,917	63
Mixteca	1,497,874	1,294,063	86
Valles Centrales	865,991	629,381	72
Costa	1,130,943	651,739	57
Total	9,045,024	6,248,554	69

Source: Agricultural census (INEGI 2016).

Village politics and governance

Social organization in Indigenous Oaxaca combines long-held values and customs with normative structures influenced by the State. As Ramos Pioquinto (1988: 9) notes, most local communities are characterized not only by language but also specific sets of economic, socio-political, and cultural relations – relations that are sustained by a peasant economy, and a village and territorial governance system that mixes traditions of pre-Hispanic political organization with institutions imposed by colonial governments during the Colonia (Cancian 1965; Carrasco 1961).

Most villages in Oaxaca are self-governed by customary practices, legislated by a general community assembly, and enforced through three primary institutions:

1   The Municipal Executive, or *Cabildo*, headed by a Municipal President, with certain judicial powers exercised by the *sindico* municipal, which is charged with enforcing municipal decrees. The administration typically includes a town mayor (*alcalde constitucional*), a secretary, and up to half a dozen 'councilmen' (*regidor de hacienda, regidor de salud, regidor de educacion*). Traditionally, there are *suplentes* (assistants) for each officer, delegated to stand in for them when absent. Assisting these officials are the *topiles* who make themselves available for routine tasks in the service of the *cabildo*, as well as for the local *comandante de policia* (police commander). The Municipal Executive is complemented and aided by citizen-led committees, whose number, composition and function varies from community to community, but generally advise on essential services such as village infrastructure (*obras*), education, health, transportation, and civic and religious celebrations. In many communities, those serving on committees are considered 'cargos menores' (lesser cargos), although some may involve significant responsibility and/or time commitments. The Municipal Executive reports on its activities to the membership-at-large within the Asamblea General de Ciudadanos (Citizens Assembly).

2   The Commissioner for Communal Property (*Comisariado de Bienes Comunales*) is responsible for assuring the integrity of the community's common property, most notably forests and water bodies and associated resources. In accordance with Federal Agrarian Law, the Comisariado is charged with executing the orders and wishes of the Asamblea General de Comuneros (Assembly of Commoners), overseeing administration of the common property resources within the community's territory, and representing the community in related dealings with external actors, including the state. The Comisariado typically consists of a President, a Secretary, and a Treasurer, and three *suplentes*. These six incumbents are elected by the Assembly of Commoners and traditionally serve for a period of three years, before being replaced by a newly elected set of incumbents.

3 The Surveillance or Oversight Council (*Consejo de Vigilancia*) is a three-person committee charged with surveillance/monitoring of communal lands, providing oversight of the *Comisariado de Bienes Comunales*, and maintaining peace, harmony and respect among village inhabitants.

These bodies administer and oversee most civic and communal activities, services and infrastructure projects that take place within the localities where resident community members live and on the lands that the community has title to (their territory). Their offices are typically housed in a municipal palace or administrative building located in the village centre (Figure 2.1). Throughout this book, we use the generic term 'village authorities' to refer to these bodies. Each of the posts or positions of responsibility that comprise these bodies are called *cargos*, and the cargo system is explained in detail in the next section.

Communities also have committees or councils responsible for the maintenance of village churches or temples, and the organization of religious services, festivities, and other rites of passage. Likewise, most communities also have councils of elders, variably known as *consejos de ancianos, de principales, consultivos* or *caracterizados*, which the village authorities can consult with and seek advice from. They are often called upon when the community is trying to

Figure 2.1 Offices of the municipal and communal authorities, Zapotec community of San Juan Evangelista Analco, Oaxaca.

Source: photo credit: Jim Robson.

resolve a conflict or debating a particularly sensitive issue. Elder councils comprise senior community members who have gained the respect of their peers due to their communal service record.[3]

Institutions of collective work and communal service

Indigenous Oaxacans organize their collectives, get work done, and staff the above-mentioned administrative positions through three specific social institutions: the *cargo*, the *tequio*, and the *asamblea*. We look at each of these in turn.

Cargos

The 'traditional' or 'classic' cargo system is a structure made up of tasks, implemented through political mechanisms of organization, and designed to underpin the functioning, cohesion, and harmony of community life. Wolf (1955, 1957) characterized MesoAmerican peasant communities as closed corporate entities,[4] where collectivity was made possible through possession of a shared territory, and where community members expressed their allegiance (to serve the common good) through exercising rights and meeting service obligations. The cargo system provides the main mechanism by which members accomplish this – offering civil, communal, and religious service to their community. In doing so, the system helps to maintain the kind of social-hierarchical structure that allows for semi-autonomous political function.

Cargos are divided into two main categories of position: *topiles*, which constitute lower-level positions within the hierarchical system, and higher-level positions that belong to the municipal or communal authorities charged with overseeing the administration of community life. It is tradition in many places that cargos follow a ladder or *escalafon* system, by which community members only occupy an authority-level cargo once they have completed all topil-category cargo obligations.[5] Young adults traditionally begin at the bottom of the ladder and, pending satisfactory performance, gradually move up to perform other cargos such as community policeman, lieutenant, church singer, or sacristan, and then high-level administrative cargos such as Mayor, Alderman, Common Property Commissioner, and Municipal President.

In some regions of Oaxaca, such as the Mixteca, an additional form of communal service is seen in the practice of *mayordomías*, where a small number of community members are each year given the responsibility to organize and oversee their village's patron saint celebrations. These mayordomías fall into two classes of seniority – 'grandes or mayores' and 'chicas or menores' – with the latter normally awarded to individuals yet to fulfil all of their topil-level cargo responsibilities, and the former awarded to those who have completed at least one cargo within a village authority.

These cargos and mayordomias essentially serve as a checklist by which the collective can assess the performance (and thus status) of individual members through the course of their lives. The names and number of cargos will vary from community to community, but the structure and mechanism by which they are assigned and by which good performance is rewarded tends to be similar across localities and regions. Some religious cargos are for life, such as musicians, lay ministers, and choir singers. In all other areas of civic and communal duty, cargo positions are held for a set period of time – generally 12, 18, or 36 months. At the end of their term, outgoing incumbents are replaced by the candidates newly elected by the assembly. Traditionally, all cargos are unpaid. Some cargos constitute part-time positions, allowing incumbents to combine cargo duties with their normal daily work activities. Others, however, require a full-time commitment, meaning that for a one, two, or even three-year period, the cargo-holder will be unable to earn much money to help support their family.

Adapted over centuries of colonial and post-colonial governments, the cargo system provides a frame of political and moral reference by which community authority and power, community integrity, the practice of political autonomy, and the defence of territorial rights and borders are exercised. Allegiance to and participation in the system is driven by an underlying set of ideals, norms, and cultural mores (Cancian 1965; Carrasco 1961; Greenberg 1981; Medina 1995).

Tequio

As Bray (2010) notes, 'if these cargo functions were not onerous enough, there are also traditional community physical labour service obligations, called tequios'. The word 'tequio' derives from the Náhuatl term, *tequitl*, which means work or tribute. Along with cargos and mayordomías, the practice of tequio operationalizes and gives meaning to the ideals of collective work and communal service in Indigenous Oaxaca. It brings together village rights-holders to work collectively on community projects or infrastructure improvements that require the labour of large numbers of people. These jobs can take place in or around the village where people live (i.e. school renovations, laying of sewage lines, building and maintaining roads) or on the communal lands they share access to (i.e. tree planting, fighting forest fires, maintaining territorial borders). While its roots lie in pre-Hispanic Mexico, tequio changed during the colonial period from a strictly religious-based practice to something more secular that could meet the additional labour needs of civic and communal life. Communities will call upon their members to perform tequio on a daily or weekly or monthly basis, dependent upon the resources available and village needs. All able-bodied active *ciudadanos* and *comuneros* are expected to participate in these labour obligations and, over the course of a year, they can easily account for 40–50 days of work. Tequios are overseen by the municipal authorities, neighbourhood organizations, agrarian authorities, or other administrative bodies responsible for the project that collective labour is being used for.

Beyond the instrumental value of getting work completed, tequio provides an opportunity for village residents to spend time together and build relationships. In this way, they are valued as de facto mini-assemblies – an additional, informal space by which rights-holders can discuss and debate upcoming or pressing community issues.

The Asamblea

Collective work also takes place in the institution of the General Assembly – considered the maximum decision-making authority in Indigenous Oaxacan communities. The assembly constitutes the formal space that brings community members together to make important decisions that affect their lives as individuals and as a collective. It is here that members discuss, debate, consider, and decide between courses of action and to elect individuals from among their peers to perform cargos within areas of civic or communal governance, or to serve on the various committees by which other community projects and initiatives are carried out. This can include naming people to oversee the provision of village health and education services, administering community-based enterprises (i.e. ecotourism), organizing the community's annual patron saint festivities, maintaining the village church, and looking after the community's water supply. In most Indigenous communities in Oaxaca, two categories of assembly exist: the Asamblea General de Ciudadanos (Citizens Assembly), where community members come together to make decisions about life in or around the village where they live; and, the Asamblea General de Comuneros (Commoners Assembly), where common-property rights-holders meet to make decisions about the community's territory and natural resources. Both types of assembly are normally held three or four times a year, with extraordinary meetings called when the need arises.

Usos y Costumbres *as governance framework*

The institutions of the cargo, tequio, and assembly operate within a framework of customary governance known as *usos y costumbres* (uses and customs), which constitute a set of written and unwritten rules and general principles used by Indigenous communities and municipalities in Oaxaca[6] to organize their members and collective lives. Oaxaca's 570 municipalities account for over one-fifth of Mexico's total, and because so many of these municipalities are small (consisting of one or two communities), and so many function under the *usos y costumbres* system, an important (and highly valued) closeness and synergy has formed between civic and communal (territorial) governance in many rural areas (Robson 2010; Walker and Walker 2008).

The system is essentially a codification of the normative structures that have existed among Indigenous peoples in Oaxaca (and Mexico more widely) since pre-colonial times, but have evolved through the vagaries of centuries of hispanization and integration with mainstream Mexican society. In Oaxaca, *usos y costumbres* was formally recognized by the State as an 'internal, normative system' of local governance in the mid-1990s, which has subsequently afforded communities an important degree of autonomy by which to structure

Table 2.3 Election strategies in communities governed under *usos y costumbres*

Election strategy	Explanation
Raised hand	The members of the community raise their hands for the candidate or candidates they choose.
Blackboard	The names of the candidates are written on a blackboard. The members of the community general assembly make a mark indicating their preferred candidate.
By ovation	The names of the candidates are called out and those in favour of each candidate provide their ovation. The candidate with the loudest call of support is elected.
By platoon	Voters congregate behind their preferred candidate. The candidate with the largest team of supporters is elected.

Source: www.ieepco.org.mx.

participation in collective life. Incumbents of the aforementioned cargos are elected by their peers in accordance with local custom (Table 2.3), rather than through affiliation to a particular political party. Similarly, office-holders are accountable to the assemblies of community members rather than any outside entity, including state or federal government.

Such a system allows community memberships the freedom to devise and approve the norms and rules-in-use that govern many activities that take place locally. For example, while bound by Mexican agrarian and environmental law, most Indigenous Oaxacan communities maintain control over land use and resource harvesting through their own communal *estatutos* or written laws.[7] Such an autonomous system exhibits many of the characteristics of polycentric governance (Alcorn and Toledo 1998; Chapela 2005), with users able to experiment with rule combinations, apply local knowledge, obtain rapid feedback from their own policy changes, and learn from the experience of other parallel units. Because local officials are elected by resource users, communities can self-evaluate their actions, and community institutions are recognized by higher levels of government in Mexico, the system meets several of the criteria associated with successful commons management (see Agrawal 2001; Ostrom 1990).

The ideology of collective work and communal service

Political-social organization and governance among Oaxacan Indigenous communities is embedded in the communalist ideology of 'comunalidad' (Martínez Luna 2010: 110). Comunalidad is not a theoretical category but rather an ideal that inhabits and inspires the everyday practice of community life in Oaxaca (Robson *et al.* 2018). In this way, it becomes an important aid to help our understanding of how and why people act the way they do in these places (Martínez Luna 2010: 143), including their decision-making in response to change.

Comunalidad is expressed through the act of being communal, which in turn creates the conditions by which community belonging and identity are achieved (Díaz Gómez 2003). As such, it can only be understood through practice, through participation in the social institutions of the asamblea, the fiesta, cargo, and tequio, and through being active on the land as customary territory (Díaz Flores 2001; Martínez Luna 2010). Through participating in communal govern-ance and collective work, citizens remain active and can access the rights of community membership: to cultivate the land, propose motions and vote in the asamblea, or access resources from the communal territory (Kraemer Bayer 2003: 40). Participation in these institutions also allows village political struc-tures to develop horizontally, and for new generations to be 'educated' in com-munity life. As community members move from childhood to adolescence and then onto adulthood, they learn to live with each other in the shared space of the communal territory. This act of living as a collective is celebrated each year in the *fiesta* and through the ideals of *convivencia*, exchange, and reciprocity.

Cohen (2004a, 2004b) believes that it is allegiance to comunalidad that has allowed so many communities in Indigenous Oaxaca to successfully maintain a sense of independence and uniqueness that belies their involvement in global markets and transnational processes. This, he argues, points to the strength of *usos y costumbres*, and the underlying institutions of collective work and com-munal service. While the impact of (outside) political agents and global/ regional trade networks, among other sources of influence and change, have impacted and shaped the conformation of such communitarian relations, the cargo system has shown remarkable resilience to remain a central component of life in rural Indigenous Oaxaca in contemporary times (Cohen 2004b; Robson *et al.* 2018).

Yet, a social phenomenon such as migration maintains the potential to alter, possibly transform, such structures and underlying ideologies, especially when pressures and stresses accumulate over extended periods of time and collective resources are slowly depleted. A central concern among Oaxacan communities is whether the institutions of the cargo, tequio, and asamblea – which enable their collective action problems to be resolved – can adapt to a reduced labour pool as people leave villages to live elsewhere.[8] Physical presence in the home village has not only been seen as wholly necessary for participation in these institutions, but also underpins long-standing traditions of oral history, lan-guage, and 'knowing the land'. In addition, the experience of migration can affect new meanings among community members – who are now tasked to navigate across Indigenous and non-Indigenous value systems – and potentially exacerbate tensions between collective work and communal service obligations, on the one hand, and the needs and self-interest of a broad and diversifying membership, on the other (see Garibay 2007; Merino Pérez 2004).

At the same time, while shrinking or stagnating resident populations may challenge community capacities to strike a balance between the maintenance and reinvention of traditions, these are arrangements that have long stood the test of time. As noted, they have persisted while modifying over generations, and should be expected to evolve further in response to new conditions and challenges. In addition, it is by no means inevitable that people will break ties with their communities of origin if and when they choose to live elsewhere. As we will see in Chapter 3, migration has the power to support, even subsidize, rather than dismantle traditional governance systems.

Such questions lay at the heart of the ethnographic research that we conducted in Oaxaca, Mexico, and the US, to investigate if and how communities adapt economically, politically, and territorially so as to incorporate migration into the fabric of their daily lives and organizational structures, and to allow community cohesion and relevance to be maintained.

Notes

1 The first evidence of human presence in Oaxaca dates to 10,000 BC. Barabas *et al.* (2003) describe how small family bands left behind a nomadic hunter-gatherer existence to form the first permanent settlements around 1500 BC – to coincide with success in domesticating maize, bean and other cultivars.

2 Communities staff two agrarian authorities that are responsible for the administration of local common property resources (land, trees, water) – the *Comisariado de Bienes Comunales* (Common Property Commissioner) and *Consejo de Vigilancia* (Surveillance or Oversight Council). However, governance authority lies with the *Asamblea General de Comuneros* (General Assembly of Commoners), where local comuneros (commoners, or common property rights-holders) meet to take decisions collectively.

3 For example, in one of the communities where we have worked, Santiago Comaltepec, the 'consejo de ancianos' is comprised of older *comuneros* who have occupied important positions within the community and completed their communal obligations or 'service' with distinction. Members have to: (i) be born in the community; (ii) be honest; (iii) complete at least six years of service (*cargos*); and (iv) attend 90 per cent or more of communal assemblies during their years of active service.

4 Central to this idea of community as closed corporation was its collective form of decision-making – 'closed' in the sense that the resources it depended upon, such as land, were available exclusively to its members, with access denied to those who were not part of the community.

5 That's not to say that all the men who have financed village fiestas or have occupied a majority of cargos can automatically assume the most important positions in the village, such as Municipal President, Mayor, or Common Property Commissioner. Ideally, only those that have performed their service obligations with distinction can expect to be elected to the highest-level cargos by their peers.

6 In 2017, the Instituto Estatal Electoral y de Participación Ciudadana de Oaxaca (IEEPCO) recorded that 417 of 570 municipalities in Oaxaca were governed in accordance with *usos y costumbres*, with the remaining 153 (55 of which are considered Indigenous) electing authorities through a political party system. The 417 municipalities governed under *usos y costumbres* account for 1,397,807 or 37 per cent of Oaxaca's population.

7 *Estatutos* (Statutes) regulate the socioeconomic and environmental activities within the community, including use of and access to territorial resources, in both general and specific terms.

8 This is the opposite of Cancian's (1965) work in Chiapas, which documented the dilemma associated with too many people to choose from to serve in the *cargo* system.

References

Agrawal, A. 2001. Common property institutions and sustainable governance of resources. *World Development*, 29(10): 1649–1672.

Alcorn, J. and V. Toledo. 1998. Resilient resource management in Mexico's forest ecosystems: the contribution of property rights. In: Berkes, F. and C. Folke (eds), *Linking Social and Ecological Systems: Management Practices and Social Mechanisms for Building Resilience*. Cambridge, UK: Cambridge University Press.

Bailón Corres, J. 1999. *Pueblos indios, élites y territorio*. Mexico City, Mexico: El Colegio de México.

Barabas, A.M., M.A. Bartolomé, and B. Maldonado (eds). 2003. *Los pueblos indígenas de Oaxaca: Atlas etnográfico*. CONACULTA/INAH.

Boege, E. 2008. *El patrimonio biocultural de los pueblos indígenas de México: hacia la conservación in situ de la biodiversidad y agrodiversidad en los territorios indígenas*. Instituto Nacional de Antropología e Historia (INAH)/Comisión Nacional para el Desarrollo de los Pueblos Indígenas (CDI). Mexico City: Mexico.

Bray, D. 2010. The community as entrepreneurial firm: common property capitalism in Mexican forest communities creates jobs, competes in global markets, and conserves biodiversity. *Americas Quarterly*, February 15, 2010.

Cancian, F. 1965. *Economics and Prestige in a Maya Community: The Religious Cargo System in Zinacantan*. San Francisco: Stanford University Press.

Carrasco, P. 1961. The civil–religious hierarchy in mesoAmerican communities: pre-Spanish background and colonial development. *American Anthropologist*, 63(1961): 486–497.

Chapela, F. 2005. Indigenous community forest management in the Sierra Juarez, Oaxaca. In: Barton Bray, D., L. Merino Perez and D. Barry (eds), *The Community Forests of Mexico: Managing for Sustainable Landscapes*. Austin, TX: University of Texas Press.

Cohen, J.H. 2004a. *The Culture of Migration in Southern Mexico*. Austin, TX: University of Texas Press, 2004.

Cohen, J.H. 2004b. Community, economy and social change in Oaxaca, Mexico: rural life and cooperative logic in the global economy. In: Otero, G. (ed.), *Mexico in Transition: Neoliberal Globalism, the State and Civil Society*. London: Zed CONABIO-CONANP-TNC-PRONATURA-FCF/UANL. 2007. *Análisis de vacíos y omisiones en conservación de la biodiversidad terrestre de México: espacios y especies*. Comisión Nacional para el Conocimiento y Uso de la Biodiversidad, Comisión Nacional de Áreas Naturales Protegidas, The Nature Conservancy-Programa México, Pronatura, AC, Facultad de Ciencias Forestales de la Universidad Autónoma de Nuevo León, México. Mexico City, Mexico.

CONAPO. 2010. Índices de marginación por entidad federativa y municipio, 2010. Accessed April 2, 2018 at: www.conapo.gob.mx/es/CONAPO/Indices_de_Marginacion_2010_por_entidad_federativa_y_muncipio.

CONEVAL. 2016. Consejo Nacional de Evaluación de la Política de Desarrollo Social. Accessed August 12, 2017 at: www.coneval.org.mx/coordinacion/entidades/Oaxaca/Paginas/Pobreza-2016.aspx.

Cué, G. 2011. *Plan estatal de desarrollo 2011–2016*. Oaxaca de Juárez, Oaxaca: Gobierno del Estado de Oaxaca.

Díaz Flores, F. 2001. Comunidad y comunalidad. *La Jornada Semanal* 314: March 12, 2001.

Díaz Gómez, F. 2003. Comunidad y comunalidad. In: Rendón Monzón, J.J. (ed.), *La Comunalidad*, pp. 59–69. Oaxaca: Consejo Nacional para la Cultura y las Artes, Fondo Editorial Tierra Adentro.

García-Mendoza, A.J., M. De Jesús Ordóñez and M. Briones-Salas (eds). 2004. *Biodiversidad de Oaxaca.* Mexico City, Mexico: Instituto de Biología de la UNAM, Fondo Oaxaqueño para la Conservación de la Naturaleza, and the World Wildlife Fund.

Garibay, C. 2007. *El dilema corporativo del comunalismo forestal.* CIESAS No. 23.

González, R.J., 2001. *Zapotec Science: Farming and Food in the Northern Sierra of Oaxaca.* Austin, TX: University of Texas Press.

Greenberg, J.B. 1981. Religión y economía de los chatinos. Mexico City, Mexico: Instituto Nacional Indigenista.

Hunn, E.S. 2008. *A Zapotec Natural History.* Tucson, AZ: University of Arizona Press.

INEGI. 2009. *Anuario Estadístico, 2009.* Accessed July 14, 2017 at: http://internet.contenidos.inegi.org.mx/contenidos/productos/prod_serv/contenidos/espanol/bvinegi/productos/historicos/2104/702825201111-1/702825201111-1_1.pdf.

INEGI. 2010. *Censo general de población y vivienda, 2010.* Accessed July 11, 2015 at: www3.inegi.org.mx//sistemas/iterm5000/.

INEGI. 2015. *Principales resultados de la Encuesta Intercensal 2015: Oaxaca.* Aguascalientes, Mexico: Instituto Nacional de Estadística y Geografía (INEGI).

INEGI. 2016. *Actualización del marco censal agropecuario.* Accessed October 30, 2017 at: www.inegi.org.mx/est/contenidos/proyectos/agro/default.aspx.

INEGI 2017. *Catálogo Único de Claves de Áreas Geoestadísticas Estatales, Municipales y Localidades.* Accessed May 13, 2017 at: www.inegi.org.mx/geo/contenidos/geoestadistica/CatalogoClaves.aspx.

Kraemer Bayer, G. 2003. *Autonomía indígena región Mixe, relaciones de poder y cultura política.* Mexico City, Mexico: Universidad Autónoma de Chapingo, Plaza y Valdés.

Martin, G.J. 1993. Ecological classification amongst the Chinantec and Mixe of Oaxaca, Mexico. *Etnoecologia,* 1: 17–33.

Martínez Luna, J. 2010. *Eso que llaman comunalidad.* Oaxaca de Juárez, Oaxaca: Colección Diálogos. Pueblos originarios de Oaxaca; Serie; Veredas.

Módulo de Condiciones Socioeconómicas de la ENIGH (MCS-ENIGH). 2010. Condiciones Socioeconómicas-Oaxaca-2010. Aguascalientes, Mexico: Instituto Nacional de Estadística y Geografía (INEGI). Accessed March 15, 2017 at: www.beta.inegi.org.mx/proyectos/enchogares/modulos/mcs/2010/default.html

Módulo de Condiciones Socioeconómicas de la ENIGH (MCS-ENIGH). 2012. Condiciones Socioeconómicas-Oaxaca-2010. Aguascalientes, Mexico: Instituto Nacional de Estadística y Geografía (INEGI). Accessed March 15, 2017 at: www.beta.inegi.org.mx/proyectos/enchogares/modulos/mcs/2012/default.html

Módulo de Condiciones Socioeconómicas de la ENIGH (MCS-ENIGH). 2014. Condiciones Socioeconómicas-Oaxaca-2010. Aguascalientes, Mexico: Instituto Nacional de Estadística y Geografía (INEGI). Accessed March 15, 2017 at: www.beta.inegi.org.mx/proyectos/enchogares/modulos/mcs/2014/default.html

Medina, A. 1995. Los sistemas de cargos en la Cuenca de México: una primera aproximación a su trasfondo histórico. *Alteridades* 9(1995): 7–23.

Merino Pérez, L. 2004. *Conservación o deterioro.* Mexico City: Instituto Nacional de Ecología.

Murat, A. 2017. *Plan estatal de desarrollo 2016–2022.* Oaxaca de Juárez, Oaxaca: Gobierno del Estado de Oaxaca, 2017.

Ordóñez, M. de J. and P. Rodríguez. 2008. Oaxaca, el estado con mayor diversidad biológica y cultural de México, y sus productores rurales. *Ciencias*, 91(Mayo 2008): 55–64.

Ostrom, E. 1990. *Governing the Commons: The Evolution of Institutions for Collective Action*. Cambridge, UK: Cambridge University Press.

Ramos Pioquinto, D. 1988. *Migración y sistema de cargos en la reproducción social de la comunidad campesino-indígena de Zoogocho, Oaxaca, de 1940 a 1987*. Oaxaca de Juárez: Universidad Autónoma Benito Juárez de Oaxaca.

Robson, J.P. 2007. Local approaches to biodiversity conservation: lessons from Oaxaca, southern Mexico. *International Journal of Sustainable Development*, 10: 267–286.

Robson, J.P. 2010. *The Impact of Rural–Urban Migration on Forest Commons in Oaxaca, Mexico*. Unpublished PhD Thesis, University of Manitoba. Canada.

Robson, J.P., D.J. Klooster, H. Worthen, and J. Hernández-Díaz. 2018. Migration and agrarian transformation in Indigenous Mexico. *Journal of Agrarian Change*, 18(2): 299–323.

SERBO. 2010. SERBO (The Society for the Study of Biotic Resources of Oaxaca). Accessed April 22, 2010 at: http://serboax.org/oaxaca/biodiversidad-de-oaxaca/.

Walker, D.M. and Walker, M.A. 2008. Power, identity and the production of buffer villages in 'the second most remote region in all of Mexico'. *Antipode*, 40(1): 155–177.

Wolf, E. 1955. Types of Latin American peasantry: A preliminary discussion. *American Anthropologist* 57(3): 452–471.

Wolf, E.R. 1957. Closed corporate communities in Mesoamerica and Java, *Southwestern Journal of Anthropology*, 13(1): 1–18.

3 Migration dynamics and migrant organizing in rural Oaxaca

Jorge Hernández-Díaz and James P. Robson

Introduction

> Los Angeles is where most of the work is, and where most of our people leave to ... my husband went there because there is no money here ... it is not enough [to live on] and so he left to earn a better wage ... my eldest daughter also went, got married over there and now lives with her family in Texas, while my other two daughters are in Los Angeles. They left to work and experience a new way of life. He [the husband] sends me about US$300 a month but my daughters don't send money ... they have their own families to support and nothing spare to send us. They tell me that life is more difficult over there, [that] they have to pay for everything and there are a lot of expenses ... here it is easier because we have our own home. My daughters cannot visit because they do not have papers and they cannot risk leaving their children.
>
> (Female resident, La Esperanza (Santiago Comaltepec), 2008)

In a single quote, this member of the Chinantec community of Santiago Comaltepec encapsulates several of the dynamics that characterize migration and the migratory experience in Indigenous Oaxaca: the importance of social networks; the varied push and pull factors that encourage people to leave their villages; the role of remittances in household economies; life in the US for undocumented workers; and, the impact of out-migration on family unity. Restricted employment opportunities and low wages have encouraged hundreds of thousands of Oaxacans to migrate to other parts of Mexico and the US in recent decades (Bezaury 2007), turning Oaxaca into a net exporter of migrant labour (INEGI 2009). For 2010, Oaxaca was reported as having 'elevated out-migration' for internal migration flows (to other parts of Mexico) and was ranked tenth (of 31 Mexican states) for US-bound migration intensities, with a grading of 'high' (CONAPO 2010).

This chapter provides a summary of historical and contemporary migration flows from rural Oaxaca to multiple destinations in Mexico and the US. We focus on migration dynamics in the two regions – Sierra Norte and Mixteca (Figure 3.1) – where the research for this book was conducted. Combined, these

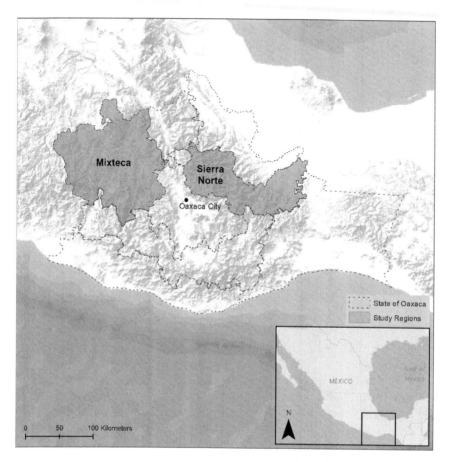

Figure 3.1 Location of the Sierra Norte and Mixteca regions, Oaxaca.

Source: map produced by Lisa Benvenuti, Center for Spatial Studies – University of Redlands.

two regions account for many of the dynamics that characterize the story of migration from rural Oaxaca more broadly.

We then introduce the idea of the TransBorder Corporate Community, which conceptualizes how community life is stretched across state and national borders as migrants self-organize to establish organizations and formal linkages back to their places of origin, and enable them, despite physical absence, to maintain agency in village development and governance.

The chapter thus provides essential context to a number of the themes discussed in greater detail in our subsequent case study and discussion chapters.

Evolving migration histories and dynamics

Migration from the Sierra Norte

Oaxaca's Sierra Norte (northern highlands) region covers an area of $9347\,km^2$, or 9.8 per cent of state territory. This is a rugged, highland region that has been identified as a priority area for biodiversity conservation at the national level (CONABIO-CONANP 2007).

Five Indigenous groups – Zapotecos, Chinantecos, Mixes, Mazatecos, and Cuicatecos – have lived in the Sierra Norte since pre-Hispanic times. Administratively, the region is divided into 68 municipalities, 74 officially registered communal territories (agrarian communities) and 35 ejido land-holdings, and three districts (Villa Alta, Mixe, and Ixtlan de Juarez) (Table 3.1). Despite variation among these communities and sub-regions, communitarian ideals continue to dominate and permeate village political structures (Díaz Gómez 2003; Martínez 2013), with most municipalities and communities governed under the *usos y costumbres* system (see Chapter 2).

While some Sierra Norte communities continue to maintain village economies based on subsistence agriculture and domestic forestry, many are in transition with an increasing dependence on the market economy, the service industry, commercial resource extraction, and migrant remittances (Martínez Romero 2005; Robson 2010). As such, they resemble what Kearney (1996) described as 'post-peasant communities' – organizations intermeshed with traditional arrangements that combine different sources of income with complex forms of reproduction in an interconnected, globalized world (Schuren 2003; Wolf 1982). The region has seen thousands of people join migration streams to Oaxaca City, other parts of Mexico, and the US over the past 60–70 years.

Migration streams and changing dynamics

During the first half of the twentieth century, migration from the region was largely sporadic, and modest in intensity. This included the temporary migration of adult males from left-leaning communities during the Mexican Revolution (1910–1917), and the seasonal migration (during the 1930s, 1940s, and

Table 3.1 Number of agrarian communities and *ejidos* in the Sierra Norte

District	No. of ejidos	No. of agrarian communities
Ixtlán	3	33
Villa Alta	0	17
Mixe	32	24
Total	**35**	**74**

Sources: Secretaria de Desarrollo Agrario, Territorial y Urbano (SEDATU) and the Registro Agrario Nacional (RAN) (2018).

1950s) of men and women to work in the coffee groves, sugarcane plantations, and pineapple plantations of lowland Oaxaca and Veracruz (before returning to their villages to attend to harvests and ceremonial life) (Ludy Molina 1991; Maldonado Alvarado 2011). For most of this period, however, permanent forms of migration were rare, with few local people seeing a need to leave their lands and villages to obtain the food and other resources required for sustenance (Maldonado Alvarado 2011).

In the 1940s, young people from a number of Zapotec communities in the region began to leave for growing urban centres – principally Oaxaca City and Mexico City – to work in the burgeoning service sector. In Mexico City, many Zapotec girls found work as maids and domestic servants in middle- to upper-class households (Ramos Pioquinto 1988: 50–51). By the end of the 1950s, migration from Indigenous Oaxaca to Oaxaca City and Mexico City (and its surrounding conurbation) had become well established, driven in part by rising rural populations, greater investment in urban areas, and opportunities for higher education (Ludy Molina 1991). Zapotecs of the Sierra Norte were an important part of this stream, and as migrant networks consolidated,[1] it became easier for others to leave for work or schooling.[2,3] Migrants often settled in the same neighbourhoods in destination centres, leading to the establishment of migrant community enclaves. In Mexico City, Indigenous migrants from Oaxaca, including the Sierra Norte, settled in relatively large numbers in the 1950s through 1970s on the edges of the capital (Kuroda 1994: 501). Here, they would congregate and socialize and, in some cases, establish organizations or clubs of migrants.

An important shift in migration dynamics began to take place in the late 1960s and early 1970s, when internal migration began to lose prominence to new migration streams to the US. In Mexico, US-bound migration had begun soon after the Second World War, when demand for agricultural labour attracted large numbers of workers from Mexico to participate in the so-called *Bracero* Program, which ran for 20 years from 1944 to 1964.[4] While the vast majority of these migrants returned to their home villages in Oaxaca, the experience proved instructive. When the *Bracero* Program ended, Indigenous Oaxacans began to travel to the US, not as legal farm workers but as undocumented wage labour migrants. Some looked for opportunities in the agricultural heartlands of central and southern California, but many headed to growing urban conurbations, notably Los Angeles.

From the Sierra Norte, Zapotecs were the first to join these migrant streams, followed some time later by Chinantec and Mixe migrants. While these streams did not establish themselves until the late-1970s and into the 1980s, flows intensified steadily over time. Indeed, by the mid-1980s, the US had overtaken Mexico City as the destination of choice for many would-be migrants. Some who had left for Oaxaca City, Mexico City, and northern Mexico in the 1960s and 1970s moved onto the US once networks there were established. For much of this period, crossing the Mexican–US border was relatively straightforward:

[...] my sister arrived because we had a cousin in Mexico who took people across the border at that time, and he got in contact with her and said 'listen, the bosses of this lady need four workers', and for that reason by brother came, my sister and some other people. The northern towns of Sonora and Chihuahua were established but us southerners had yet to arrive ... those from Guerrero, Chiapas, Oaxaca ... we still didn't know about that. But it was really easy [to cross into the US] ... I remember that I arrived on the Saturday to Tijuana and they said to me 'we're going to have some tacos and then we go'. Well we went to get some dinner, then joined the line, and by 9pm we were there [in California], we got in just like that, there was no control, no restrictions at the border.

(Ezequiel, migrant from Yatzachi el Bajo, Los Angeles, 2016)

The intensification of US-bound streams was tied to economic and policy changes taking place in both Mexico and the US at the time. The Mexican economy underwent macro-structural realignment in the early 1980s, leading to the devaluation of the peso in 1982. The financial crisis and economic recession that ensued prompted many tens of thousands to head north, attracted by increased US demand for wage labourers (Kearney 1996; Zabin 1992) and a stark differential in earning potentials.[5] Economic opportunities in rural Mexico at this time were very limited, with most villagers in the Sierra Norte still heavily dependent on subsistence activities (Table 3.2).

Migrants crossed into California, Arizona, and Texas throughout the late 1980s and into the 1990s (Fox 2004; Fox and Besserer 2004). Many settled in these southern states, especially in and around Los Angeles, although some

Table 3.2 Primary economic activities among our study communities in 1980

Municipality	Economically active population	Population primarily involved in agriculture, livestock, hunting
Tezoatlán de Segura y Luna	4753	2482
Santa María Yavesía	386	127
San Pablo Macuiltianguis	736	522
San Juan Evangelista Analco	261	168
Santiago Comaltepec	965	465
San Juan Quiotepec	1189	720
San Bartolomé Zoogocho	345	221
Santiago Zoochila	198	118
Santa Ana del Valle	876	205
San Baltazar Yatzachi el Bajo	659	389
Santa María Yalina	215	98
San Felipe Usila	3909	2435
San Martín Itunyoso	856	388
Coatecas Altas	1843	1312

Source: INEGI (1980).

headed up the Pacific Coast into Oregon and Washington States (Stephen 2002). Other streams were established that took migrants to large urban centres – notably New York and Chicago – in the north (Smith 2006). Most migrants during this period were men, either single or with dependents back in Mexico and Oaxaca.

A significant moment arrived in 1986, when the US Federal Government introduced the Immigration Reform and Control Act (IRCA)[6] to try to limit further illegal immigration. As part of the Act, an 'amnesty' (the opportunity to apply for legal resident status) was offered to undocumented migrants who had arrived prior to 1982 and had evidence that they had been working during the intervening period. Almost three million migrants applied for, and secured, their papers this way (Runsten and Kearney 1994: 7), which in turn gave them the right to bring family members in Mexico to join them. Subsequently, the migrant population shifted from being predominantly adult males, to include large numbers of women and children.

Although IRCA was designed to close the door to further undocumented migration, the inability of the US to secure its extensive southern border meant that many thousands of migrants continued to make the journey every year throughout the 1990s and into the 2000s. For much of this time, crossing the border was still relatively easy and, while expensive, not prohibitively so. This allowed circular migration dynamics to continue – whereby migrants would spend time in the US, return to Oaxaca for a period, and then head north again when savings ran low. The need for cash had become more pro-nounced following signing of the North American Free Trade Agreement (NAFTA) in 1994, which had further disadvantaged struggling farmers in southern Mexico who now competed with subsidized US corn and other agri-cultural imports (Mann 2004).

US-bound migration from the Sierra Norte reached its peak in the late 1990s and early 2000s, with a sharp decline setting in from the mid-2000s onwards. This change had been driven by increased enforcement at the US–Mexican border, which has made crossings both prohibitively expensive and more pre-carious (Massey, Durand, and Pren 2015). It was also influenced by the global economic recession of 2008–2009, which hit the US hard – reducing demand for wage labour, especially in the sectors (i.e. construction, hospitality) where undocumented migrants often worked. This 'closing' off of the US–Mexican border not only halted the plans of would-be migrants in Mexico, but also put a stop to circular migration dynamics and effectively turned migration into a 'one-way trip' (after Fox 2007) for millions of undocumented Mexicans living north of the border.

As of 2015, an estimated 1,203,680 Oaxacans were living in the US (López 2016). A number that roughly equates to 40 per cent of Oaxaca's state popula-tion. While Oaxacans are found living across the US, the majority are in Cali-fornia, with smaller populations in Texas, New York, Arizona, Colorado, Illinois, and Oregon (Alarcón Acosta et al. 2014). Migrants in the US represent all 16 of Oaxaca's Indigenous groups, and include large numbers of Zapotecs and

Chinantecs from the Sierra Norte, with smaller populations of Mixe. Fox and Rivera-Salgado (2004: 10) reported as many as 50,000 to 60,000 Zapotecs (from Oaxaca's Valles Centrales and Sierra Norte regions) living in and around downtown Los Angeles.

Migrations from the Mixteca

The Mixteca comprises 155 municipalities, distributed across three subregions – the Mixteca Alta, Mixteca Baja, and Mixteca de la Costa. A total of 465,991 people were resident in the Mixteca in 2010, with just over a third (160,335) speaking an Indigenous language (CIEDD 2012). The region is home to Indigenous Mixtecos, Triquis, Chochos, Ixcatecos, Amuzgos, Popolocas, and Nahuas, as well as communities of Afro descent (Romero Frizzi 1996; Spores 1984). While rich in cultural heritage, the region's natural resource base is limited when compared with the heavily forested Sierra Norte. Seasonal migration has long been a component of local livelihood strategies – a response to soil degradation, population pressure on a limited resource base, unfavourable climatic conditions (particularly the impact of periodic and severe droughts), and limited local wage labour opportunities (Aguilar Medina 1980; De La Peña 1950; Sanders 1975).

Migration streams and changing dynamics

During the first half of the twentieth century, many Mixtecos left for work in Tapachula, Chiapas, as well as in the sugarcane fields of Veracruz. More permanent forms of migration from the Mixteca took hold in the 1940s and 1950s (Butterworth 1975; De La Peña 1950; Sanders 1975) as local people were recruited to meet growing labour demands in Mexico City and Puebla (López and Runsten 2004: 284), and support a rapidly growing agro-industry in northwestern Mexico (Nagengast and Kearney 1990). While the 1960s saw Mixtecos leave for Puebla and Mexico City, the 1970s saw new streams established to Sonora, Sinaloa, and Baja California, where Mixtecos began to find work in a booming agro-industrial sector (Velasco 1998).

　While most early migrants were men looking for work to sustain their families in Oaxaca, the 1980s witnessed the movement of families to growing enclaves in Mexico's north (Mines, Nichols, and Runsten 2010; Velasco 2002). In the Culiacán, Navolato and El Carrizo valleys of Sinaloa, 60,000 hectares of land were converted for horticulture in the 1990s, with each hectare requiring an average of four migrant workers. As many as 240,000 workers would arrive each year, with over one-fifth (40,000–50,000) from Oaxaca, and most of these Mixtecos. In Baja California, migrants congregated in the San Quintín Valley (Garduño, García, and Morán 1989: 52) where 10,000 hectares of agricultural land employed close to 30,000 people, 70 per cent of whom were Mixtecos (Guzmán and Lewin 1999: 244). In Baja California Sur, the migrant population numbered 20,000 to 25,000. Around one-third were Oaxacans, again with Mixtecos prominent (PIRCS 1998: 22). While many were temporary or circular migrants, returning annually to their places of origin, a significant minority remained permanently in northern Mexico to establish Mixteco settlements in the region (Hernández-Díaz 2001).

For much of this period (1960s–1980s), migration from the Mixteca to the US was sporadic at best, although sojourns into northern Mexico were important for establishing a base and migratory experience from which US-bound migration streams would later become possible (O'Connor 2016: 93). When agriculture began to be heavily promoted in central California, growers and investors cast their eyes towards the ready-made, trained workforce in northwestern Mexico, who were subsequently recruited to make the trip north (Velasco 2002; Zabin 1997).

By the late 1980s, Mixteco migration dynamics had come to incorporate two major streams: one to northwestern Mexico and one to the Western US, notably California, where an estimated 45,000–55,000 Mixtecos established themselves (Pinzón 2007: 185). This enclave was consolidated further following the IRCA 'amnesty' of 1986. Farm workers were generally more able to provide proof of employment than those who had settled in US cities (Fox and Rivera-Salgado 2004). For Mixtecos living and working in the agricultural heartland of central California, IRCA was transformative:

> Well, the amnesty began in 85 but given the process, it really began to be implemented in 87 and that was when several [of us] qualified and could begin to bring in our families ... we're talking 1988, 1989, 1990 ... those that had been [in the US] for a certain number of years [could apply for legal status] and then you could bring the family ... it's really then that you started to see this influx of whole families.
>
> (Antonio, Migrant from Santa Maria Tindu, in Madera, California, 2015)

> The amnesty of 87 had a huge impact, people started to bring their whole families over ... that's when they abandoned their lands [back home], the house was left empty, only the grandparents stayed and then there came a moment when they passed away and the land and the houses were completely abandoned.
>
> (Miguel, San Martin Itunyoso, 2015)

While the most sizeable Mixtec migrant communities established themselves in central California, additional populations of Mixtecos settled in San Diego County – across from popular border crossings in the Tijuana area (Runsten and Kearney, 2004: 54) – as well as northern California, Oregon, and Washington state (París 2003: 65).

Summary

Migration has become a defining feature of family and community life in rural Oaxaca (Alvarado Juárez 2008; Cohen 2004; Velasco 2002), and a driver of demographic, sociocultural, and economic change (Bustamante *et al.*, 1995). For two of Oaxaca's most prominent migrant-sending regions – the Mixteca and the Sierra Norte – four migration streams stand out: to the Metropolitan Zone of Mexico City; to the expanding agricultural zones of northern Mexico (Sinaloa, Baja California and Sonora); to growing urban conurbations in the US (Los Angeles, Chicago, New York); and, to agricultural producing zones in California. While the Mixteca is known for sending temporary and permanent agricultural workers to northern Mexico and the US (Cohen 2004; Stephen 2007; Zabin *et al.* 1993), migration from the Sierra Norte is more associated with streams to large urban centres in the two countries – streams established first by highland Zapotecs, then later joined by Chinantecos and Mixes (Ramos Pioquinto 1992).

For both regions, migration has ebbed and flowed over time in response to macro-economic and political changes. Internal migration streams lost prominence in the 1970s and 1980s, with US wage labour migration taking over. After two decades of intense flows, US-bound streams have since experienced sharp declines.

The emergence of translocal migrant communities

Migration from Oaxaca has led to the creation of important migrant enclaves in Oaxaca City, Mexico City, Northwest Mexico, and US destination centres. Among the most notable aspects of Indigenous migration dynamics in Oaxaca is the degree to which migrants integrate into new social contexts while maintaining, even recreating, ties with their communities of origin. Consequently, migrant-sending communities in Oaxaca have come to inhabit a transterritorial, socio-political space, which can subsequently redefine the parameters of community identity and belonging, as well as civic and communal governance and political participation. Zapotecs, Mixtecos, and Chinantecos have been among the most successful of Oaxaca's Indigenous migrants in establishing strong, cohesive communities in other places, gaining a great deal of scholarly attention in the process (Kearney 1995, 2000; Kearney and Besserer 2004; Ramos Pioquinto 1988; Stephen 2007; Schütze 2014; Smith 2006).

As Levitt (2004) notes, 'the assumption that people will live their lives in one place, according to one set of national and cultural norms, in countries with impermeable national borders, no longer holds true'. In the 1990s, the term 'transnationalism' became widely used in the social sciences to describe 'the processes by which immigrants forge and sustain multi-stranded social relations that link together their societies of origin and settlement' (Basch, Glick Schiller, and Szanton-Blanc 1994: 7). In the Mexican context, commentators have since debated how to conceptualize trans-migrant activity, where communities are connected to each other through ties of kinship, *compradazgo*, and trans-border forms of cooperation such as hometown associations. Recently, increased emphasis has been placed on the concept of *translocalism*, rather than 'transborder' or 'transnational', to reflect how both international and internal (within-country) dynamics shape many communities' migratory experiences (Cohen 2013; Greiner and Sakdapolrak 2013). Writing about the Oaxacan experience, Stephen (2007: 65) has defined translocal as the 'movement of place-specific culture, institutions, people, knowledge, and resources within several local sites and across borders – national and otherwise'.

While the idea of transnationalism or translocalism can suggest a more or less permanent state of being between two or more locations, the reality tends to be more fluid, so that

> some people may spend a good part of their lives engaging in this state of being, others may live for longer periods of time in one place or another, and others still may leave their home communities only one time or never ... [but] all of the people are living within a transnational social field.
>
> (Stephen 2007: 21)

As Levitt (2001, 2004) notes, there are times when migrants are more focused on their communities of origin, and times when they are more involved in their places of reception. In this way, migrants climb two different social ladders, moving up, remaining steady, or experiencing downward mobility, in various combinations, with respect to both sites (Stephen 2007).

Yet the regular activities of a few can still combine with those who participate periodically to potentially transform the economy, culture, and everyday life of sending communities and regions. Through the establishment of home-town associations and other types of migrant organization, migrants have constructed social fields that cross geographic, cultural and political borders, and allow the translocal (or transnational or transborder) community to have an effective impact on specific issues in places of origin, bypassing the state or national dimension (Ostergaard-Nielsen 2003; Sassen 1991). In this way, migrants become much more than workers in a global division of labour (for capitalist production). Rather, they may function as significant political and social actors in both the place where they reside and the place where they come from.

Traditions of migrant organizing

In rural Oaxaca, 'community' is often conceptualized as a collection of extended families, living in a specific place or territory, that are connected through kinship, the act of being neighbours, shared social values and cultural norms, and a common vision of the world that allows for such values and norms to be accepted (Hernández-Díaz 2013). Scholars have used such ideas to identify and explain new configurations of collectivity within the emergent transnational or translocal territorial space, utilizing terms such as 'transnational corporate community' (Kearney 1995; Smith 2003), 'transnational social fields or spaces' (Faist 2005; Glick-Schiller *et al.* 1992; Levitt and Glick Schiller 2004), 'transnational communities' (Besserer 1999; Kearney 1995), and 'transnational governance'

(Kearney and Besserer 2004). For the late Michael Kearney, such configurations function as de-territorialized entities that serve to extend the reach of the community corporation beyond municipal or territorial borders, to encapsulate the places where community members reside and remain active.

Within such spaces or fields, community processes become predicated upon the establishment of reciprocal relations connecting migrants and villagers. As migrants form enclaves in destination centres, they establish social and economic ties with their *paisanos* (countrymen and women) that can enhance senses of communal belonging and identity (Bacon 2006; Kearney 1995; Smith 2006). Velasco Ortiz (2005: 13) saw these ties as being instrumental in helping Oaxacan collectives to maintain themselves in a time of globalized change – creating the forms of socio-political organization that could knit together a potentially disparate community membership (Aguilar Orea 2012: Wence 2012; Ruvalcaba Oliver and Torres Robles 2012) and enable migrant groups to act as agents of community development (Franzoni and de Lourdes Rosas 2006).

Distance from 'home'[7] makes it rare for more than a small minority of migrants to participate directly in local governance institutions, the general assembly, and the different bodies and committees that administer multiple aspects of community life in rural Oaxaca. For individuals unable to participate in person but keen to remain 'active' members of their community, the establishment of migrant associations and organizations – known by a variety of names, including 'organizaciones *de pueblo*', '*clubes de oriundos*', and '*clubes sociales comunitarios*' (Fox and Rivera-Salgado 2004) – have allowed migrants to self-organize in support of their home community. Over time, through their activities, connections, and fundraising, these organizations enable 'active' migrants in 'sister' communities in Mexico and the US to collaborate with village authorities on development initiatives and governance tasks inside and outside of the customary territory (López Vallejo-Olvera 2013: 27).

Different factors converge to provide a rationale for organizing in this way, including migrants' nostalgia and belonging, family connections, sense of moral obligation to the community of origin, religious beliefs, and self-interest (Lanly and Valenzuela 2004). In some instances, several factors come into play. At other times, a single reason may trigger self-organization:

> In the 1980s, we started to arrive and at that time [some migrants] began to suffer misfortune, some of the paisanos died and so we all got together because we all knew each other and knew where each of us lived, anyway we all chipped in and raised enough money so we could send the body back to the village to be buried there. It was at this point that we felt the need to get organized as a group, when someone like that was in need of support ... [later] ... I went to a meeting and there were several people who wanted to organize into a mesa [management board], to find a way to continue to participate in the social development of our people but from here ... in whatever way possible, to propose changes to help our hometown in its development and to help it to continue to function through

usos y costumbres. So that some way or another, life would continue there
... because as citizens we are custom-bound traditionalists

(Elfego, Migrant from Santa Ana del Valle, in Los Angeles, CA, 2015)

As migrant organizations were established, institutional links were forged with
village authorities in Oaxaca. In many cases, links became formalized through
migrant management boards, or *mesa directivas*. Typically comprised of three to
six positions, these boards are staffed by migrants akin to how *cargos* are assigned
in the community of origin, with incumbents elected by their peers to serve for
a set period of time, before being replaced by others from the migrant community. These *mesas* create communication channels between migrant groups
and village authorities, help to coordinate migrant fundraising activities, oversee
the collection of migrant 'cooperaciones' (fees levied by the home village), and
often organize migrant involvement in annual patron saint celebrations and
festivities.

Regardless of the activities undertaken, considerable commitment is required
on the part of participating migrants, both in terms of time and finances:

It's an enormous investment because we have all these events, they do six,
maybe six to eight dances a year, where we raise funds [for the migrant community or for the home village], and so that means a lot of planning,
looking for the bands to play, and then booking a place, advertising the
event, making sure everything is legal, there's this to do, that to do ... hon-
estly, it's a lot of work.

(Antonio, migrant from Santa Maria Tindu, in Madera, CA, 2015)

In some cases, migrant organizations have been sufficiently proactive and politically astute to even mobilize actors from outside the community sphere to
support village needs:

When we started the organization, there was a lot of unhappiness with the
government [in Oaxaca] and a lot of resentment felt towards the community [of origin]. We, or at least some of us, when we were involved, we
felt it wasn't fair that we work so hard in support of the community, but
there wasn't much given in return. So we used that feeling to develop a
strategy ... we took US$10,000, raised through donations among the
migrant community, and we went to Oaxaca, we organized a press conference and we said [to the government] 'we are migrants and we are going to
knock on the Governor's door to tell him that we brought this US$10,000,
and we want the State Government to match those funds to support a
drinking water project in our community.'

(Antonio, Migrant from Santa Maria Tindu, in Madera, California, 2015)

It should be noted that not all migrant organizations are or were established
with the express goal of supporting their communities of origin. Prior to the

1990s, Burgess (2006: 139) reports that many organizations began as social or sporting clubs, and only later evolved into more philanthropic, political, or development entities. Migrants have always congregated in their places of residence for ritual celebrations, basketball games and tournaments, and social gatherings and parties, whether in honour of their community of origin's patron saint or those of a more civil nature, such as weddings and baptisms. A shared Indigenous language often connects migrants during these encounters, providing a sense of safety, nostalgia, and ability to express one's self and culture. These gatherings, which migrant organizations continue to promote, build camaraderie and a sense of identity in places that few first-generation migrants may ever consider their true 'home'.

Migrant umbrella associations

In places where many Indigenous Oaxacans are based, migrant organizations and clubs have sometimes come together to form second-level migrant associations or coalitions. While individual organizations are critical for providing on-the-ground support in communities of origin, their participation in translocal institutional spaces takes place within a context of evolving Mexican and US economic and immigration policies. Membership of migrant associations or coalitions offers organizations access to forms of social, economic, and political capital that can help them function within an often complex and fraught landscape.

In California, these associations include the Frente Indígena de Organizaciones Binacionales (FIOB), Organización Regional de Oaxaca (ORO), Unión de Comunidades Serranas de Oaxaca (UCSO), Coalición de Organizaciones y Comunidades Indígenas de Oaxaca (COCIO), Red Internacional Indígena de Oaxaca (RIIO), and Federación Oaxaqueña de Comunidades y Organizaciones Indígenas de California (FOCOICA). As Fox and Rivera-Salgado (2004: 19) note, these second-level associations and coalitions have helped new ethnic identities to emerge out of the migratory experience, and for an Oaxacan migrant civil society in California to coalesce.

The Organización Regional de Oaxaca (ORO) was among the first to be established, formed in 1988 by Oaxacan migrants living in Los Angeles. Currently registered as a not-for-profit organization, in 2017 it comprised eight member groups and affiliated communities of origin,[8] and works predominantly to preserve and strengthen Oaxacan Indigenous culture. In recent times, it has also begun to support educational opportunities for second- and third-generation migrants. It organizes the Guelaguetza de ORO in Los Angeles County each summer. As Natividad, from an ORO member organization, OPAM, explains:

> We belong to ORO because they help their member communities ... ORO supports us in the matter of ... when we have a cultural activity they put us in contact with the other communities that want to participate with their dances. When they do their Guelaguetza they invite all the communities to

take part, to present their dance and they give [each of us who participate] a small donation, an economic donation, it's not much but it is a donation and it brings us together.

ORO, however, rarely involves itself in political issues, and some early members split to form the Frente Indígena de Organizaciones Binacionales, originally the Frente Mixteco Zapoteco Binacional (FM-ZB), in 1991. The FM-ZB became the Frente Indígena Oaxaqueño Binacional in 1994 (Domínguez Santos 2004: 72), and then later the Frente Indígena de Organizaciones Binacionales (FIOB) when new members from outside of Oaxaca joined. FIOB was the first Oaxacan migrant coalition to get involved in transnational political activism, making demands of consecutive Oaxacan Governors to provide greater resources for rural development and infrastructure projects in migrant-sending villages, as well as supporting the rights of Mixteco migrants in the Valle de San Quintín, Baja California Norte, to unionize. FIOB provided financial support to the 'Casa de la Cultura Oaxaqueña' in Los Angeles, as well as the 'Casa del Trabajador Migrante' in the Valle de San Joaquín and in San Diego County (FIOB 1992).

The Federación Oaxaqueña de Comunidades y Organizaciones Indígenas de California (FOCOICA) is another important umbrella organization. Established in 2001, its goal is to unify Oaxacan migrant organizations in California, preserve Indigenous Oaxacan sociocultural values, and secure political representation (of Oaxacan Indigenous migrants) among government authorities in Mexico and the United States (FIOB 2001). Much of FOCOICA's work has focused on building relationships with Oaxaca's State Government, through which it has promoted 3×1-funded development projects[9] in communities of origin, as well as encouraging Oaxaca's government to sponsor the annual Guelaguetza festival held in Los Angeles.

Final reflections

The movement of people away from rural Oaxaca over a 70-year period, but particularly since the 1970s, has produced a 'culture of migration' among Oaxaca's Indigenous population (Cohen 2004). Migration has become a way of life, a rite of passage for some, and even a self-perpetuating phenomenon (see Portes and DeWind 2007) that can see continued flows explained independently of the causes that led to initial movements.

While migration has the potential to weaken community organization, it can also support it, changing it in some instances. This attests to the power of Indigenous *comunalidad* (see Chapter 2), which continues to permeate the everyday practice and thoughts of a broad and geographically dispersed community membership. Migrants may have chosen to live away from the home village but many have shown a willingness to invest time and money in support of community customs, communal governance structures, and village development. Maintained by social networks and trans-local institutions that connect them to their home communities (Velasco Ortiz 2002), Indigenous Oaxacans living in

Oaxaca City, Mexico City, northern Mexico, and the United States have established institutional and philanthropic ties with their *paisanos* back home, providing channels to help reduce or mitigate the negative impacts of migration on village life and governance.

However, while migrants form new collectivities, that's to say, sister communities in Mexico and the US (Massey *et al.* 1991), they function in accordance to their own dynamic and cannot be considered permanent. In experiencing life in a new place and cultural context, migrants forge new conceptions of community, with the social relations that stretch beyond geographical and political borders often acquiring a different character to those internal to the territorial-bounded space of the traditional community sphere. The continued support of migrants is by no means guaranteed, and this is one of the complexities of change (following migration) that we look to make sense of in the case study and discussion chapters that follow.

Notes

1 Massey defined these networks as 'sets of interpersonal relations that link migrants or returned migrants with relatives, friends or fellow countrymen at home' (Massey 1990: 7), which reduced the costs and uncertainty of migration (Curran and Rivero-Fuentes 2003; Davis *et al.* 2002). While Hirabayashi (1993) noted how networks would serve to trigger further migration, Curran and Rivero-Fuentes (2003) found that migrant networks were more important for international than internal migration streams.

2 Zapotec communities in the Sierra Juarez sub-region of the Sierra Norte are notable for the number of young people who left in the 1950s and 1960s to pursue studies (as an alternative to wage labour migration) in Oaxaca City, Puebla, and especially the Mexico City area, where they could access preparatory and university-level education not available in rural Oaxaca at that time. Initially, it was mainly boys who left for school, but by the 1970s girls were starting to do so also (Hirabayashi, 1993).

3 Some migrants would eventually return to Oaxaca, often fluent in Spanish and constituting a link between the home village and growing centres of urban power. Communities recognized this, often giving returnees jobs as translators or fast-tracking them into local governance positions that involved liaison with external actors and agencies.

4 In 1956, an estimated 15,558 Oaxacans took part in the Bracero Program, or 1.1 per cent of the state population (Runsten and Zabin 1995).

5 The difference in average wages between Oaxaca and California is seven-fold, while in Baja California and in Mexico City, wages are on average 30 per cent higher than in Oaxaca (Cué 2011: 310).

6 Also known as the Simpson–Mazzoli Act or the Reagan Amnesty.

7 Direct involvement is much easier for migrants residing in Oaxaca City than for those living further afield, including the US.

8 The affiliated groups and organizations are: Comunidad Tlacolulense en Los Ángeles (COTLA), Organización para la Ayuda Macuiltianguense (OPAM), Comunidad de San Marcos Tlapazola, Comunidad de San Bartolomé Quialana, Comunidad de Santa Ana del Valle, Ballet Folklórico Nueva Antequera, Ballet Folklórico Huaxyacac, Grupo Folklórico Monte Albán, Grupo Folklórico Mis Raíces, and Grupo Folklórico Princesa Donají.

9 *Tres por uno* (3×1) is a programme run by the Mexican Ministry of Social Development (SEDESOL) (www.sedesol.gob.mx/work/models/SEDESOL/Transparencia/TransparenciaFocalizada/Programas_Sociales/pdf/3x1_para_migrantes.pdf), which provides

matching government funds for migrant groups outside of Mexico to support social development and infrastructure projects in their communities of origin. For every peso raised by participating migrant groups, each level of government in Mexico (Municipal, State and Federal) will provide an equal amount of funding.

References

Aguilar Medina, J.I. 1980. La Mixteca oaxaqueña. Una zona de emigración. In: Nolasco, M.A. (ed.), *Aspectos sociales de la migración en México*, pp. 155–185. México, DF: Secretaría de Educación Pública, Instituto Nacional de Antropología e Historia.

Aguilar Orea, L.A. 2012. Una transición sufrida hacia la reconfiguración de la comunidad transnacional de Ixpantepec Nieves. Mexico, DF: Universidad Autónoma Metropolitana.

Alarcón Acosta, R., L. Escala Rabadán, and O. Odgers Ortíz. 2014. *Mudando el hogar al norte: Trayectorias de integración de los inmigrantes mexicanos en Los Ángeles*. Tiijuana, BC: El Colegio de la Frontera Norte.

Alvarado Juárez, A.M. 2008. Migración y pobreza en Oaxaca. *El Cotidiano* 23(148): 85–94.

Bacon, D. 2006. *Communities without Borders: Images and Voices from the World of Migration*. Ithaca, New York: Cornell University Press.

Basch, L., N. Glick Schiller, and C. Szanton-Blanc. 1994. *Nations Unbound: Transnational Projects and the Deterritorialized Nation State*. New York: Routledge.

Besserer, F. 1999. Estudios transnacionales y ciudadanía transnacional. In: Mummert, G. (ed.), *Fronteras fragmentadas*. Michoacán, México: El Colegio de Michoacán, Centro de Investigación y Desarrollo del Estado de Michoacán.

Bezaury, J.A. 2007. Organized coffee producers: mitigating negative impacts of outmigration in Oaxaca, Mexico. *Mountain Research and Development*, 27(2): 109–113.

Burgess, K. 2006. Filantropía de migrantes y gobernanza local. In: Merz, B.J. (ed.), *Nuevas pautas para México: observaciones sobre remesas, donaciones filantrópicas y desarrollo equitativo*, pp. 125–155. Cambridge, UK: Cambridge University Press.

Bustamante, J. 1995. *Estado actual de la migración interna e internacional de los oaxaqueños*. Oaxaca, México: Consejo Estatal de Población.

Butterworth, D. 1975. *Tilantongo: Comunidad mixteca en transición*. Mexico City, DF: Instituto Nacional Indigenista, Secretaría de Educación Pública.

Cohen, J. 2004. *The Culture of Migration in Southern Mexico*. Austin, TX: University of Texas Press.

Cohen, J. 2013. Latin America: internal migration. In: Ness, I. (ed.), *The Encyclopedia of Global Human Migration*. London, UK: Blackwell.

CIEDD. 2012. *Carpeta Regional Mixteca: Información Estadística y Geografía Básica*. Oaxaca de Juarez, Oaxaca: Centro de Información Estadística y Documental para el Desarrollo (CIEDD).

CONABIO-CONANP. 2007. *Análisis de vacíos y omisiones en conservación de la biodiversidad terrestre de México: espacios y especies*. Comisión Nacional para el Conocimiento y Uso de la Biodiversidad, Comisión Nacional de Áreas Naturales Protegidas, The Nature Conservancy-Programa México, Pronatura, AC, Facultad de Ciencias Forestales de la Universidad Autónoma de Nuevo León, México. Mexico City, Mexico.

CONAPO. 2010. Índices de marginación por entidad federativa y municipio, 2010. Accessed April 2, 2018 at: www.conapo.gob.mx/es/CONAPO/Indices_de_Marginacion_2010_por_entidad_federativa_y_muncipio.

Cué, G. 2011. *Plan Estatal de Desarrollo 2011–2016*. Oaxaca de Juárez, Oaxaca: Gobierno del Estado de Oaxaca.

Curran, S. and E. Rivero-Fuentes. 2003. Engendering migrant networks: the case of Mexican migration. *Demography* 40(2): 289–307.

Davis, B., G. Stecklov, and P. Winters. 2002. Domestic and international migration from rural Mexico: disaggregating the effects of network structures and composition. *Population Studies* 56(3): 291–309.

De la Peña, Moisés, T. 1950. Problemas sociales y económicos de las Mixtecas Vol. II. Mexico City, DF: Instituto Nacional Indigenista.

Díaz Gómez, F. 2003. Comunidad y comunalidad. In: J.J. Rendón Monzón (ed.), *En La Comunalidad*, pp. 59–69. Oaxaca, Mexico: Consejo Nacional para la Cultura y las Artes, Fondo Editorial Tierra Adentro.

Domínguez Santos, R. 2004. The FIOB experience: internal crisis and future challenges. In: Fox, J. and G. Rivera-Salgado (eds), *Indigenous Mexican Migrants in the United States*, pp. 69–80. La Jolla, California: UCSD.

Faist, T. 2005. Espacio social transnacional y desarrollo: Una exploración de la relación entre comunidad, Estado y mercado. *Migraciones Internacionales* 2005: 1–34.

FIOB. 1992. www.fiob.org. 7 de Diciembre de 1992. http://fiob.org/1992/12/pliego-de-dedemandas/ (last accessed April 8, 2016).

FIOB. 2001. www.fiob.org. 3 de Marzo de 2001. http://fiob.org/2001/03/funda-federacion-oaxaquena/ (last accessed May 14, 2016).

Fox, J. 2004. Introducción, una mirada retrospectiva a la migración transnacional mixteca. In: Escárcega, S. and S. Varese (eds), *La ruta Mixteca: El impacto etno-político de la migración transnacional en los pueblos indígenas de México*, pp. 15–37. Mexico City, DF: Universidad Nacional Autónoma de México.

Fox, J. 2007. *Accountability Politics: Power and Voice in Rural Mexico*. Oxford, UK: Oxford University Press.

Fox, J. and River-Salgado, G. 2004. *Indigenous Mexican Migrants in the United States*. Center for US–Mexican Studies; Center for Comparative Immigration Studies.

Fox, J. and G. Rivera-Salgado. 2004. Introducción. In: Fox, J. and G. Rivera-Salgado (eds), *Indígenas Mexicanos Migrantes en los Estados Unidos*, pp. 9–74. Mexico City, DF: Miguel Ángel Porrúa.

Franzoni, J. and M. de Lourdes Rosas. 2006. Migración internacional y prácticas políticas transnacionales: agentes de cambio en dos comunidades rurales. *Estudios Sociológicos* 24(70): 221–241.

Garduño, E., E. García, and P. Morán. 1989. *Mixtecos en Baja California: El caso de San Quintín*. Mexicali: Universidad Autónoma de Baja California.

Glick-Schiller, N., L. Basch, and C. Blanc Szanton. 1992. Transnationalism: A new analytic framework for Understanding migration. *Annals of the New York Academic Sciences* 1992: 1–24.

Greiner, C. and P. Sakdapolrak. 2013. Translocality: concepts, applications, and emerging research perspectives. *Geography Compass* 7: 373–384.

Guzmán, E. and P. Lewin. 1999. Los migrantes oaxaqueños: escenarios, interlocutores y estrategias para el desarrollo social. In: *Memoria del Coloquio Nacional sobre Políticas Públicas*. Oaxaca, Mexico: Gobierno del Estado de Oaxaca.

Hernández-Díaz, J. 2001. Reclamos de la identidad: la formación de las organizaciones indígenas en Oaxaca. Oaxaca, Mexico: Miguel Ángel Porrúa, Universidad Autónoma Benito Juárez de Oaxaca.

Hernández-Díaz, J. 2013. Comunidad, migración y ciudadanía: Avatares de la organización indígena comunitaria. Oaxaca, Mexico: Miguel Ángel Porrúa, Universidad Autónoma Benito Juárez de Oaxaca.

Hirabayashi, L.R. 1993. *Mountain Zapotec Migrant Associations in Mexico City.* Tucson, AZ: University of Arizona Press.

Hirabayashi, L.R. 1987. On the formation of migrant village associations in Mexico: Mixtec and Mountain Zapotec in Mexico City. *Urban Anthropology* 12: 29–44.

INEGI. 1980. X *Censo General de Población y Vivienda, 1980.* Estado de Oaxaca-Volumen I-Tomo 20, Mexico 1984. Aguas Calientes, Mexico: Instituto Nacional de Geografía e Informática (INEGI).

INEGI. 2009. *Perspectiva estadística: Oaxaca.* Instituto Nacional de Geografía e Informática (INEGI). Centro de Información. Oaxaca City, Mexico.

Kearney, M. 1995. Local and the global: the anthropology of globalization and transnationalism. *Annual Review of Anthropology* 24(1995): 547–565.

Kearney, M. 1996. *Reconceptualizing the Peasantry: Anthropology in Global Perspective.* Critical Essays in Anthropology Series. Texas: Westview Press.

Kearney, M. 2000. Transnational Oaxacan indigenous identity: the case of Mixtecs and Zapotecs. *Identities: Global Studies in Culture and Power* 7(2): 173–195.

Kearney, M. and F. Besserer. 2004. Gobernanza municipal en Oaxaca en un contexto transnacional. In: Fox, J. and G. Rivera-Salgado (eds), *Indígenas Mexicanos Migrantes en Los Estados Unidos,* pp. 483–501. Mexico City, Mexico: Miguel Ángel Porrúa.

Kuroda, E. 1994. Mesutiisoka to senjuumin shakai (Mestisaje and Indigenous Society). Tokyo, Japan: Estuko Kuroda.

Lanly, G. and B.M. Valenzuela. 2004. Introducción. In: Lanly, G. and B.M. Valenzuela (eds), *Clubes de migrantes oriundos mexicanos en Estados Unidos. La política transnacional de la nueva sociedad migrante,* pp. 11–37. Guadalajara, Mexico: Universidad de Guadalajara.

Levitt, P. 2001. Transnational migration: taking stock and future directions. *Global Networks* 3(1): 195–216.

Levitt, P. 2004. *Transnational Migrants: When 'Home' means more than One Country.* Migration Fundamentals Feature. Migration Information Source: Fresh Thought, Authoritative Data, Global Reach. Accessed online at: www.migrationinformation.org/Feature/display.cfm?id=261

Levitt, P. and N. Glick Schiller. 2004. Perspectivas internacionales sobre migración: conceptualizar la simultaneidad. *Migración y desarrollo,* 2004: 60–91.

López Vallejo-Olvera, M. 2013. Marco teórico conceptual de la gobernanza global. In: López-Vallejo Olvera, M., A. Bárbara Mungaray Moctezuma, F. Quintana Solórzano, and R. Velázquez Flores (eds), *Gobernanza global en un mundo interconectado,* pp. 19–27. Mexico City, Mexico: UABC-AMEI-UPAEP.

López, F. and D. Runsten. 2004. El trabajo de los mixtecos y los zapotecos en California. In: Fox, J. and G. Rivera-Salgado (eds), *Indígenas Mexicanos Migrantes en los Estados Unidos,* pp. 277–309. Mexico City, DF: Miguel Ángel Porrúa.

López, V. 2016. Migración: 1,203,680 paisanos de Oaxaca viven en Estados Unidos. *Todo Oaxaca, El oriente contenido con rumbo,* 13 de Enero de 2016: www.eloriente.net/home/2016/01/13/migracion-1203680-paisanos-de-oaxaca-viven-en-estados-unidos/.

Ludy Molina, V., 1991. La Migración Indígena y Sus Efectos al Interior de la Comunidad de Origen. *Etnia y Sociedad en Oaxaca* 71.

Maldonado Alvarado, B., 2011. Comunalidad and the education of Indigenous peoples. In: B. Maldonado Alvarado (ed.), *Comunidad, Comunalidad y Colonialismo en Oaxaca:*

La Nueva Educación Comunitaria y su Contexto. Oaxaca, Mexico: Colegio Superior para la Educación Integral Intercultural de Oaxaca.

Mann, C.C. 2004. *Diversity on the Farm: How traditional crops around the world help to feed us all, and why we should reward the people who grow them*. New York: Ford Foundation.

Martínez Luna, J. 2013. *Textos sobre el camino andado* (Vol. I). Oaxaca de Juárez, Oaxaca: CSEIIO.

Martínez Romero, A.E. 2005. Las tendencias migratorias y la de los comuneros del impacto de la migración en la organización tradicional, relacionada con el manejo forestal comunitario en el Distrito de Ixtlan, Oaxaca. Unpublished thesis. Facultad LatinoAmericana de Ciencias Sociales (FLACSO), Mexico City, Mexico.

Massey, D.S. 1990. Social structure, household strategies, and the cumulative causation of migration. *Population Index* 56: 3–26.

Massey, D.S., R. Alarcón, J. Durand, and H. González. 1991. *Los ausentes: El proceso social de migración internacional en México occidental*. Mexico City, DF: Alianza Editorial Mexicana y Consejo Nacional para la Cultura y las Artes.

Massey, D.S., J. Durand, and K.A. Pren. 2015. Border enforcement and return migration by documented and undocumented Mexicans. *Journal of Ethnic and Migration Studies* 41(7): 1015–1040.

Mines, R., S. Nichols, and D. Rusten. 2010. *Indígenas de México en la Agricultura de California*. Available online at: www.indigenousfarmworkers.org/es/final_report.shtml (last accessed March 11, 2017).

Nagengast, C. and M. Kearney. 1990. Mixtec ethnicity: social identity, political consciousness, and political activism. *Latin American Research Review* 25(2): 61–91.

O'Connor, M.I. 2016. *Mixtec Evangelicals, Globalization, Migration, and Religious Change in an Oaxacan Indigenous Group*. Boulder, CO: University Press of Colorado.

Ostergaard-Nielsen, E. 2003. The politics of migrants' transnational political practices. *International Migration Review* 37(3): 760–786.

París, M.D. 2003. Migración, violencia y cambio cultural: los triquis en el Valle de Salinas. *Reencuentro* 37: 64–70 (Universidad Autónoma Metropolitana).

Pinzón, P. 2007. Políticas migratorias en el estado de Oaxaca. In: Fernández de Castro, R., R. García Zamora, R. Clariond Rangel, and A. Vila Freyer (eds), *Las políticas migratorias en los estados de México, una evaluación*, pp. 183–218. Mexico: Miguel Ángel Porrúa, Universidad Autónoma de Zacatecas, Cámara de diputados LX legislatura.

PIRCS. 1998. Diagnóstico sobre los jornaleros agrícolas en Baja California Sur, La Paz. Programa de Investigación Rural en Ciencias Sociales. La Paz: Instituto Nacional Indigenista, Universidad Autónoma de Baja California Sur.

Portes, A. and J. DeWind. 2007. *Rethinking Migration: New Theoretical and Empirical Perspectives*. New York: Berghahn Books.

Ramos Pioquinto, D. 1988. Migración y sistema de cargos en la reproducción social de la comunidad campesino-indígena de Zoogocho, Oaxaca, de 1940 a 1987. Oaxaca de Juárez: Universidad Autónoma Benito Juárez de Oaxaca.

Ramos Pioquinto, D. 1992. La migración por micro-regiones en la Sierra Norte de Oaxaca. In: Corbett, J., M.A. Musalem Mehry, O, Ríos Vásquez, and H.A. Vásquez Hernández (eds), *Migración y etnicidad en Oaxaca*. Nashville, TE: Vanderbilt University Publications.

Romero Frizzi, M. de los Ángeles. 1996. *El sol y la cruz los pueblos indios de Oaxaca colonial*. Mexico City, Mexico: Centro de Investigaciones y Estudios Superiores en Antropología Social, Instituto Nacional Indigenista.

Runsten, D. and M. Kearney. 1994. *A Survey of Oaxacan Village Networks in California Agriculture*. California: California Institute for Rural Studies.

Runsten, D. and M. Kearney. 2004. Encuesta sobre las redes de los pueblos oaxaqueños en la agricultura de California. In: Escárcega, S. and S. Varese (eds), *La ruta mixteca*, pp. 41–76. Mexico City, Mexico: Programa Universitario México Nación Multicultural en México CEIICH-UNAM.

Runsten, D. and C. Zabin. 1995. *Changing Face*. Available online: https://migration.ucdavis.edu/cf/more.php?id=64 (last accessed May 6, 2016).

Ruvalcaba Oliver, D. and C. Torres Robles. 2012. *Excluidos y ciudadanos, las dimensiones del poder en una comunidad transnacional mixteca*. Mexico City, Mexico: Juan Pablos Editor, Universidad Autónoma Metropolitana-Iztapalapa, Comisión de Derechos Indígenas.

Sanders, T.G. 1975. Migration from the Mixteca Alta. *North America Series II* 5: 1–16.

Sassen, S. 1991. *The Global City: New York, London, Tokyo*. Princeton, NJ: Princeton University Press.

Schuren, U. 2003. Re-conceptualizing the post-peasantry: household strategies in Mexican *ejidos*. *Revista Europea de Estudios LatinoAmericanos y del Caribe* 75: 47–63.

Schütze, S. 2014. Purhépechas in Tarecuato and Chicago: shifts in local power structures through transnational negotiations. *Latin American Perspectives* 41(3), 75–89.

Smith, R.C. 2003. Transnational localities: Community, technology and the politics of membership within the context of Mexico and U.S. migration. Vol. 6 of Comparative Urban and Community Research. In: Guarnizo, L.E. and M.P. Smith (eds), *Transnationalism from Below*, pp. 196–238. New Brunswick, Canada: Transaction Publishers.

Smith, R.C. 2006. *Mexican New York: Transnational Lives of New Immigrants*. Berkeley: University of California Press.

Spores, R. 1984. *The Mixtec in Ancient and Colonial Times*. Oklahoma: University of Oklahoma Press.

Stephen, L. 2002. Globalización, el Estado y la creación de trabajadores indígenas 'flexibles': trabajadores agrícolas mixtecos en Oregón. *Relaciones XXIII*, 90: 114–189.

Stephen, L. 2007. *Transborder Lives: Indigenous Oaxacans in Mexico, California and Oregon*. London, UK: Duke University Press.

Velasco Ortiz, L.M. 1998. Identidad cultural y territorio: una reflexión en torno a las comunidades transnacionales entre México y Estados Unidos. *Región y sociedad* 15: 105–130 (El Colegio de Sonora).

Velasco Ortiz, L.M. 2002. *El regreso de la comunidad: migración indígena y agentes étnicos. Los mixtecos en la frontera México-Estados Unidos*. Mexico: El Colegio de México, El Colegio de la Frontera Norte.

Velasco Ortiz, L.M. 2005. *Desde que tengo memoria: Narrativas de identidad en indígenas migrantes*. Mexico City, Mexico: El Colegio de la Frontera Norte, Fondo Nacional para la Cultura y las Artes.

Wence, N. 2012. *El pequeño gobierno. Una comunidad transnacional mixteca en la lucha por conservar su gobernabilidad*. Mexico City, Mexico: Juan Pablos editor, Universidad Autónoma Metropolitana-Iztapalapa, Comisión de Derechos Indígenas.

Wolf, E.R. 1982. *Europe and the People without History*. Berkeley, CA: University of California Press.

Zabin, C. 1992. La incorporación mixteca al mercado de trabajo agrícola de California: un breve ensayo contextual. *Current Issues Brief*, pp. 5–21 (San Diego, Center for U.S.–Mexican Studies UC-San Diego, INI, California Institute for Rural Studies).

Zabin, C. 1997. U.S.–Mexico economic integration: labor relations and the organization of work in California and Baja California agriculture. *Economic Geography* 73(3): 337–355.

Zabin, C., M. Kearney, A. García, D. Runsten, and C. Nagengast. 1993. *A New Cycle of Poverty: Mixtec Migrants in California Agriculture*. Davis, CA: The California Institute for Rural Studies.

Part II
Empirical case studies

4   Avatars of community

The Zapotec migrants of the Zoogocho micro-region

Jorge Hernández-Díaz

Summary

The Zoogocho micro-region is a consortium of Zapotec Indigenous communities bound by political union and cultural ties. Small in size and lacking the timber resources of neighbouring communities, they were among the first villages in the Sierra Norte to take part in migration streams to other parts of Mexico and the US. In this chapter, they present a set of illustrative cases that introduce the theme of change following migration, and what change means for the institutions and forms of communitarian life that have long defined life in rural Oaxaca.

Methods

The chapter draws on empirical research that the author conducted during multiple visits to the region between 2004 and 2016. Initial research focused on the history of the *Unión de Pueblos del Sector Zoogocho* (The Union of Zoogocho Sector Towns). These early visits helped to establish relationships with municipal authorities and local leaders, and highlighted the degree to which migration was shaping village life. This formed the focus for subsequent trips, where research was conducted in collaboration with authorities in Yatzachi el Bajo, Yatzachi el Alto, and San Bartolomé Zoogocho. In the summers of 2015 and 2016, trips were made to Los Angeles, California, in order to interview migrants from these communities, who provided further insights into the migratory experience, migrant–village ties, and institutional responses to migration.

Setting

The Zoogocho micro-region (Figure 4.1) comprises seven Indigenous Zapotec municipalities,[1] and 15 individual communities (Table 4.1), located in an area of rugged, mountainous terrain approximately 115 km (by road) from the state capital, Oaxaca City.

In the 1990s, these communities formed the *Unión de Pueblos del Sector Zoogocho* (The Union of Zoogocho Sector Towns),[2] a unique example of

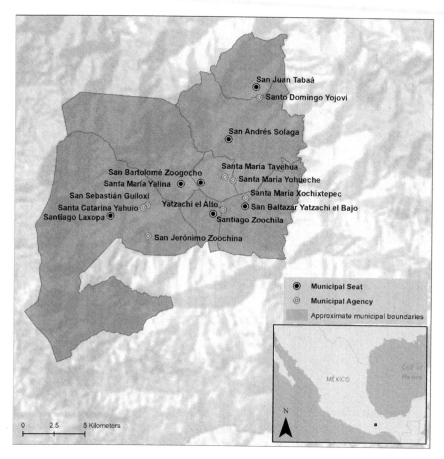

Figure 4.1 The municipalities and localities of the Zoogocho micro-region.

Source: map produced by Lisa Benvenuti, Center for Spatial Studies – University of Redlands.

intercommunal and municipal collaboration (Hernández-Díaz 2004). Formally established to cooperate on village development and livelihood strategies, the *Unión* comprises a General Assembly (or *Llin Lhawe*) and a management board that works with technical personnel to oversee inter-village projects and initiatives.

While part of a consortium, the 15 member communities are governed independently of one another in accordance with their own territorial needs and customary laws (Bautista Cruz 2017). While all promote *cargos* (local governance posts), *tequio* (collective, unpaid labour) and *gozona* (reciprocity), known in other Oaxacan regions as *guelaguetza*, each community membership participates in these social institutions differently.

Table 4.1 The member communities of the Unión de Pueblos del Sector Zoogocho

Community	Municipal status	District	Municipal home
San Andrés Solaga	Municipal Seat	Villa Alta	San Andrés Solaga
Santa María Tavehua	Agency	Villa Alta	San Andrés Solaga
Santo Domingo Yojovi	Agency	Villa Alta	San Andrés Solaga
San Baltazar Yatzachi el Bajo	Municipal Seat	Villa Alta	San Baltazar Yatzachi el Bajo
Yatzachi el Alto	Agency	Villa Alta	San Baltazar Yatzachi el Bajo
San Jerónimo Zoochina	Agency	Villa Alta	San Baltazar Yatzachi el Bajo
Santa María Yohueche	Agency	Villa Alta	San Baltazar Yatzachi el Bajo
Santa María Xochixtepec	Agency	Villa Alta	San Baltazar Yatzachi el Bajo
San Bartolomé Zoogocho	Municipal Seat	Villa Alta	San Bartolomé Zoogocho
San Juan Tabaá	Municipal Seat	Villa Alta	San Juan Tabaá
Santa María Yalina	Municipal Seat	Villa Alta	Santa María Yalina
Santiago Zoochila	Municipal Seat	Villa Alta	Santiago Zoochila
Santiago Laxopa	Municipal Seat	Ixtlán de Juárez	Santiago Laxopa
Santa Catarina Yahuio	Agency	Ixtlán de Juárez	Santiago Laxopa
San Sebastián Guiloxi	Agency	Ixtlán de Juárez	Santiago Laxopa

Migration, demographic change, and remittance trends

From 1930 to 1960, a general trend of population growth unfolded across Oaxaca's Sierra Norte region (de Grammont 2009; Narro *et al.* 1984), a result of shifts in rural development policy, elevated birth rates, enhanced access to medicine, and general improvements in the public health system. While this pattern was seen in three of the seven municipalities in the Zoogocho micro-region (the more populous Solaga, Yatzachi el Bajo, and Laxopa), the micro-region's smaller municipalities experienced a 10–25 per cent decline in population during this same period (Figure 4.2) – indicative of how out-migration had taken hold earlier there than in many other parts of the Sierra Norte (Durand and Massey 2003: 161).

Migration intensified in the 1960s. While these dynamics included internal migration streams – mainly to Mexico City, with some movement to Oaxaca City – US-bound streams became particularly significant at this time and through to the early 2000s. The Immigration Reform and Control Act (IRCA) or 'Simpson Rodino Law' of 1986 added critical momentum to flows north. As Sánchez and Mejía (2014) explain, IRCA resulted in the legalization of several million Mexican migrants, and many US-based migrants from the Zoogocho micro-region were among this number – paving the way for family members in Oaxaca to join them.[3] Most of the migrants who left the micro-region for the US settled in the Los Angeles area.

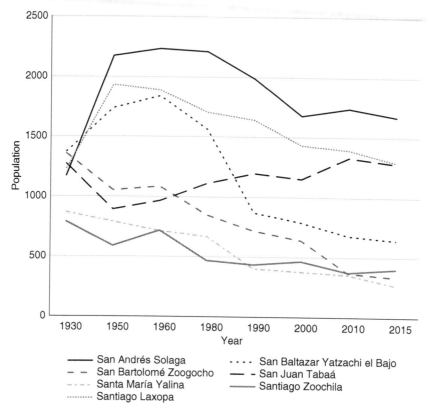

Figure 4.2 Population change in the Zoogocho micro-region (1930–2015).
Source: INEGI (2018).

Dynamics changed again about 10–15 years ago, as US-bound rates fell sharply because of economic recession in the US and an effective closing off of the US–Mexican border. This change coincided with a decline in migrant remittances received by Zoogocho micro-region households between 2000 and 2010 (Table 4.2).

Such a decline is explained by reduced migration rates and thus an aging out of remittance ties among migrants with decades living in the US, as well as the number of whole families that migrated from the late 1980s onwards, and thus fewer reasons to send money back to the home village.

As Figure 4.2 shows, migration over time has had a striking impact on village demographics in the micro-region. Resident populations in five of seven municipalities declined by 40–60 per cent from 1960–2015, with the total regional population falling from 9436 in 1960 to 5887 in 2015 (INEGI 2018). Only San Juan Tabaá's population increased during this period. Prolonged periods of out-migration have left many communities with small, disproportionately female,

Table 4.2 Migration remittance trends for the Zoogocho micro-region (2000–2010)

Municipality	Number of households (2000)	Number of households (2010)	% of households receiving remittances (2000)	% of households that receive remittances (2010)
San Andrés Solaga	540	483	28.15	32.51
San Baltazar Yatzachi el Bajo	257	226	28.40	25.66
San Bartolomé Zoogocho	125	131	14.40	7.63
San Juan Tabaá	270	328	1.11	13.41
Santa María Yalina	109	100	11.01	27.00
Santiago Zoochila	116	96	23.28	14.58
Santiago Laxopa	365	366	4.38	1.64

Sources: CONAPO (2000, 2010).

aging populations. For example, 2010 census data show that Yatzachi el Bajo had the highest proportion of seniors per capita of any municipality in Mexico. As migration rates abated in the 2000s, village populations have levelled off or stabilized.

History of migrant organizing

As Chapter 3 of this book shows, a trend among Oaxacan communities has been for many first-generation migrants to invest time and energy in building and maintaining ties with their communities of origin and often self-organize in support of those back home.

Organizing of this kind has been enshrined in local community statutes. For example, in 1973, the *Asociación para el Progreso de Yatzachi el Bajo* created a document that – under the motto, 'for a better tomorrow' – called for migrant associations to be established in the diaspora, thereby creating a mechanism by which active migrants were more likely and could more easily invest in community-level projects and activities.

Migrants from the Zoogocho micro-region settled predominantly in southern California, many in and around downtown Los Angeles. Table 4.3 lists the many hometown associations, regional migrant organizations, migrant community brass bands, and sports teams that these migrants have established.

All seven municipalities – although not all 15 communities – have, or have had, *mesas directivas* (hometown associations or management boards) established in US and Mexican destination centres. In most cases, these *mesas* comprise a President, Vice-President, Secretary, Treasurer, Events Secretary, and Announcers (Assistants), who raise funds through organizing raffles, food sales, basketball tournaments, concerts (see Figure 4.3), dances and other types of social events (*kermes*). A portion of the funds raised are sent to village authorities in Oaxaca to help finance local festivities, sporting activities, or to contribute to the cost of repatriating ill or deceased members of the migrant community.[4]

Table 4.3 Zoogocho micro-region migrant organizations, clubs, and bands in California

Community	Name of Migrant Organization or Musical Band/Group
San Andrés Solaga	Banda Solaga USA-OAX, Organización Social Solaga Oaxaca
Santa María Tavehua	Banda juvenil de Tavehua, Fundación cultural Tavehua – Los Ángeles
Santo Domingo Yojovi	Organización de Voluntarios de Santo Domingo Yojovi
San Baltazar Yatzachi el Bajo	Banda (YEB) Yatzachi el Bajo en Los Ángeles, California
Yatzachi el Alto	Banda (YEA) Yatzachi el Alto en Los Ángeles, California
San Jerónimo Zoochina	San Jerónimo Zoochina LA
Santa María Yohueche	Santa María Yohueche LA
Santa María Xochixtepec	Banda de música de Xochixtepec
San Bartolomé Zoogocho	Unión Social Zoogochense, Banda Filarmónica de Zoogocho de Los Ángeles, California
San Juan Tabaá	Mesa Directiva de San Juan Tabaá en Los Ángeles, CA.
Santa María Yalina	Organización Renacimiento Yalinense US, Banda Cerro de Agua
Santiago Zoochila	Banda Santiago Zoochila de Los Ángeles
Santiago Laxopa	–
Santa Catarina Yahuio	Banda Juvenil SC Yahuio, Comité Pro-Mejoramiento de Santa Catarina Yahuio, Oax
San Sebastián Guiloxi	Banda Filarmónica de San Sebastián

These migrant collectivities have contributed significant monies to development and infrastructure projects in their communities of origin. Indeed, much of the work undertaken by the *Unión de Pueblos del Sector Zoogocho* has only been possible because of migrant support:

Associations were formed in Oaxaca, Mexico and Los Angeles. They were well organized, strengthened [over time] and [...] supported the community. It's because of them that we have [basketball] courts, a theatre ... because there is no government money [for those kinds of things] ... it's money from migrants that makes these things possible.

(Jorge, resident and citizen of Yatzachi el Bajo)

They help us with the cemetery. We made it bigger, which was needed because we were almost burying the dead elsewhere. Now we are raising funds for another communal kitchen, and we have support of them [the migrants] for that.

(Salvador, resident and citizen of Santa María Tavehua)

Over time, however, and as migrant communities have become multi-generational, there has been a gradual shift in focus away from the community of origin, with migrants beginning to limit collective investments in village life

Figure 4.3 The Banda Filarmónica of San Bartolomé Zoogocho playing at a social event
   in downtown Los Angeles, California.

Source: photo credit: Jim Robson.

in Oaxaca. They continue to support the annual patron saint festivities, but
have become less inclined to provide funds in other areas. In some cases, organizations of active migrants appear in decline, not helped by the fall in US-bound
migration, which translates into less 'new blood' to drive organizational renewal.
In 2014, Yatzachi el Bajo's mesa directiva in LA disbanded in large part for this
reason.

As migrants restrict the support that they can or are willing to provide, collective energies are being devoted to building links among migrants in places
of residence. Music has been one way that migrants have looked to achieve
this. The band Solaga USA-OAX, the philharmonic band/orchestra
Zoochileña, the band of Zoochina, the band Cerro de Agua, the band YEA,
the youth band of Tavehua in Los Angeles, and the band YEB, were all set up
in the early 1990s to create more togetherness among migrants living in Los
Angeles, and in particular to help the sons, daughters, and grandchildren of
first-generation migrants cultivate a sense of Zapotec *serrano* (highland) identity and custom.

Migration and customary governance

While the monies sent by migrants have materially benefited home villages in the Zoogocho micro-region – enabling investments in productive projects and helping local families to feed, clothe, and educate themselves – the absence of so many community members has stressed the structures around which life in these places revolve, presenting significant challenges to reproducing local systems of communitarian organization and governance. The fiestas, the tequio, the gozona (reciprocal relations) and the local cargo system have all undergone change.

The way by which local collectivities approach the ideals and practice of communal service has shifted as the realities of life for many community members has altered. Essentially, community memberships comprise those who have not migrated, those who migrated but have now returned, and those who remain absent but are keeping the door open to a possible future return. Gregorio, a comunero from Yatzachi el Bajo, is one of several retired migrants who return each year from the US to their home village:

> The people left gradually, first to Oaxaca City, then to Mexico City and then, in the 1960s, they went to the US. Because of that the village is as it is today [empty] ... because of all the families that made a life for themselves away from here. And for the youngsters who were born elsewhere, well it's unlikely that they will return ... they're used to life there, there are so few young people here ... most of us are old now.

With the hardening of US immigration and border policies, the circular migration dynamic common in the 1970s, 1980s, and much of the 1990s, is no longer feasible for those without papers. Today, few migrants return in person to comply with cargo obligations or other forms of communal service. González Rojas (2016) reports how 10 to 15 years ago, community collectives began to really suffer from the problem of too few village residents. At this point, it became difficult for villages to cover the 20–40 cargo positions needed to maintain civic and communal governance.

Faced with this reality, community assemblies took to discussing, debating, and developing policies to set out what migrants could do to alleviate these pressures, and to ensure that their own rights as community members were maintained. Table 4.4 summarizes the range of different policies that communities have developed, including the specific roles that migrant organizations and management boards are expected to play.

While some communities have set strict tequio and cargo obligations for migrant members, others have been more flexible around the terms of community citizenship for non-village residents (Hernández-Diaz 2013) – allowing migrants to send support (cooperaciones) from afar or to comply indirectly with the ideals of mutual support that underpin local ideals of Indigenous comunalidad (see Chapter 2). Even in places where migrants are routinely named to serve cargos, such as in Yatzachi el Bajo, the means by which obligations are met can alter over time:

> For a while now, migrants have been asked to pay for cargos. [The burden of doing cargos] was encouraging people to migrate because there weren't enough people living in the village to cover them ... so the migrants with families in the village were given the obligation to do cargos even though they [the husband] weren't around and the women couldn't do them because of having kids [to look after]. So, they had to hire and pay someone else to do the cargo. At first, they would have to hire another family member but now they're able to hire anybody who has a house or something else in the community ... so they look for someone who can do the cargo and they pay them, so it gets done and that means they're covered [have met their obligations] and okay to return.
>
> (Jorge, Yatzachi el Bajo)

In San Bartolomé Zoogocho, migrants are regularly appointed to perform municipal cargos, and in most cases a substitute can be hired to do this on their behalf. An exception concerns high-level cargos, such as Municipal President, which must be performed in person by those named by the community assembly. In Santa María Tavehua, migrants were originally expected to return to perform any municipal cargo they were named for, but this proved unworkable and the payment of substitutes is now permitted.

Interview data suggests that such obligations work best when clear, enforceable sanctions (for non-compliance) exist. In some cases, communities have been known to disconnect essential services (i.e. electricity, water) from the homes that migrants own in the home village, or they revoke a migrant's rights to the lands where their home is built or where crops are grown and livestock pastured. Sanctions are normally most effective when dealing with migrants who hold material assets and interests in the home village.

As they make institutional changes in response to migration, communities slowly alter or reconfigure some of the mechanics of communal participation and cooperation. On the one hand, this points to the flexibility and adaptability of traditional governance structures. On the other hand, such responses may weaken or devalue the ideals and norms around which life in the micro-region has long been based. In addition, while migrants can help to subsidize the cargo and tequio systems, and thus alleviate the burden of village governance, the research suggests difficulties in maintaining such contributions over time. Many of the first-generation migrants who hold strong ties to the community of origin (often having participated in collective work and communal service institutions prior to leaving the home village) are now reaching 'retirement' age and reducing their involvement in migrant organizations and activities. As they take a step back, overall migrant interest and investment in hometown affairs may diminish.

Table 4.4 Municipal governance obligations for migrants from the Zoogocho micro-region

Municipality	Migrant obligations	Role of migrant organization(s)	Mesa directiva
San Andrés Solaga	To join their nearest solagueña migrant organization and make regular contributions (cooperaciones). More than six-months of non-residence in the village sees migrants temporarily forfeit their communitarian rights.	The Organización Social Solaga-Los Ángeles oversees the collection and sending of migrant cooperaciones to the home community.	There is no mesa directiva, but the organization maintains a register of migrant contributions.
San Baltazar Yatzachi El Bajo	When young men leave to work outside the municipality, their wives replace them in tequios and cargos, or a substitute is hired to perform the work in their stead.	To oversee the collection and sending of migrant's (voluntary) cooperaciones to the home community.	Yatzachi el Bajo had a mesa directiva in LA, but disbanded. The mesa of Yatzachi El Alto in L.A. continues to function.
San Bartolomé Zoogocho	Migrants are not forced to participate in tequios or the asamblea, but are expected to make regular contributions (cooperaciones), and can be named to do cargos.	Migrants in both Mexico and the US send their cooperaciones through the closest migrant organization.	There is a mesa directiva in LA and Mexico City with formal links to the asamblea and is permitted to name migrants to perform cargos in the community of origin.
Santa María Yalina	Migrants are not forced to participate in tequios or the asamblea, but are expected to make regular contributions (cooperaciones).	Migrant cooperaciones are collected and sent by the Organización Renacimiento Yalinense en Los Ángeles, California.	No mesa directiva. Migrant contributions are collected and sent by the organization in LA.
Santiago Zoochila	Women replace absent husbands in the tequio or by paying a substitute. Migrants maintain status as citizens by being active in their nearest migrant organization and through sending cooperaciones when asked to do so.	No migrant organization in the US. One in Mexico City – the APZO (Asociación Pro-Santiago Zoochila). It holds events to raise funds to support activities and projects in the home community.	No mesa directiva. Active migrants send their contributions direct to the municipal authority in Zoochila.

San Juan Tabaá	Migrants maintain rights as citizens as long as they pay for missed tequios and send *cooperaciones* to the community when asked to do so. Migrants are expected to join the migrant organization if one exists in the city/region where they reside, and to serve on the *mesa directiva* if elected to do so.	Tabaá has migrant organizations in LA, Mexico City, and Oaxaca City.	There are *mesas directivas* in LA, Mexico City, and Oaxaca City. They collect tequio fees, organize fundraising events to help finance public works and annual festivities in the home community, and generate funds to support the migrant community.
Santiago Laxopa	Compliance with community obligations, including cargos, is voluntary. However, after six-months of non-compliance, migrants forfeit rights in the village and lose voice and vote in village decision-making.	Laxopa has two migrant organizations: the Asociación de Laxopeños in LA, and the Frente Unido Seis Hojas in Mexico City. They collect migrant *cooperaciones*, which are used to fund development and infrastructure projects in the home community, and patron saint festivities.	There is no mesa directiva. Rather, migrant contributions are sent via the organizations or with a family member or friend visiting the community.

Migration and women as political actors in local governance

In Oaxaca, Article 3 of the *Ley de Sistemas Electorales Indígenas del Estado* recognizes and guarantees the rights of Indigenous communities and peoples to self-determination and, as an expression of this right, the autonomy to decide upon the forms of *convivencia* and political organization to govern themselves. As part of this freedom to govern, they can elect – in accordance with their own normative systems – the authorities or representatives to enact locally-determined policies.

While they are free to commit to the equal participation of men and women, the reality is that women have not historically had a role in formal institutions proportionate to their numbers. In recent years, however, this has begun to change, with many communities in the Zoogocho micro-region creating opportunities for local women to take a more active role in village governance and decision-making.

In some cases, this enhanced role has been borne more out of demographic necessity[5] than an overt commitment to gender equality:

> This is something that's been around for a long time now and has come about because, well ... for example, with the health committee I remember it was always us [women] that took on that role. I mean, we all need a health service and they [the men] said that it's not a difficult job so the women can do it and, anyway, there aren't enough of us [men] around.
>
> (Concepción, Yalina, 2016)

In other cases, however, enhanced female participation reflects a recent Federal electoral mandate, implemented by the *Instituto Estatal Electoral y de Participación Ciudadana de Oaxaca* in 2014, that set targets for female involvement in municipal governance across Mexico. San Bartolomé Zoogocho, for example, elected its first ever female Municipal President in July 2017. As an unprecedented political development for the community, it triggered a structural change in the local cargo system and created controversies among the membership:

> The decision was taken to invite women because they [the federal government] were demanding it ... a letter arrived from IEEPCO saying that we had to have women in the town hall, that it was necessary to have at least one woman. They [the men] weren't happy about it at first because they aren't used to having women telling them what to do ... they asked 'how it could be possible to have a woman in the *cabildo*?' They said that it could be arranged some other way and suggested that things be put on hold. They then held a meeting with just women, and they said that only single women could participate. They [the assembly] said it wasn't right that married women participated because that would mean they couldn't attend to their husbands' needs and meet their obligations as women ... they said, 'how is

it possible for the woman, you know … the wife … to be elected without fulfilling other cargos in the town hall?' But [because of the new law] at the meeting we received instructions that we would be eligible [to work in the town hall] without doing the cargos that are normally required.

(Beatriz, San Bartolomé Zoogocho, 2016)

The full implications of the federal mandate are still to be seen. As they take effect, these new legal requirements are butting up against beliefs and behaviours that are deeply embedded within local patriarchal–societal structures. In the Zoogocho micro-region, evidence points to splits and divisions regarding how the political participation of women could and should unfold. Yet these changes remain a highly significant development that affects how the cargo system is perceived, challenging the widely-held view that such positions are the domain of men only.

The feminization of village governance also impacts the communal service obligations that are set for migrants. In San Andrés Solaga, for example, when a husband or adult son migrates, they are required to integrate themselves into the local migrant organization (if there is one) and remain active in that organization, so that the wife or mother in the home community remains free of any obligation. In San Juan Tabaá, wives can pay additional *cooperaciones* (fees) on behalf of an absent husband or son, which then frees the family of further communal service (González Rojas 2016: 280). Both these municipalities, however, have sizeable resident populations, such that labour shortfalls (for governance) are less pronounced here than in some neighbouring communities. In villages with fewer people, women can have no choice but to take on more prominent roles. In Yalina in 2016, for example, two women sat on the town council. In San Bartolomé Zoogocho, in 2018, the town council was evenly split in terms of male and female incumbents.

These cases are a reminder of how change following migration can incentivize organizational structures to adapt to new realities. In an Indigenous Oaxacan context, it is women who can be particularly affected as they: administer migrant remittances, take on the role of head of household, and become more involved in the political life of their communities. Indeed, the realities of contemporary village life, combined with the government's push to feminize municipal governance, are such that it may become routine (perhaps within the space of a single generation) to see women enter and shape village politics and administration as much as men do.

Conclusions and reflections

In the Zoogocho micro-region, US-bound migration streams began before border and immigration policies hardened, allowing more migrants to acquire legalized immigration status. Yet, in a current climate of deportations, increased border restrictions, and reduced family ties in Oaxaca, circular migration has fallen dramatically in recent years. The end to circular dynamics may mark a (general) decline in translocal or transborder communities, as the connections between migrant and home communities are weakened, as evidenced by declining remittances and the difficulty in maintaining migrant organizations and hometown associations. While migrants establish summer or fiesta homes in their community of origin, and form musical bands in California, these linkages are more cultural in nature, and not well placed to underpin village development and governance.

As most migrants in the US struggle to comply fully with their collective work and communal service obligations, communities are relaxing the terms of membership for absentees – to find new ways for migrants to contribute from afar. Migrant *cooperaciones* (fees), the paying of substitutes to perform cargos, and levying fines for missed tequios provide examples of how community citizenship can be adapted while still falling under the auspices of customary governance structures and institutions.

With few migrants set to return to the home village, communities in the Zoogocho micro-region are exploring alternatives to help maintain local populations and customary territories. Seniors and elders, who under normal circumstances would be exempt from carrying out cargos, continue to do so. The dearth of young people has seen some communities offer incentives (e.g. local school scholarships) to attract young families from other places. Several have seen families arrive from the neighbouring Mixe region (to the east), fast-tracking them into membership of a Zapotec community and its organizational structures and hierarchy. In Yatzachi el Bajo, houses built by migrants as holiday retreats or retirement homes are now cared for by Mixe immigrants, who are slowly repopulating a village ravaged by migration. Little by little, they are being permitted to acquire rights as new community citizens.

Similarly, household and community economies in the micro-region have changed substantively in recent decades. Subsistence agriculture dominated the local sphere up until the late 1980s, but milpa production systems have contracted, following periodic droughts and the labour shortages associated with migration. A new productive landscape has emerged as local people look for new ways to make a living. These include collective enterprises tied to commercial forestry in Laxopa and charcoal production in Yalina, as well as family-level initiatives based on agave cultivation and mezcal production in Laxopa, Zoochila, and Yatzachi el Bajo, and pottery production in Tabaá and Tavehua.

Such changes form part of a suite of coping responses and longer-term adaptations that rural communities in Oaxaca can be expected to enact or experiment with following changes driven by or associated with migration – both expected and necessary if their Indigenous collectivities are to endure and find a place for themselves in the wider world.

Notes

1 Municipalities are divisions of Oaxaca's political geography conceptually similar to a canton or US county. An Agencia is a political subdivision of the municipality, and

the civic authorities elected in an agencia are dependent on those in the municipal seat. Municipalities often contain private properties and agrarian communities. These communities are collectively-held territories governed by customary law, where commoners have obligations to serve cargos and tequios, an assembly of commoners elects members to represent them, and in which water, forest, agricultural land, and house plots are owned collectively, with differing degrees of family usufruct recognized by the community. See Chapter 2.

2 The *Unión de Pueblos del Sector Zoogocho* was formally established in 1991 to cooperate on village development and livelihood strategies. It comprises a central body – a General Assembly (or *Llin Lhawe*) – and a board that works with technical personnel to oversee management of the program. A regional fund, based in San Andrés Solaga, raises monies to support development projects among member communities.

3 In Yatzachi el Bajo, for example, as many as 80 to 90 per cent of US based migrants are estimated to be legal residents (Worthen 2012).

4 By constructing formalized links with the *asamblea* in their community of origin, these mesas help to create a translocal community governance structure, further helping active migrants to maintain traditions and contribute to the development of the home village. They provide clear evidence as to how migration expands the social field of Oaxacan Indigenous communities (after Stephen 2007) and highlights the need for researchers to adopt a binational and sectoral lens for their analyses.

5 All of the municipalities in the Zoogocho micro-region had more female than male residents in 2015 (CDI 2015).

References

Bautista Cruz, M. 2017. *Memoria histórica de Tapa-baa. La defensa de la tierra, los espacios sagrados y los principios de la vida comunal en San Juan Tabaá, Oaxaca, México* (Second Edition). Mexico City, Mexico: Universidad Nacional Autónoma de México.

CONAPO. 2000. Migration Intensity Index, 2000. Accessed at: www.conapo.gob.mx

CONAPO. 2010. Migration Intensity Index, 2010. Accessed at: www.conapo.gob.mx

CONAPO. 2010. Obtenido de índice de marginación por entidad federativa y municipio. Accessed at: www.conapo.gob.mx/es/CONAPO/Indices_de_Marginacion_2010_por_entidad_federativa_y_municipio. Consejo Nacional de Población.

de Grammont, H. 2009. La desagrarización del campo mexicano. *Revista de Ciencias Sociales* 50: 13–55.

Durand, J. and D. Massey. 2003. *Clandestinos, migración México-Estados Unidos en los albores del siglo XXI*. Mexico City, Mexico: Miguel Ángel Porrúa.

González Rojas, A. 2016. *Monografías de comunidades zapotecas Xhon y Xidza de la Sierra Norte de Oaxaca: Catálogo de comunidades indígenas del Estado Libre y Soberano de Oaxaca*. Oaxaca de Juárez: Secretaría de Asuntos Indígenas del Gobierno del Estado de Oaxaca.

Hernández-Díaz, J. 2013. *Comunidad, migración y ciudadanía: avatares de la organización indígena comunitaria*. Oaxaca, Mexico: Miguel Ángel Porrúa, Universidad Autónoma Benito Juárez de Oaxaca.

Hernández-Díaz, J. 2004. Desarrollo regional de los pueblo Zapotecas del Sector Zoogocho en Oaxaca. In: García del Castillo, R. (ed.), *Gestión local creativa: experiencias innovadoras en México*, pp. 75–88. Mexico City, Mexico: Centro de Investigación y Docencia Económica (CIDE).

INEGI. 2015. *Principales resultados de la encuesta inter-censal 2015: Oaxaca*. Aguascalientes, Mexico: Instituto Nacional de Estadística y Geografía (INEGI).

INEGI. 2018. Archivo histórico de localidades geo-estadísticas. Accessed at: http:// geoweb2.inegi.org.mx/ahl/

Narro, J.R., M. Urbina Fuentes, R. Castro, J.L. Palma, and Y. Palma Cabrera. 1984. Evolución reciente de la mortalidad en México. *Comercio Exterior* 34(7): 636–646.

Sánchez, L. and L. Mejía. 2014. Remesas confrontan a expertos en migración. Accessed April 9, 2016 at: http://archivo.eluniversal.com.mx/: http://archivo.eluniversal.com. mx/estados/2014/impreso/remesas-confrontan-a-expertos-en-migracion-96944.html.

Stephen, L. 2007. *Transborder Lives: Indigenous Oaxacans in Mexico, California and Oregon.* Durham, US Duke University Press.

Worthen, H. 2012. *The Presence of Absence: Indigenous Migration, a Ghost Town, and the Remaking of Gendered Communal Systems in Oaxaca, Mexico.* Unpublished PhD Dissertation, University of North Carolina at Chapel Hill, USA.

5 Santa María Tindú

The tip of a melting iceberg

Dan Klooster

Summary

Following a dynamic historical relationship between the local economy, migrant labour opportunities, and US immigration policy, a disproportionately elderly village population of 500 Mixtec Indigenous people is linked to communities of migrants in the US and Mexico that number close to 4500 individuals. Many of those migrants support the religious and civic functions of the village through participation in a hometown association that leverages Mexican governmental matching grants for collective remittances. Some return to serve cargos. Thus, the village of Santa María Tindú is the visible, rooted tip of a much larger translocal community. However, as US-based migrants age and their families in the US become more firmly rooted in their California and Oregon communities, their associations are beginning to shift their focus away from the village of origin and more toward their US-based communities. Meanwhile, declining population and a reduction in agriculture has opened up opportunities for conservation in a rugged area no longer used for milpa agriculture or for grazing goats.

Methods

Santa María Tindú was visited from March 26 to 31, 2015. Formal, semi-structured interviews were conducted with village authorities and other community members, including many returned US migrants. Interview guides covered personal and family migration histories, migration status, the influence of village rules on migration and migrants' role in local governance, and the community's conservation strategy. In addition, Klooster, Robson, and Hernández-Díaz visited Madera, California from August 21 to 24, 2015 to conduct additional interviews and to observe social events organized by the community of people from Santa María Tindú (Tindureños) who live there. These methods revealed a pattern of migration, translocal community governance, and community development which is quite consistent with those discovered by a more in-depth ethnography from a decade earlier (Gil Martínez de Escobar 2006). Interviews were recorded with jot notes and daily write-ups in the system described by Bernard (2017). Pseudonyms are used throughout.

Setting

Santa María Tindú (see Figure 5.1) lies in the Mixtec region of Oaxaca, two hours by paved road from Huajuapan de Leon. Currently, the village is inhabited by 533 people in 205 households.[1] The resident population is disproportionately elderly. In addition to Spanish, Mixtec is still spoken by a minority of residents, and English is often heard. Bordered on two sides by the Mixtec River, the community collectively owns 8500 ha of mountainous territory. The village and an agricultural area dedicated to pasture and *milpa* are at 1900 metres above sea level. In contrast with most other places in the region, the community is blessed with springs that provide ample water for domestic use and some for irrigating small groves of temperate fruit trees. In addition to a treeless agricultural area, the community's territory encapsulates canyon lands along the Rio Mixteco, stony badlands, and a rocky mountain reaching 2500 metres above sea level. These areas provide firewood, building materials, and palm fibre for weaving hats, baskets, and mats.

Gil Martínez de Escobar (2006) portrays Santa María Tindú as a transnational community exercising agency in its own development process. The transnational community of Tindú consists of perhaps 5000 people, of which 3000 live in Madera, Bakersfield and Santa Maria in California, 1000 in Oregon, 500 in the village itself, and another several hundred residing elsewhere in Oaxaca and the rest of Mexico. Village authorities recognize 763 comuneros who collectively own the 8500 ha territory, and are responsible for governing it.

Figure 5.1 Santa María Tindú seen from the Cerro de la Mano.

Source: photo credit: Dan Klooster.

They estimate that 400 of these comuneros live in Madera, Bakersfield, and Santa Maria in California, 120 live in Santa María Tindú, 100 in Oregon, and 60 elsewhere in Mexico.[2] Comuneros living elsewhere participate in formal hometown associations which function as part of the village governance system, and Mayordomos canvas the community's nodes in Madera and elsewhere to raise funds for the village fiestas. Tindú's hometown association in Madera, California, is formally recognized by the Mexican federal government, and its collective remittances have received federal, state, and municipal matching grants for a number of important village development and infrastructure projects.

Family income from migration has created a village landscape of concrete and brick houses, including some impressive structures that stand empty, in a permanent state of construction. Thanks in part to collective remittances, the community's roads are paved, a health clinic has refrigerators and an ambulance, a local infrastructure carries water to almost every house, a sewer system carries effluent to a sewage treatment plant that discharges to an artificial wetland for additional filtration, and a recently-equipped water bottling plant promises to generate bottled water sales in the near future.

Migration history

Population

Migration has wrought tremendous change on the community. The censused population in Santa María Tindú reached a high of nearly 1500 in 1980, but fell to just 471 by 2010 (Figure 5.2).

In the early 1980s, Tindú's school had 30 to 40 children in each grade, two kindergarten teachers, 13 primary school teachers. In 1987, the school had 17 teachers and a principal. In 1990, the graduating sixth grade class had 32 students, none of whom now live in Tindú full time. In 2015, enrolment had dropped to nine in kindergarten, 20 in grades 1 through 6, and six in a television-supported junior high, serving grades 7 to 9. Four teachers serve these 35 students. Because of migration, the village in Mexico has become something like the tip of an iceberg; it is the visible component of a much larger community membership that live elsewhere, especially the US where Tindureño migrants number about 4000 people.

Migration pre-IRCA

Santa María Tindú's settlement pattern reflects changing labour demands in North America, the influence of US immigration policy, and the historical social networks bringing people together in specific areas. Since the early twentieth century, migration was essential for family livelihoods, supplementing domestic agricultural activities. In the 1940s, migrants sought seasonal work harvesting sugar cane, coffee and cotton in Veracruz, later adding Sinaloa to a seasonal migration circuit (see Chapter 3 for migration histories from the

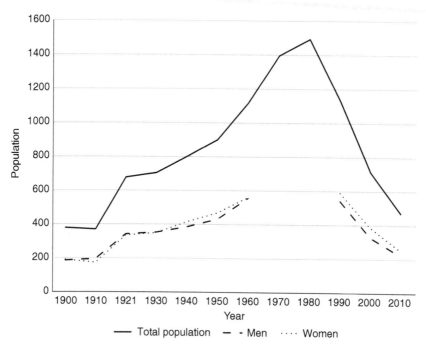

Figure 5.2 Population change in Santa María Tindú (1900–2010).

Source: INEGI n.d.

Note
1921 (rather than 1920) is used on the x-axis as it is the year recorded by INEGI, in recognition of the census that decade being carried out a year late.

Mixteca). In the 1950s, migrants began to reach the US through the Bracero Program, and continued doing agricultural work in the US without work permits after that program ended in 1964 (Gil Martinez de Escobar 2006).

During this period of cyclical migration, families in Tindú continued to plant corn, beans and squash, tend animals, and weave hats and baskets from the local palm. Men would leave in May, after village festivals were over, and seek seasonal work in Veracruz, Sinaloa, and later the US. In October, they would return to Tindú. The situation that residents described at this time is analogous to that of San Jeronimo Progreso, as observed in 1980 (Stuart and Kearney 1981). This nearby Mixtec community also depended on peasant agriculture and hat weaving. Crop production was sufficient to feed only 250, but the population at that time was 1450. Hats sold for about 11 cents, and a weaver could produce only two a day. 'For most households, migration is the only alternative to starvation' (Stuart and Kearney 1981: 70). As in Santa María Tindú, seasonal migration to sugarcane fields in Veracruz gave way to destinations in northern Mexico and the US. The border was relatively porous at the time, making cyclical migration common. One 36-year-old had been to the US 11 times (Stuart and Kearney 1981).

Similarly, elders living in Tindú describe this period as one in which migration provided income needed for family obligations and productive investments. Valentin, age 90, was one of the first Tindureños to participate in the Bracero Program. He reached the US at age 18, 'during the war with the Germans'. Later he established residency in Tijuana and was able to enter the US with his border residency documents. 'I went to the US for a long time', he told me. 'You suffer, but you learn things. That's why my children were able to get ahead.' His seven children established themselves as professionals, including an accountant, an engineer, and a dentist. None live in the village. In Tindú, Valentin also owns a comfortable brick house and a ranch with spring water and 500 fruit trees. Lucio, age 74, migrated for the first time in the 1950s, at age 13. He earned money in Veracruz and Sinaloa while his wife, Sofia, stayed in Tindú to tend the family's herd of 20 goats. The couple had 10 children, of whom three survived. 'When our children got married, we didn't have any money. I suffered a lot,' she said. 'There wasn't any money, but we had lots of expenses.' In 1992, in his early 50s, Lucio migrated to the US and found work picking apples in Washington State. Because he was able to buy three steers for each of his children's weddings, he considers his migration to have been extremely successful. 'The whole town came to eat,' he told me proudly. Lucio also owns land for planting and pasture in Tindú (see Figure 5.3).

Figure 5.3 Santa María Tindú's population is disproportionately elderly.

Source: photo credit: Dan Klooster.

Migration post-IRCA

The Immigration Reform and Control Act (IRCA) of 1985 began to change this pattern. This law granted work permits and legalization opportunities to undocumented immigrants with a work history. A pattern of mostly men coming and going to support families in Tindú declined, because with legalization, immigrants were able to bring their families to the US as well.

> We are talking about 88–89–90 when those who already met certain years with the permit could then bring the family, it was the opportunity for whole families to come.
>
> (Antonio, migrant leader, Madera, CA)

Family migration continued through the 1990s, both legal and, especially for youth, without documents (Gil Martínez de Escobar 2006: 71). Building on existing social networks, they established permanent communities in the Californian cities of Madera, Fresno, Santa Maria, and Bakersfield, in the Oregon communities of Woodburn, Hillsboro, and Silverton, and in Seattle, Washington, and elsewhere (Gil Martínez de Escobar 2006: 73). Two-thirds of Tindureños were legal residents in the US by 2005, and half of those acquired residency directly through IRCA (Revilla López 2010: 113). Community leaders estimate that the clear majority of Tindureños currently live in Madera, California.

Return migration

In 1995, Tindureño migrants formed an association in Madera, California to coordinate collective remittances to their village of origin, and other associations formed later in Oregon and in Huajuapan de Leon, Oaxaca State. Participation in migrant associations maintains a right to return. All those born in Tindú are citizens, but to become a comunero with rights to the land, wood, and water in the village commons, you must petition the village assembly. Returned migrants who have been active in a migrant organization in the US, paying their annual quotas and serving cargos in the US, should have no problem being accepted. If they have not been active with an organization of Tindú migrants, however, they would have to correct any arrears in their membership dues to migrant organizations. Even to live in the village and drink water from the public water system built with local *tequio* and cooperation from migrant organizations, they would have to be up-to-date with migrant dues. As Natalio put it, the first thing you do when you return from the US is to go see your family. Next, you see the authorities. They will say 'welcome to the village of your birth, how did it go in the states?', and then they discuss what you will pay for water, electricity, and your obligations for *tequio*.

Tindú has a disproportionate number of elders. Those who are able, continue to farm, to care for goats and cattle, and to weave hats and baskets, even though the prices are low and buyers rare. Remittances from grown children established in the US are an essential part of their livelihood. Natalio has plans for a trans-border life in his retirement. Currently a US legal resident, with the ability to come and go, he is studying to become a US Citizen so he can maintain contact with his four US-born daughters even after retiring to Tindú. 'When you are old, you can't work in the United States, but I can take care of my father's lands. I'm the oldest son,' he said. As a retiree in Tindú, he would plant corn, take care of cattle, walk a lot, get exercise, enjoy fresh air, a relaxing environment, and a cool healthy climate. In the US, he'd live in a noisy city with a very harsh climate, sleep too much, watch a lot of TV, get sick, and die more quickly. He expects to retire with $700 a month in social security payments, and that will go much farther in Santa María Tindú than in the US. Natalio's uncle, Daniel (age 74), is already living this period of a transborder life. He returned to Tindú to care for an aging mother-in-law, knowing it was a one-way-trip since he lacks residency papers. 'I've returned for forever. I have a little savings, and my sons send me money from over there [the US],' he says. When it rains, their fields produce enough corn for a whole year. 'I'm content here. Because of my age, they won't give me work [in the U.S.] anymore.'

Leaders of the migrant community in Madera have also noticed that those who have returned to Tindú are people who have lived most of their lives in the US, but are now retired. They have roots in Tindú, but grandchildren north of the border. Antonio told us during interviews in California:

> My father for example, goes there for five months, three months, then he comes back here … it is already very complicated to define or say that someone is going to stay [in Tindú], but we are seeing that the people who are now retiring are the ones who stay longer in the community.

The village also hosts about 10 deportees. Such deported young men working on construction projects contrast with other Indigenous youth due to their dress, their unaccented street English, body piercings, and numerous tattoos.

> Those deported guys arrived and started to cause problems in the community, like graffiti. There started to be a few thefts from empty houses. The community absorbed them and said ¡hey! We don't want you to keep doing your stuff from over there, here in the village. It was a message that helped a lot, and they realized, wow! Since the organization has achieved so much, it's not worth it to destroy what has been accomplished. Currently those kids go and cut firewood, sell it in the village, and that's how they make a living.
>
> (Antonio, community leader, Madera California)

A contrasting example is El Pelón, a heavily tattooed 22-year-old man who left the community with his family as a three-year-old, but returned to Tindú in 2009 to be with his father and brothers. In 2012, he abandoned a cargo of *policía* to return to the US, where he was arrested, jailed for three years, and deported back to Mexico. Upon his return, he got into a drunken fight with another village member seeking revenge for a beating El Pelón had given him three years earlier.

I asked village authorities Javier and Lucero if a person like El Pelón can find a place in the village. 'Only if he finds his path,' they answered,

> The community has a lot of tolerance. We know each other and we are all family, but it can come to a point where we say, 'you can't be here'. It would depend on how violent the person is, and how many, or how important the cargo is that he abandoned.

Some deportees, such as Caín, age 30, seem well-integrated into community life. He left the community for the US at age three, but was deported in 2012 because, as he put it in unaccented English and with a culturally-astute baseball reference, 'I stole a base and got called out.' Now he serves cargos in a Mayordomía.

Crossing the US border without legal documents has become more and more difficult since 2000 and cyclical migration by the undocumented is no longer practical. Residents of Tindú mention the high cost of paying smugglers and the mortal danger of crossing deserts as reasons not to migrate to the US without papers. The undocumented do not return voluntarily, unless they plan to stay.

Migration and village governance

As an Indigenous *comunidad agraria* and an *agencia* of the *municipio* of Tezoatlán de Segura y Luna, community governance in Tindú requires 12 municipal *cargos*, 12 communal *cargos*, a group of 20 *policias* who rotate through the activities of providing security at community events, and 32 posts on committees for the school, the health clinic, roads, and other public goods and services. In addition, two *Mayordomos* occupy 10 villagers who gather funds and coordinate the village's main ritual celebrations. Eighty-six unpaid governance positions are an enormous burden for a resident population of 120 comuneros in 205 families. 'Tindú currently faces a significant problem, which is the lack of people to serve cargos due to migration' (Gil Martínez de Escobar 2003: 6).

However, the village relies on its extended community of migrants for support. Santa María Tindú has 'an emergent transnational community government' (Gil Martínez de Escobar 2006: 2), in which the local village government is linked to formal member associations of migrants, such as *La Organización Tindureña de Huajapan de León*, the *Mesa Directiva* in Madera, California (which includes satellites in Santa Maria and Bakersfield, California), and the *Comité Seccional* in Oregon. Migrants build and maintain their village membership by serving cargos and paying dues to these nodes of Tindú's translocal governance structure.

Migrant organizations name their own leadership in assemblies that take place in Madera or Oregon. The assembly of comuneros in Santa María Tindú then ratifies those choices to give them legitimacy and authority. These recognitions bear the stamp of the official community seal, held by the Alcalde Unico Constitutional.

> We take up important matters here [in Madera] and in Oregon and the votes get sent to the community. So, I would say we are a community, but not a common ordinary community … we are so connected to the community [of origin] that the president of the migrant association says, 'hey listen, there is this problem in the community, this is what happened.' We have reunions here, minutes are taken, and you contact the community. So, we are very connected.
>
> (Antonio, migrant leader in Madera, California)

Similarly, when the community assembly debates issues of special significance, such as the establishment of a community protected area, it informs the community's various migrant associations. In that example, migrant leaders in the US responded that they would respect the will of the community assembly.

Migrants also play a central role serving cargos. The assembly notices who returns for family visits and selects them for the next year's cargos. This process takes advantage of the community's relatively high proportion of documented migrants; the undocumented are unlikely to be called upon.

Natalio, age 53, exemplifies this. He left for Madera, California at age 14 and stayed there for 24 years, without returning once. His work supported his parents, who remained in Tindú. He acquired residency papers through marriage in 1987, and has a US family with four children and four grandchildren. He returned to Tindú for the first time in 2001, to see his parents. Since 2004, he has lived and worked in Madera from April to October and in Tindú during the late fall and winter. This schedule allows him to care for his aging parents and serve the community. He has served four cargos: Topil, Tesorero de Bienes Comunales, Suplente de Alcalde, and currently, Alcalde Unico Constitucional. He takes breaks from these cargos during the summer to return to the US and work. This example conforms to the model that Gil Martínez de Escobar (2006: 227) observed 10 years earlier; the village relies on its migrants to return and serve cargos, and it accepts some interruptions to their cargo service as they return to the US for seasonal work.

Migration and village development

In addition to their essential role in buying food and clothing, covering educational expenses, and paying medical costs, remittances have improved the housing stock. The road was unpaved until the 1970s, and electricity was absent until then. In 1950, an adobe house or log cabin was a luxury, and most roofs were made of palm. Many houses were so flimsy, you could buy one, pick it up, and move it to another location. In 1970, census data showed that 60 per cent of the houses in Santa María Tindú had dirt floors. By 2010, the rate had dropped to 23 per cent, and by 2015 the few remaining log cabins were essentially museum pieces.

> Before, there weren't any concrete houses. The situation was one of poverty. Now, migrants make their houses, and there has been a tremendous change. There are nice houses, with bathrooms, ceramic tiles, all the services, with nice kitchens.
>
> (Valentin, resident of Tindú, age 90)

Construction funded by migrants provides young local men with important opportunities to earn income. Figure 5.4 provides an example of the change in Tindú's built landscape.

Collective remittances have also transformed the village's public infrastructure. Migrants pay annual quotas of US$60 to their local committee, all contributions are recorded on lists that are shared with the village authorities in Tindú. Out of 400 comuneros in Madera, 203 contribute. Out of 100 in Oregon, more than 80 contribute. Committees in the US also raise funds for specific purposes by holding collections, parties, and sporting events. Entrance fees of $15 or $20 can generate up to US$10,000 for community projects.

> We have achieved a change. We've sent millions of pesos – US$50,000 a year! Our projects include sewers, drinking water, electricity, street paving, an ambulance, a bridge, [improvements to] the cemetery, the water purifying and bottling plant. We've supported it all. Refrigerators to store medicine in the clinic. We've supported a lot!
>
> (Jaime, former president and vice president of the *Mesa Directiva* in Oregon)

Figure 5.4 House in Santa María Tindú under construction by a migrant living in Oregon.
Source: photo credit: Dan Klooster.

Other projects noted by a migrant leader in Madera include municipal buildings, a central plaza, the church, and a tilapia fish-farming project. Such collective remittance projects are visible throughout the village. Metal signs above paved streets acknowledge the joint investments of migrants with federal, state, and municipal funds through the 3 × 1 Program for Migrants, operated by the federal Secretariat of Social Development.

A state agency, the Oaxacan Institute of Migrant Support (IOAM, Instituto Oaxaqueno de Atención al Migrante), has also supported 3 × 1 projects in the village. Rufino Domínguez, IOAM's director, visited Santa María Tindú to review some of these investments and to promote the idea of additional productive projects such as fruit tree orchards and roadside restaurants. 'We have to generate employment in our country so that people can exercise the right to not migrate,' he said.

The showcase initiative was a project to purify and bottle spring water, which was approved by the village assembly, supported by leaders in the migrant community in Madera, and successfully submitted to the 3 × 1 programme to receive matching funding. Reverse osmosis technology and bottling equipment enabled the production of bottled water. As of 2015, however, the operation did not have the licence to sell this water, due to a lack of storage facilities that were separate from the production laboratory space. Work on a storage facility was generating construction jobs for local men.

Past and current experiences suggest that migrant investments in productive projects will face significant challenges. Unlike public works, productive projects require more than physical infrastructure, but also social organizations able to hire, fire, and direct workers, to account for flows of money, and to manage planning, purchasing, and marketing activities over multi-year cycles. Neither village governance structures, migrant associations, nor the majority of government or NGO development assistance organizations are well equipped to transfer these kinds of skills. The water bottling project already has tensions between the chief of the administration committee and the village authorities to whom he (a young deported migrant) must answer. He complains about not being paid and points out problems of project design.

Gil Martínez de Escobar (2006) described a fish farm funded by the Rotary organization. Although not officially a collective investment by migrants, it required donations from the migrant associations in California and Oregon to replace missing contributions required from the local Rotary organization in Huajuapan. The tanks stand empty and abandoned now, testament to the failure of a project with no clear marketing plan, a training programme inaccessible to the illiterate community members selected to manage the operation, errors in constructing water lines, and the expectation that fish farm managers live isolated from the rest of the village to tend the tanks even though no housing or compensation was provided. Another barrier to success of that project came from the fact that the village does not typically consume fish.

None of the collective remittances from migrant associations cover ritual celebrations, but Tindureños can demonstrate their religious convictions and cultural citizenship by participating in one of the two *mayordomias*, which support the village's main ritual celebrations honouring the Immaculate Conception, Our Father Jesus of Nazareth, and others. Each *mayordomia* consists of a mayordomo and four diputados, who typically live in the US because that is where the money is. They raise money from volunteers and organize the contracting of bands and purchasing of fireworks and food. The core body of donor/volunteers form *hermandades*, each with 50 or 60 members who contribute $300 or $400 each. The mayordomo and the diputados each contribute significantly more.

Reorienting translocal governance and development goals

An internal debate is forming within the Tindureño migrant community about the objectives of their organizations. On one hand there are those who favour maintaining the expensive ritual celebrations in Santa María Tindú and keeping the migrant organization focused on the needs of their community of origin in Mexico. These are mostly older pioneer migrants and the original beneficiaries of IRCA. Members of this group often join the brotherhoods that form the mayordomías and raise large sums of money to support the lavish patron saints' festivals in Santa María Tindú.

On the other hand there are younger people who arrived in the US as children and are more oriented toward US culture. They continue to identify as Tindureño and wish to maintain their Hometown Associations in California and Oregon, but redirect these to meet community needs in the US. In contrast with their neighbours in the brotherhoods and mayordomias, this group believes that their money would be better spent on the social development needs of Tindureños living in Madera.

> We must make people aware that in reality we are not benefiting anyone from the community, because all those funds that are collected over a long time on the basis of our hard work get burned up in fireworks in one hour. The band arrives, plays for one hour and goes away, and there goes $10,000 dollars!
>
> (Miguel, Home Town Association President, Madera, California)

Migrant associations are beginning to reduce the emphasis on collective remittances in favour of projects to benefit their members in the US. In Madera, for example, in addition to the base $60 contribution to support projects in Santa María Tindú, hometown association members are expected to give $40 for domestic projects.

> We are modifying the investment ratios: A percentage for over there and a percentage for back here, because remember that here we have a project to give scholarships. We also have the idea of investing in a vehicle to get around in, a car or minivan or something. We will also want to buy some

kind of furniture and space for storage. So, you see the mesa directiva has a lot of dreams, a lot of projects, and so we really do need money here [in Madera].

(Miguel, Home Town Association President, Madera, California)

Our children are not going to return here. We are working for scholarships, to promote sports and youth activities. Our children are no longer coming back here; we're thinking about the future citizens [in the United States].

(Jaime, leader of the Oregon migrant community)

Migration and conservation

In the 1970s and early 1980s, the village population peaked at 1500 and the seasonal migration of the time supported household livelihoods that included agriculture and livestock. Since then, the planted area and the number of sheep, goats, and cattle have declined. This is most notable in the area known as Sata Yuki N'daa, 'Behind the Cerro de la Mano', a rugged mountainside sloping steeply down to the Rio Mixteco. In the past, it was used for growing slash-and-burn corn and squash on steep fields. A fabric map of the community territory, dating to 1947 or 1948, estimated that 15 per cent of the 'Sata Yuki N'daa' area was agricultural. Farming continued there into the 1970s. The area was also rented as a seasonal foraging area to transhumant goat herders moving their herds of thousands of goats from Putla, on the Pacific coast to markets in Tehuacán, Puebla. This continued through to the 1980s. Since the exodus to the US during the 1990s, however, it has only been used by a few community members as a source of medicinal herbs.

In 2013, the village assembly accepted a proposal from the National Commission of Protected Areas to declare 625 ha as a Voluntary Conservation Area, and confirmed this acceptance with migrant associations. The revegetating conservation area now shelters ocelot, jaguarundi, puma, deer, and numerous threatened and endangered plants (ADN Sureste 2014). Other than occasional temporary employment clearing fire breaks, the project generates no direct monetary benefit to the community, although ecotourism is a possibility in the future. Nevertheless, communal authorities say that it will generate benefits for the community's grandchildren:

As I see it, I have a vision that the conservation area will have positive impacts. There will be more trees, more rain. It will provide us with more good air and animals. There will be more deer, like in Oregon. It'll be good for us. There will be animals like panther, cola pinta, deer, coyote, tejon, racoon, fox, javelina, ocelot … right now it doesn't bring us anything, but in the future, it can give us recreation and tourism. Right now, it's only conservation for the animals, there's no economic benefit.

(Javier, President of the Office of the Common Property Commissioner)

Conclusion

In Santa María Tindú, US migration policy shapes transborder connections. Seasonal migration once complemented a farming community of 1500, but in the 1990s, two-thirds of the population left to establish their families in the US. This pattern of immigration in Tindú corresponds to changing US immigration policy. Interviewees repeatedly identified IRCA of 1986 as a watershed event, which converted a cyclical, seasonal pattern of migration supporting resident families, to one where entire families moved once a family member was able to establish permanent residency in the US. Currently, increased border enforcement means that undocumented Tindureños living in the United States are not willing to leave and that young men and women in Tindú are unlikely to risk the trip north. Thus, cyclical migration between Tindú and the US is only available now to a select group of migrants who have already established legal residency or citizenship in the US.

Meanwhile, a large population of migrants remains connected to the village of origin. The 500 people living in the village of Santa María Tindú are part of a community of approximately 4500 Tindureños living elsewhere. The largest concentration lives in Madera, CA, with important groupings in Oregon, other California cities, and elsewhere in Mexico. Most villagers do not live in their home village, and this pattern also holds for the rights-holding comunero who own the 8500 ha of collective private property surrounding the home village.

The village is like the tip of an iceberg; it is the visible root and remnant of a much larger translocal community. Tindú relies heavily on an extensive migrant community to breathe life into a remnant village. Collective remittances from the translocal community of Tindureños fund collective infrastructure and welfare projects in the home village, family remittances go to house construction, and *mayordomías* transfer money from the migrant community to fund the village's cycle of ritual celebrations.

Migrant investments, often leveraged by municipal, state, and federal funds through a matching grant programme, have transformed the infrastructure of the village. Migrants have poured their savings into concrete houses, replacing traditional dwellings of log, adobe, and cane. They also purchased the first ambulance in the region, paved village streets, built bridges over gulleys where neighbours had been swept away in floods, installed spring-fed drinking water systems, sewers, and a sewage treatment plant. Productive investments, however, have been much more difficult. A fish farm failed, and a water-bottling project shows problems in its planning process and management structure.

Migrants formed formal hometown associations that are linked to village governance structures, and which participate in village decision-making. These organizations provide arenas for the members of a translocal community to establish and exercise their community membership even when they live far outside of the physical limits of the community's collectively-owned territory. Some migrants also contribute to village governance by returning to serve cargos.

The long-term future of connections between the village and the translocal community is uncertain, however. The resident population is disproportionately elderly. Census data for 2010 record only 10 per cent of the village population under 15 and 50 per cent over 60 (INEGI 2010). Only 35 children are enrolled in the local K-12 school.

In the near future, the village's future population will be supplemented by deportees, many who left the village as children. More numerous, however, will be seasonal and permanent retirees from some of the 1000 IRCA-era migrants, who are currently 45 and older. They grew up in Tindú, and some will be attracted to a nostalgic retirement community with a pleasant climate and an extremely low cost of living. In the next decades, they are likely to add a significant number of returning migrants to the community. Eventually, however, connections between the migrant and resident populations are likely to weaken. On the one hand, the closing of the border and a small and aging resident population means the village will stop contributing to the US migrant community. On the other hand, the aging IRCA-era migrant population will inevitably decrease. Similarly, connections with the Hometown Associations have been strong since the 1990s, and have changed little over the last decade, but these Associations are beginning to reduce their focus on their village of origin in order to address the needs of a new generation of Tindureños rooted in the US and unlikely to ever return to Santa María Tindú.

Thus, we see a kind of reorientation of the translocal community away from supporting the community of origin and towards supporting families and communities in the US, with less and less thought of permanent return. This also happens with other Oaxacan Home Town Associations; contributions to village governance, collective remittances for community development, and contributions for patron saint celebrations decline. It suggests the ephemerality of translocal community governance, a theme that is explored in greater detail in Chapter 11.

Meanwhile, migration creates new conservation opportunities. Migration has opened up new land use opportunities for areas marginal to agriculture and the community has established a Voluntary Conservation Area under the auspices of the National Commission of Protected Areas. Although the economic impact has been minimal, community leaders recognize intangible benefits from conservation.

Notes

1 This figure is from village authorities. The 2010 census counted 471 individuals in the village.
2 A census in 2003 recorded 1056 '*ciudadanos*' (or citizens, and a less exclusive category than comunero) for an estimated total population of 2500. Approximately 40 per cent of these ciudadanos lived in the village, 26 per cent were in Madera, 20 per cent in Oregon, and the rest spread out across locations in the US, Baja California, and other parts of Mexico (Gil Martínez de Escobar 2003).

References

ADN Sureste. 2014. Certifican a 625 hectáreas como ANP en Santa María Tindú, Oaxaca. September 13, 2014. Available at http://adnsureste.info/certifican-a-625-hectareas-como-anp-en-santa-maria-tindu-oaxaca-1357-h/.

Bernard, H.R. 2017. *Research Methods in Anthropology: Qualitative and Quantitative Approaches*. London: Rowman & Littlefield.

Gil Martínez de Escobar, R. 2003. Estrategias de desarrollo transnacional de una comunidad indígena oaxaqueña: Santa María Tindú. Presented in *el Primer Coloquio Internacional sobre Migración y Desarrollo: Transnacionalismo y Nuevas Perspectivas de Integración*, Universidad Autónoma de Zacatecas, pp. 23–25. Available at http://meme.phpwebhosting.com/~migracion/primer_coloquio/3_4.pdf.

Gil Martínez de Escobar, R. 2006. *Fronteras de pertenencia. Hacia la construcción del bienestar y el desarrollo comunitario transnacional de Santa María Tindú, Oaxaca*. Mexico City, Mexico: Juan Pablos Editores-Universidad Autónoma Metropolitana. (No. 307.097 274 G5).

INEGI. 2010. Censo de Población y Vivienda 2010. Principales resultados por localidad (ITER) Available at www3.inegi.org.mx/sistemas/iter/default.aspx?ev=5.

INEGI. n.d. Archivo Histórico de Localidades Geoestadísticas (Historical Archive of Geostatistical Localities), Santa María Tindú. Accessed May 25, 2018. http://geoweb2.inegi.org.mx/ahl/realizaBusquedaurl.do?cvegeo=205490015.

Revilla López, U. 2010. *Trabajadores agrícolas Mixtecos en el Valle de San Joaquín, California*. Doctoral Thesis in Social Studies. Universidad Autónoma Metropolitana, Unidad Iztapalapa, Mexico.

Stuart, J and M. Kearney. 1981. Causes and effects of agricultural labor migration from the Mixteca of Oaxaca to California. *Working Papers in US–Mexican Studies*, 28. Program in United-States–Mexican Studies, University of California-San Diego, La Jolla, CA.

6 Children of the wind

Migration and change in Santa María Yavesía

Mario Fernando Ramos Morales and James P. Robson

Summary

In the Zapotec community of Santa María Yavesía, migrants are asked to recognize and respect their roots and to maintain a social contract with the home collective. Migrants have been an important source of moral and financial support for the community, from funding its annual festivities and investing in village health and education services, to helping to deal with an ongoing agrarian conflict with neighbouring territories. This chapter explores the significance of migrant–community linkages over time, from watershed moments in Yavesía's recent past to a contemporary context in which active migrants are few in number and limited in the support they can provide. The chapter highlights the significance of migration to destinations within Mexico, as well as legal, seasonal labour migration to the US.

Methods

This chapter draws on ethnographic research conducted over different periods by Ramos Morales and Robson. In the case of Ramos Morales, who is a citizen of Yavesía, the work draws on direct observations and participation in community institutions and assemblies over a 16-year period (2002–2018), and interviews during this same period with municipal and communal authorities, and with migrants and their families and migrant organizations in Mexico City, Los Angeles, and Chicago. In the case of Robson, interviews with village authorities, community members, and returned migrants were conducted in Yavesía during the period 2014–2015, with individual and group interviews held with migrants, migrant leaders, and migrant organizations in Oaxaca City, Mexico City, Los Angeles, and Chicago during the period 2014–2016.

Setting and introduction

Santa María Yavesía (hereafter referred to as Yavesía) (Figure 6.1) is an Indigenous Zapotec community and municipality, located in the Sierra Juarez, a subregion of the Sierra Norte of Oaxaca.

Figure 6.1 Homes and landscape in Santa María Yavesía.
Source: photo credit: Jim Robson.

The community was first settled in AD 600, and is home to 9140 hectares of heavily forested lands. Its people have long maintained a strong attachment to multiple elements of the local environment, in particular forest and water. Until recently, regular rituals were held in honour of the *Dios Guzio*, the God of Lightening and Rain, and of Fertility, central components to the cosmovision of the *Benne Shoora* Zapotec who make Yavesía their home (Ramos Morales 2013). Local economic activities are centred on agriculture and orcharding.

Customary Indigenous law (*Usos y costumbres*) remains the system around which civic and communal governance in Yavesía is structured (see Chapter 2). The General Assembly is the maximum authority in the community, and is where all major decisions are made. Tequio is the institution of collective, unpaid labour used to carry out work in the community for the common good. Village cargos form the internal, normative system by which community plans are implemented, and cover religious, civic, and communal aspects of village life. Together, active participation in the asamblea, and the performing of tequio and cargos when called to do so, form the basis of the social contract that community members are expected to adhere to in return for receiving the benefits of village life.

In this case study, we explore Yavesía's past relationship with migration to highlight the role of migrants in supporting their communities of origin at times of need or to enhance the cultural development of their collectivities despite physical absence from the home village. We argue that prior experiences constitute a form of institutional memory that the community can draw upon as contemporary challenges present themselves. However, the emergence of new migrant profiles, changing migration dynamics, and deteriorating migrant–village relations may reduce this possibility in the future.

Migration history (1940–present)

Migration is a fact of life in the Sierra Juarez, an area first settled by families and kin groups that travelled from Monte Alban and other principal centres in Oaxaca's Valles Centrales during the classic (200 to 900 CE) and post-classic (900–1519 CE) periods (Ramos Morales 2013). In Yavesía, little is known about early migration dynamics in and out of the village, but oral histories suggest that notable out-migration first emerged in the initial decades of the twentieth century. However, most early streams were sporadic, local, and often seasonal in nature, and it wasn't until the 1940s that flows became more significant and migration extended to places beyond Oaxaca's borders. It is this period, post-1940, that we focus on here, identifying six distinct phases (Table 6.1).

Different migration profiles or types emerge across these phases. Phases 2–4 saw an important *permanent migration* dynamic emerge, where people left with little intention of returning to live in their home village. This was more evident among internal (within Mexico) than US-bound streams. Permanent absence often implied disconnection from the community of origin, so such a dynamic contributed not only to village population loss but also fewer community members willing to participate in local governance institutions. During Phase 4, a form of *semi-permanent* migration also emerged, particularly among undocumented migrants living in the US. Sometimes tied to people leaving without a clear long-term plan, it is a dynamic also shaped by subsequent changes in migrants' personal situations in destination centres, as well as the effective 'closing' off of the border for US-based migrants without papers. Such individuals cannot be considered permanent absentees, since even those with decades living north of the border can face possible deportation. Finally, Yavesía has experienced an important *temporary-legal labour migration* dynamic that sets it apart from many communities in the region (see Phase 5). This stream began in the mid-1990s and enables significant numbers of adult men to travel to multiple destinations in the US to work for five to six months per year (from April to October).

Table 6.1 Key phases of out-migration from Santa María Yavesía (1940s–present day)

Phase 1 (1940s–1950s) The Bracero Program	Temporary, legal migration to the US, to work mainly in agriculture. Once contracts ended, most Braceros returned to Yavesía. A small number stayed and settled (without papers) in the US. Compared with some other communities in the region, relatively few men from Yavesía participated in the programme. However, it was an instructive experience, introducing members to life north of the border.
Phase 2 (1950s–1970s) Student migration to Mexico City	Migration of young people to Mexico City, many in order to continue their studies. Many stayed on to raise families in Mexico City, although some have since returned to Yavesía and Oaxaca.
Phase 3 (1960s–1980s) Female migration to Mexico City and northern Mexico	This involved the migration of women to Mexico City (often to find jobs as domestic workers) and to Tijuana and Mexicali (in Mexico's north) to work in the growing number of assembly plants there. The exodus was in part due to a high female population in Yavesía at the time. Because the main productive activities of farming, orcharding, and mining were considered to be men's work, this meant limited livelihood opportunities for women who didn't marry. While most women left for places in Mexico, some moved on to the US once migration routes and networks became established in the 1980s and 1990s.
Phase 4 (1970s–2000s) Undocumented wage labour to the US	The undocumented wage labour migration of (mainly single) men and women to the US, with two main destination centres: Los Angeles and Chicago.
Phase 5 (1990s–present) Legal migration to US (H-2B program)	The temporary-legal wage labour migration of adult men from the community to work in different parts of the US. Began in 1996 with six participants, peaking at 60 individuals in 2014. Average participation over past few years has been 30–40 individuals.
Phase 6 (2000s–present) Student migration to Mexican cities	Significant rise in the number of young people, especially girls, leaving to further their studies in regional and national urban centres.

Migrants as key actors in community and regional development

To understand community governance in Indigenous Oaxaca, it is necessary to understand the social contract that binds community members together, structured around participation in collective work and communal service obligations. This contract stipulates that members can only exercise their civic and communal rights once obligations to the collective have been met. It is an expectation that lies at the heart of the dilemma facing both actual and would-be migrants. That is, in order to maintain a good standing in the community, non-residents must do what they can, or what is asked of them, to support the community in absentia. Unlike some other communities in the Sierra Juarez, Yavesía has yet to make written, 'legal' obligations of its non-resident members. Rather, it relies on their sense of moral commitment to the community to secure their participation, collaboration, and cooperation in village governance structures and development support. While this social contract remains front and centre in the minds of many migrants, recent research (Robson, in press) shows that growing numbers may be breaking with community expectations. Non-participation has led to resentment in the village – 'those that leave aren't named [to do cargos] and it's bad because those of us here get screwed!' – and may encourage the asamblea to create new laws to stipulate how migrants will serve their community.

Yet any erosion of migrant–community ties also highlights the remarkable investments in *comunalidad* that Yavesian migrants have made over many years, in spite of physical separation and often prolonged absences. As a village resident explained, 'service to the community remains the basis of the community and that has never changed, including among migrants … [indeed] with them it can be the opposite – being away strengthens their links to the village!'. This commitment most clearly manifests itself in the migrant organizations established in Oaxaca City, Mexico City, Tijuana, as well as Los Angeles and Chicago in the US. The actions and activities of these organizations tend to mirror how cooperation unfolds in Yavesía itself, where work groups and commissions are set up to oversee the village-level activities and enterprises that underpin the political project of communal-community life.

In the section that follows, we report on two areas of community life in which Yavesian migrants (in both instances, those living in Mexico City) have been critical: the defence of Yavesía's communal territory; and the promotion of inter-community basketball in the Sierra Juarez and among migrant communities in Mexico City.

Migration and territorial governance

In Yavesía, there are multiple reasons or factors that help to explain why people leave the village, and not all fit the classic narrative of 'poverty' as driver. For instance, in the 1950s and 1960s, significant migration stemmed from a desire of young people (encouraged by their parents) to continue into higher education, which up until the 1990s meant leaving both village and region. In the 1960s and 1970s, a gender imbalance in Yavesía's village population encouraged girls and young women – faced with the prospects of being single in a place where paid work for females was extremely limited – to look elsewhere for opportunities.

From the 1960s through to 2000, another significant push factor was an ongoing territorial conflict, at times violent, between Yavesía and the other members of an eight-village/three-community Commonwealth known as 'Pueblos Mancomunados'. Rooted in prehispanic inter-village cooperation, the Mancomunados was formally established in 1891, and constituted an arrangement by which property rights to forests and other natural resources were held and administered by a Commonwealth of communities rather than individual member communities. From 1891 through to the second half of the twentieth century, the relationship between member villages was often strained because of disagreements over how money generated from natural resource use and extraction was controlled, and the political and economic influence of regional political bosses (*caciques*). In the early 1950s, Yavesía attempted to withdraw its membership and regain control of its communal territory, but was denied by the other members of *Mancomunados*, who were supported by state and federal governments. In 1961, when the federal government officially reaffirmed (common property) title to the Commonwealth of territories, the existing tensions turned into full-blown legal/jurisdictional/territorial/ecological conflict, as Yavesía fought against logging within what it considered its own territory.

The community's fight took shape just as new migration streams (to Mexico and the US) emerged and became established. And while these conflicts contributed to an exodus of village residents, absentee members subsequently became an important source of support for Yavesía in its struggle for territorial sovereignty. A group of 25 migrants who had left for Mexico City in the 1950s and 1960s organized themselves to create the *Unión Liberal Serrana*, with the goal of funding Yavesía's legal battles to get its customary territory and statutory rights recognized. As Ramos told Robson in 2014, 'this was about providing both ideological and economic support to Yavesía in its efforts to defend and protect its forest'. Each member provided a weekly donation of around 15 pesos, or US$40 in today's money, with some contributing even more.[1] In 1964, the leader of the organization became Yavesía's communal representative, and travelled on a regular basis to Oaxaca and Yavesía to oversee legal proceedings. This same individual was instrumental in getting a territorial boundary line marked in the 1970s to show the extent of the lands that the community laid claim to. By the end of the 1990s, the community was finally in a position to name a communal representative who lived in the community. At that point, the *Unión Liberal Serrana* disbanded, considering its work to be done.

Thus, during a prolonged struggle for territorial sovereignty, it was migrants from Yavesía that were among the lead protagonists. And it is thanks to their efforts that migration is perhaps viewed in a less negative light by village residents in Yavesía than in other places. Residents are thankful to their fellow community members in Mexico City for having covered the bulk of Yavesía's legal costs, for having fulfilled the cargo of communal representative for 30-odd years, as well as the cargo of Municipal President from the end of the 1960s to the mid-1970s. Migrant support proved crucial once again in 1999 and the early 2000s, when conflict arose over logging by other members of the Commonwealth on Yavesía's community lands, and debates about the best means to combat a pine beetle infestation that affected areas of old growth forest. Migrants contributed funds to cover the cost of necessary sanitation and surveillance work in the forest,[2] and these efforts helped to reinforce social cohesion within the community.

Collectively, the work of residents and migrants in defence of Yavesía's natural patrimony has led to a strong conservationist ethic to emerge among much of the community's broad membership. Indeed, its current 'no-logging' policy sets Yavesía apart from several of its Zapotec neighbours. As a 19 year-old female village resident noted, Yavesía wants 'proper sustainable development that uses the environment only moderately ... where conservation and restoration is fundamental [to who we are]'. Robson's work in Oaxaca City, Mexico City, and the US shows that Yavesian migrants are largely supportive of this approach to conservation. Long-term absentees in the US supported the logging ban, keen that the village (they may return to) maintains a good water supply and an intact forest. Temporary labour migration to the US has also shaped community opinion, since the men who participate do so as workers for an 'integrated vegetation management' company called Progressive Solutions. Contracted to apply herbicides to rights-of-way across the US, these migrants have seen what effect herbicides can have on adjacent forests, and many return to Yavesía not wanting to see their forest lands similarly degraded. As one H-2B migrant explained, 'we want to conserve the forest so we can enjoy what we have'.

Migrants as promoters of Indigenous sports and culture

At the same time that migrants in Mexico City were supporting Yavesía in its territorial struggles, they were also pioneering the use of sport – in this case, basketball – to bring Indigenous migrants together in a celebration of custom and culture. Yavesians were among the founders of Mexico City's 'Sierra Juárez' Basketball League. As Gil Jaime Cruz Hernández, of Yavesía, explains:

> Towards the end of the 1950s a lot of us went to Mexico City to study, to work, to do a number of things, and the only time we got together was on Sundays at the Venustiano Carranza sports centre, in Balbuena. In the early days, there was already a basketball league there but it wasn't a Sierra Juárez league ... anyway, they used the centre and there weren't too many basketball courts, and the paisanos were keen to form their own league and it was logical to make it for people from the Sierra Juárez and that's how it got started ... I remember at the time that a paisano from Yavesía, Teófilo, was heavily involved in the organization and then my brother Héctor Cruz Hernández took over ... that's how the Sierra Juárez league in Mexico City came about. At the time, there were a lot of serranos who were finishing up their university studies and wanted to get together and socialize, and so they organized themselves. And there was lots of interest, lots came ... I remember the first tournaments they organized and there were a lot of strong teams that came from the region such as Xiacuí, Lachatao, Yavesía, Latuvi, and Zoogocho ... it was this group that took it upon themselves to get the league together.[3]

The *Liga Sierra Juárez* started in Mexico City in 1971. In 1975, it held the inaugural Sierra Juárez tournament, with teams representing communities from across the region.

Those living in Mexico City did not see basketball simply as a means to promote highland culture in their new place of residence, but also as a way to build links with their communities of origin. For many years now, teams have travelled each year to Oaxaca to play in the tournaments that form part of their home village patron saint festivities:

> [In the Sierra Juárez league] we had 150 teams across all categories. Israel Martínez had his team from Capulalpam ... he took them to the reserve leagues in Mexico City and then later to the major league there, and that got others hooked. Israel also liked to be a part of that scene [politics] and went about encouraging people to act on their urge to organize, to the point where we got together with Frente Revolucionario Oaxaqueño in Mexico City and the Valley of Mexico. It was that partnership that enabled us to travel each year to the Sierra and be in contact with all the people there. From that group, a bunch of us committed to going to the village of each one of our compatriots to play basketball as part of their annual festivities, but only on the condition that they reciprocated and went to play at the fiesta of another community and so on and so forth ... and that's how we ended up going to [our neighbouring communities of] Trinidad, Xiacuí, Macuiltianguis, Atepec, and Ixtlán to play basketball. We had travelled from Mexico City to play in villages across the Sierra and out of that we built a very interesting relationship that just continued to grow ... it's from those early comings together around basketball that I believe the idea for the annual Copa Benito Juárez tournament in Guelatao was born.[4]

In 1975, at the inauguration of Yavesía's Municipal Palace (Offices), Gil Jaime Cruz Hernández and colleagues from the Zapotec communities of Capulalpam de Mendez, San Pablo Macuiltianguis, and Santiago Xiacui met to discuss the idea of organizing an inter-village, inter-region basketball contest in the Sierra Juarez in the name of Lic. Benito Juárez, Mexico's first Indigenous President (1857–1858), who was born and raised in the region. The Copa Benito Juárez was born. As Gil Jaime Cruz Hernandez explains:

> I had the chance to open the remodelled Municipal Palace in Yavesía, and I was accompanied by Israel Martínez, Álvaro Alavés, Filemón,[5] Luis ... and we chatted about getting our paisanos together to organize a tournament in the region, something along the lines of how they organize the World Cup in football, where we would organize by sub-regions, and we saw the Sierra as being constituted by four regions ... and the idea would be that teams in each region would play each other and produce one winning [champion] team, and these four teams would come here and play for the inaugural Copa Benito Juárez. In 1975, Israel was in charge of contacting

the paisanos that were here [in the Sierra], and that included Vicente Montes[6] who became an important part of getting that first tournament set up. [The tournament] was all about convivencia, because in the pueblos it was clear that basketball could help make the annual fiestas even bigger events that brought more people together. I remember the one in Macuiltianguis, I'd never played a final before at 3 am and everyone was still there waiting to see who would win and for the tournament to finish so that the dancing could begin … it was very impressive to us players and from then on we became active participants in different communities' festivities.[7]

The first Copa Benito Juárez basketball tournament took place on March 21, 1977 and has been held every year since, to become one of the main cultural events in the region.

The promotion of basketball in the region, and its tie-in to village festivities, was instrumental in starting the now long-standing tradition of migrants contributing to the costs of organizing annual festivities in their communities of origin. In Yavesía, a fiesta is held in honour of the Virgen de la Concepción each and every December, and it is custom for those residents who sit on the 'Fiesta Committee' to travel in-person to Mexico City and Oaxaca City, and send written requests to migrants further afield, in order to request donations for the fiesta. Migrant support has become essential for covering the costs of food, music, tournament prize-money, and, since 2014, bull-riding (el jaripeo). A direct outcome of this support is that the annual fiesta is far more vibrant today than it was in the past, and villagers openly acknowledge that they would struggle to organize similar events without the help of permanent and temporary (H-2B) migrants. The latter group, in particular, play a key role. They organize and pay for the bull-riding event. They also pay for the musical groups that open the main dance of the fiesta. For residents and visitors alike, this event is free thanks to the patronage of these migrants. The significance of their contribution became apparent in 2017, when President Trump's anti-immigrant platform placed the H-2B programme in doubt. The men couldn't travel to the US at the end of March as was their custom, as the issuing of their visas was put on hold. It seemed likely that they would not travel at all. Upon hearing this news, the first question that many residents in Yavesía were heard raising was, 'How are we are going to hold the fiesta this year!'

Lastly, through their investments in sporting leagues, and other forms of cultural capital, migrant leaders, such as those from Yavesía, have helped to establish a tradition of inter-community interactions in the Sierra Juarez. The broader significance of this contribution cannot be underestimated. It is possible, perhaps likely, that without such developments, Indigenous forest-owning communities in the Sierra Norte would not have successfully mobilized against the renewal of forestry concessions in the 1980s (that would have seen logging rights over community forests granted to private logging and milling companies). In this way, migrants are among the key local actors who lay the groundwork to enable Oaxaca's community forestry sector to emerge (Klooster 2003)

Migration and village governance

Life in Yavesía is built upon active participation in the social institutions of tequio, cargo, and the asamblea, which combine with Zapotec territoriality and cosmovision to form the communal philosophical corpus of life, enshrined in the Zapotec-Mixe Indigenous concept of *comunalidad*. Within this context, migration (in all its varied forms) can drive transformative change, with affected communities forced to adapt customary structures in order to keep them viable and enable continued political autonomy.

From the 1940s through to the present day, the impacts of migration in Yavesía emerged gradually, almost creeping up on people. In the early years, most of those in the village would have neither felt nor seen the impact because there still seemed to be plenty of people living locally. Indeed, the more visceral impacts didn't emerge until the end of the 1980s, when population loss combined with declining fertility to produce sharp falls in the number of residents and an aging group of village residents[8] (see Figures 6.2 and 6.3).

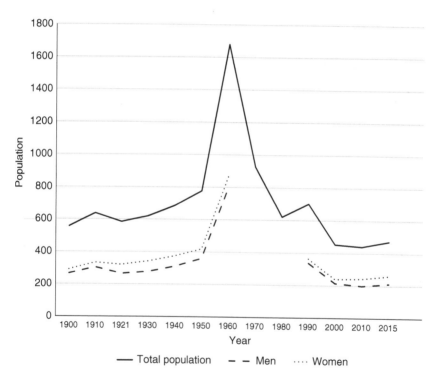

Figure 6.2 Population change in Santa María Yavesía (1900–2010).

Source: INEGI Census data (1900–2010).

Note
1921 (rather than 1920) is used on the x-axis as it is the year recorded by INEGI, in recognition of the census that decade being carried out a year late.

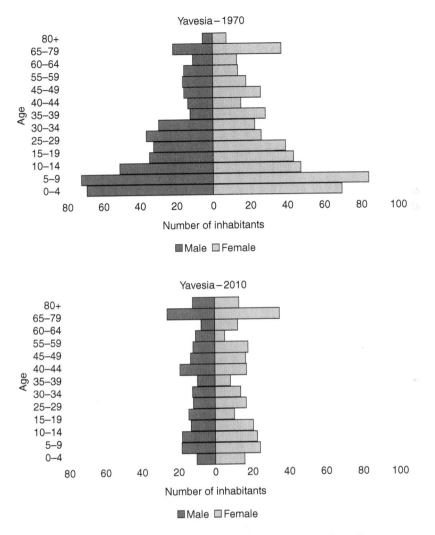

Figure 6.3 Population pyramids for Santa María Yavesía (1970 and 2010).
Source: INEGI Census data (1900–2010).

With fewer people in the village, there were suddenly fewer bodies to cover municipal, agrarian, and religious cargo demands. The cargo system began to feel overstretched. Traditionally, men would expect a number of years' rest between serving cargos, which would give them time to recover lost earnings, contribute to their family's well-being, and begin to save for their next stint of communal service. Migration put an end to that, with men rarely enjoying more than one or two years 'rest' between cargos. Over time, this has become a source of concern and frustration, with most in the village viewing communal service as a burden, rather than as a matter of pride and prestige through which status could be measured (after Martinez Luna 2013).

In recent years, long-term absentees have come forward with specific offers of support to village governance institutions. Active migrants in Mexico City, for example, have asked to be named to carry out cargos in the village. This has transpired on a number of occasions, and in most cases, migrants have chosen to pay someone from the village to perform the cargo on their behalf. In Los Angeles, a group of around 20 active migrants have been discussing the possibility of collectively financing one or two cargos per administration. With most unable to travel back to Oaxaca, and possessing only limited resources, they see this as the most practical way to 'do their bit' in support of those back home. Similar adaptations have been seen in other communities in the region, where lower-level cargos – topil, secretario, commission/committee member – have become paid positions (i.e. a substitute is hired) in those instances where the person named is residing outside of the home village. In contrast, it remains a custom for higher-level cargos (Municipal President, Common Property Commissioner, Mayor, etc.) to be performed in person by whoever was elected for the position. However, while not a 'paid' position, some communities have introduced or increased the stipend that the cargo-holder receives in an effort to lighten the load or burden of these posts (see Chapter 9).

These changes, which have unfolded more quickly in some places than in others, show that while migration reduces the resident pool of collective labour, the support of migrants can help these same systems be maintained and reproduced over time. Migration may even trigger forms of change that, in the long-run, are seen as necessary, such as forcing a collective conversation about the role of women in contemporary village life. As a comunera from Yavesía notes, 'when the husband isn't here, we are given a cargo to serve on some committee, to help the community and its people. The husband might not be here, but we are'.

In the case of Yavesía, the burden placed on local governance is less severe than it would have been thanks to the emergence of legal guestworker (H-2B) migration to the US since the mid-1990s. Of the dynamics emergent across different migration phases (see Table 6.1), temporary migration of this kind enables migrants to maintain an active presence in village life and community governance. First, Yavesía's H-2B migrants are away for short enough periods to remain part of cargo rosters. Second, they still participate directly in tequio and community assemblies for half the year, paying fines for those they miss. Several of the men who travel each year do so with a cargo obligation, hiring someone within the community, often a family member, to perform their duties while they are away. Indeed, the emergence of contract (paid) positions has turned Yavesía's cargo system into a source of migrant-funded temporary employment. The community has also adapted its tequio system so that the most substantial village and territorial infrastructure projects take place during the six months of the year when H-2B migrants are living in the village.

Despite obvious challenges, Yavesía has often found ways to navigate the worst impacts of migration and, in some instances, use it to its advantage. Where this has not been possible is in the General Assembly, where migration has shorn the collective of ideas and perspectives that would likely benefit community decision-making processes. Participation in the assembly is essentially restricted to individuals living in Yavesía. At times, resident adults have been so few in number that it has been a challenge to make critical decisions about village life and draft appropriate policies for the community to enact. Changes have been made in an attempt to mitigate this problem. For example, since 2000, those assemblies where very important decisions are to be taken – such as the election of new authorities – have been scheduled at times when the full cohort of adult men are present in the village. Even so, decisions taken in the assembly remain a function of those present, and on several occasions, conflicts have emerged with active members living outside of the home village, who struggle to get their ideas put forward for consideration. This is a particular problem for migrants living in Mexico City and the US, for whom trips back to Oaxaca are not possible or practical. Frustrations have not been eased by poor communication between migrants and village authorities, limited information being sent to migrants, and a general lack of coordination (see Chapter 11 for more on this). As problems have built up over time, significant numbers of migrants have become disillusioned (Robson, in press), and are at risk of breaking ties with the community.

These findings suggest that improving links and communication between migrants and residents is a pressing challenge that the community will need to remedy if migrant–village relations in Yavesía are to be as positive and productive in the future as they have been in the past.

Conclusions

Migration has impacted life in Santa María Yavesía in multiple ways. However, the community has often found ways to resolve associated problems by drawing on its history, its culture, and its members' sense of commitment towards their place of origin. Migrant's social and capital resources have created new arenas for the community to engage in an ongoing struggle over territory and – through sports – to form networks with other communities that not only help to maintain highland culture but also build social capital that can then underpin regional mobilization and resistance during times of crisis. This case shows how a community can remain resilient in the face of migration, and how migrants can provide the impetus to drive new processes of community-making and governance, with important environmental implications. Despite current communication challenges, and tensions between migrants' and residents' understandings of community responsibilities, past experiences have given Yavesians a degree of confidence in their collective future and their ability to debate, negotiate, and adapt in response to change.

Notes

1 One of the members of the *Unión Liberal Serrana* lost his house in Mexico City in order to raise funds for the struggle.
2 Migrants in Mexico City, for example, raised $40,000 pesos to help fund the first year of tequios to 'clean' the forest of pine beetle. It is worth noting the extent of the work carried out in the forest – between 1999 and 2009 comuneros and citizens of Yavesía together dedicated approximately 8000 days of tequio in their forest stewardship work.
3 Captured at the workshop on Guelatao and Benito Juárez held on March 18, 2017 Guelatao de Juárez, Oaxaca.
4 Captured at the workshop on Guelatao and Benito Juárez held on March 18, 2017 Guelatao de Juárez, Oaxaca.
5 Natives of San Pablo Macuiltianguis who later organized communities of the Sierra Juárez to successfully resist the renewal of forest concessions on community lands, creating a pathway for community forestry in the region.
6 Native of Santiago Xiacui (passed in the year 2000).
7 Captured at the workshop on Guelatao and Benito Juárez held on March 18, 2017 Guelatao de Juárez, Oaxaca.
8 Yavesía has always been a (relatively) small community, rarely exceeding 900 inhabitants. From 1970 to 2013, however, its resident population fell from 927 to 479, a decline of almost 50 per cent. While partly attributable to declines in fertility rates post-1970s, the shrinking of resident population also coincided with periods of moderate to elevated out-migration.

References

Klooster, D. 2003. Campesinos and Mexican forest policy during the twentieth century. *Latin American Research Review* 38(2): 94–126.

Martinez Luna, J. 2013. *Textos sobre el camino andado (Vol. I)*. Oaxaca, Mexico: CSEIIO.

Ramos Morales, M.F. 2013. *Territorio, naturaleza y proyecto de vida de la comunidad zapoteca de Santa Maria Yavesía*. Unpublished manuscript.

Robson, J.P. In press. Indigenous communities, migrant organisations, and the ephemeral nature of translocality. *Latin American Research Review*.

7 More space and more constraint
Migration and environment in Santa Cruz Tepetotutla

Dan Klooster

Summary

In the Chinantec community of Santa Cruz Tepetotutla (hereafter referred to as Santa Cruz), migration has created opportunities for forest conservation at the same time that it has stressed the institutions of village self-governance upon which forest conservation depends. In this case chapter, I look at how the community adopted coercive internal rules governing migration and member participation, maintained its self-governance ability, and developed a remarkable strategy of cultural preservation based in part on forest conservation.

Methods

This research began informally with visits in 2012 to scope the village for a field course, and in 2013 and 2014 with University of Redlands students. Each of these visits consisted of several days each, were accompanied by local guides, and included discussions and/or observations of ecotourism facilities, trails, agriculture, coffee markets, environmental service payment programmes, village governance, and migration. In March of 2015, I was able to conduct four days of formal, semi-structured focus group interviews with village authorities and individual or small group interviews with families of returned migrants. Eleven interviews in Santa Cruz reached 20 informants, including four women. Additionally, I was able to speak with a community member expelled from Santa Cruz but living in a neighbouring community, and four women and one man in an extended family of migrants from Santa Cruz living in Dana Point, California. Interview guides covered migration histories, migration status and location of children, the influence of village rules on migration, and the community's conservation strategy. One person emerged as a key informant in this process. Pablo (a pseudonym) was a member of the ecotourism committee who accompanied me on many of the interviews and participated in many of them. He is a village leader with a history of participating with NGOs doing development projects and academics doing biological surveys. Field notes covering each interview were coded to permit reading themes across informants in the method described by Bernard (2017). The resulting ethnography has a bias toward the views of current community leadership and is insufficiently detailed to uncover internal community conflicts over gender relationships or community schisms surrounding families or productive activities (see for example Mutersbaugh 1999). Nevertheless, it is sufficient to shed light on the interrelated processes of migration, conservation, and internal institutional development, which are reported here.

Setting

Located 80 kilometres North of Oaxaca City, Santa Cruz (Figure 7.1) is a Chinantec Indigenous community of some 550 inhabitants, 96 per cent of whom speak the local variant of Chinantec.

These villagers collectively own 12,372 ha of rugged terrain ranging in elevation from nearly 2900 m down to 800 m above sea level. Located on the windward side of the Sierra Madre, orographic rainfall varies from 2500–4500 mm across this terrain. Biologists identify ten vegetation types[1] in the community, mostly cloud forest but also elfin forest, pine forest, and montane rainforest. Five-hundred-and-sixty species of plants have been recorded in the area, and fauna includes jaguar, puma, ocelot, red brocket deer, spider monkey, among many other species (Anta Fonseca and Mondragón Galicia 2006).

Figure 7.1 View of Santa Cruz Tepetotutla, Chinantla sub-region, Oaxaca.

Source: photo credit: Jim Robson.

In the mid and lower elevations, community members grow corn, beans, chili, squash, tomato, and cassava on hillside *milpas*, using a slash-and-burn agricultural system in a stable agricultural area. Fields are fallowed for up to 15 years, and then the secondary vegetation is again slashed, carefully burned, and planted. Chinantecs in this region manage up to several hundred species in their fallows (Mutersbaugh 1997; Van der Wal 1998). Jungle-covered ruins of pyramids, patios, ball courts, and stone tombs containing polychrome pottery attest to human habitation going back more than 600 years.

Land for planting corn is available, and agriculture provides sufficient food for families with adequate labour power. The main cash supplement to subsistence agriculture comes from coffee production and wage labour migration to urban areas of Mexico and the United States. In the past several decades, cooperatives and village projects have also established supplementary income streams from activities such as bread baking, dairy production, ecotourism, and payment for environmental services (Mutersbaugh 1997, 1999; Bray, Duran, and Molina 2012). The community was roadless until 2004. Previously, coffee and other commodities had to be carried on the back of a person or an animal. Now, a community-owned van, or local trucks, can transport villagers and their goods to Oaxaca City in about five hours.

In the 1960s, villagers overthrew their local *cacique* who had exploited his external political and economic contacts to dominate village life. Since then, Santa Cruz has developed a rigorous village governance structure based on state-sanctioned institutions. A village assembly is the highest authority. The assembly governs both communal affairs regarding the villagers' collective properties and civic affairs linking the village to state and federal institutions. To govern communal affairs, the assembly elects a president of communal property (*presidente of bienes comunales*) and a cabinet of supporters, which is collectively known as the *comisariado*. An oversight committee (*consejo de vigilancia*) provides checks on the *comisariado*'s activities. The village is an *agencia de policia* of the *municipio* (municipality) of Usila, and so the assembly also elects a set of authorities to represent the village to civil authorities (Mutersbaugh 2002; see also Table 7.1).

History of migration

Village authorities report that in 1990 Santa Cruz Tepetotutla had a population of 1200, and very little migration. Migration exploded in the mid-1990s, when coffee prices became extremely volatile and then collapsed after the dissolution of the International Coffee Agreement and the Mexican Coffee Institute INMECAFE (Jaffee 2014). Returned migrants said that they had left with several discrete goals, which could not be met if they had stayed in Santa Cruz, especially during periods of low coffee prices. Medical debts were a frequent reason for leaving. Accidents and illnesses requiring hospitalization can quickly generate expenses far beyond what can be earned growing corn and coffee in the village and so remittances from a migrant family member can quite literally mean the difference between life and death for a migrant's mother, father, brother, sister, son, or daughter. Similarly, the village economy offers few possibilities to raise money for housing improvements or to pay for children's educational opportunities after primary school. Young families wishing to build a house or to support the educational aspirations of their children often look to migration as a way to raise the necessary capital for construction materials and hired labour. Faced with poor employment prospects in Mexico, others left for the US soon after finishing high school in Oaxaca City.

During the 1990s, the weight of village obligations also provided incentives to leave. The fall in coffee prices coincided with particularly heavy communal labour obligations (*tequio*) for roadbuilding and a powerline construction project that required approximately 3000 *tequio* work days for male heads of household, plus the crucial support work of women (Mutersbaugh 2002: 482). These were unpaid days of hard physical labour clearing jungle and carrying heavy loads on difficult mountain trails. The opportunity cost of these work days was subtracted from an already marginal baseline of subsistence corn agriculture supplemented by the cultivation of coffee, for which commodity prices had collapsed.

By the year 2000, most heads of household younger than 50 years old, and about half of all villagers, had left to find work in Mexican cities and the US. Most left with their entire families, no longer communicate with village authorities, are not recognized as community members, and are not expected to return (Mutersbaugh 2002). Between 2000 and 2010, village population dropped by one-third (Figure 7.2).

In 2015, village authorities reported that Santa Cruz had 190 resident *comuneros*, an overall resident population of 550, and 20 additional *comuneros*

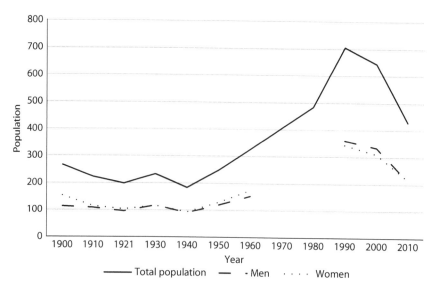

Figure 7.2 Population change in Santa Cruz Tepetotutla (1900–2010).

Sources: INEGI (1970, 1973, 1990, 2000, 2010, 2018)

expected to return eventually from their labour sojourns in New Jersey and Southern California.[2] A population pyramid based on the 2013 health clinic census (Figure 7.3) shows disproportionate numbers of elderly people and suggests missing cohorts of men and women in their prime years for working and raising families. Most of the adult children of older residents no longer live in the community: of families with five or more adult children, for example, generally only one or two remain as resident, active members of the community.

In recent years, migration to the US has reversed. No one left for the US in 2014 and only two in 2015. From 2012 to 2015, communal authorities estimate that 30 or 35 comuneros have returned with their families[3] to the village, and other migrants have returned to live and work in Oaxaca City or the regional capital of Tuxtepec. Migrants returned for a host of reasons, most commonly an illness or death in the family. Several were deported. Others returned to avoid accruing fines incurred for missed *tequios*, assemblies, and *cargos* (see below). Although there is currently no net migration to the US, it is common for villagers to pursue educational and work opportunities in Mexican urban areas.

Future of migration

In conversations about migration, villagers said migration could rise again if coffee prices fall or diseases diminish the harvest. They also note that climate change is affecting maize agriculture, and all this could create powerful incentives to migrate

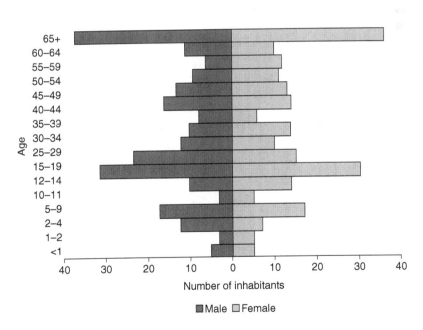

Figure 7.3 Village population pyramid (2013).

Source: Santa Cruz Health Clinic.

in the future. 'The climate is out of control. Rains come early, or they come late. Young people are looking for other opportunities,' a village leader told me in a group interview.

Mitigating such drivers are the risks and costs of crossing an increasingly dangerous border. Previous migrants say they are willing to return to the US, but only with a visa; they envy the guest worker permits held by some of their co-workers in New Jersey nurseries. Potential migrants note the dangers, difficulties and costs to cross the border, and deportees fear the jail sentences they would face if they were caught trying to re-enter the US. Potential migrants also face resistance from family members who fear for their physical safety and the moral risks of falling victim to vices such as drug and alcohol addictions.

Meanwhile, most US migrants from Santa Cruz are undocumented and have very little chance of legalizing their status under the current political climate. They face increasing insecurity, with deportation and voluntary returns seen during the Obama administration likely to continue, potentially at higher rates than before.

More space: migration and environment

Due to migration, there are fewer people farming. It requires less land to grow corn and coffee with a population of 500 than 1200 and so if the people who left in the 1990s were still present, 'We'd be doing agriculture in virgin forest', communal authorities told me. Aided by a series of environmental NGOs,[4] the community has been able to turn this conservation opportunity to its advantage.

Starting in the 1990s, academic researchers and NGOs worked with the community to promote diversification of coffee orchards and to document biodiversity and agricultural systems. These, and subsequent biological surveys, have confirmed that the region contains forests of very high conservation value and led to proposals to establish a biosphere reserve (Anta Fonseca and Mondragon Galicia 2006; Bray, Duran, and Molina 2012). In the late 1990s and early 2000s, the community worked with other NGOs and developed a forest management plan, used participatory methodologies to create a community land-use plan, promoted the cultivation of a local wild edible pacaya palm (*Chamaedorea tepejilote*) in coffee orchards and second-growth forest, and evaluated the community's social and environmental conditions using participatory methods. In the early and mid-2000s, the community worked with another NGO to form CORENCHI, a regional coalition of Indigenous communities better able to interact with governmental and non-governmental organizations in sustainable development projects and conservation proposals.

In 2003, after vigorous internal debate, the community worked with an NGO and incorporated its land use plan and participatory socioenvironmental evaluations into the community's official statutes, which they registered with federal authorities. Thus, the community now manages a territory with areas zoned for conservation, rotational slash-and-burn-and fallow *milpa* agriculture, domestic and (potentially) commercial forestry, coffee and agroforestry, environmental restoration, pasture, and the urban centre.

To govern these land use zones, village authorities can call upon their federally-recognized internal constitution, stipulating acceptable uses in each of those areas. These rules cover commoner rights and responsibilities according to zone. For example, they prohibit clearing, hunting, and extraction in the conservation zone, they require commoners to carefully monitor and control the fires used to prepare fields for planting corn, allow hunting only in agricultural areas, and limit it to common species that damage agriculture (Anta Fonseca and Mondragon Galicia 2006). In 2011, the community strengthened its conservation strategy by establishing a community protected area, in accordance with federal conservation policy (Bray, Duran, and Molina 2012).

Productive conservation as an alternative to migration

Community members now manage more than half of their territory exclusively for conservation. They value the water and biodiversity that their forests produce, but they also see it as a resource for strategies of migration management and cultural survival.

Pablo, one of the community leaders of this strategy, told me that during the participatory evaluations and discussions that took place from 2002 to 2004, they recognized the challenges and opportunities associated with migration. 'If we don't do anything, it will only be us old people left in the village!' he argued. Pablo's own daughters left for the US during this time period. 'We have to really struggle to stop migration, to conserve our own identity and community rhythm,' he told his neighbours at the time. He and several other community leaders in the early 2000s had been the attentive guides to academic researchers and the active collaborators in NGO projects during the previous decade. They were essential in the conservation and productive diversification strategies that had evolved, and came to see conservation as an integral part of a broader strategy.

> When I talk about conservation, it is not just the forest, it is our children, the mother tongue, the backyard garden, food sovereignty.... We are betting on the forest, so our children can be employed as guides, drivers, cooks. It's getting benefit from the forest.... The idea is to conserve our children and our own pueblo [village/town/people] – so our children don't risk their lives over there.
>
> (Pablo, 60-year-old community leader)

The idea is not to stop being campesinos, he told me, but to become not-so-poor campesinos through diversification.

Payment for Environmental Services (PES) is part of this strategy. Santa Cruz was an early entry into the environmental services market, selling carbon bonds on the voluntary market from 2001 to 2003. As part of CORENCHI,

Santa Cruz entered a new federal payment for a hydrological services programme. Between 2004 and 2010, Santa Cruz received US$570,000 in payments under this programme (Anta Fonseca and Mondragon Galicia 2006; Bray, Duran, and Molina 2012).

These payments have funded a collective savings fund for 180 heads of household. It helps pay some of the expenses of the *comisariado*, CORENCHI, and counterpart payments required by some government programmes. It makes a basic payment to the elderly of about 200 pesos a month, while six disabled community members receive 500 pesos a month. Funds are not distributed for living expenses, but they are available to pay for emergency medical costs, which historically could only be met by migration. In 2015, for example, a community member fell while woodcutting on a very steep slope and his injuries required treatment at a regional hospital. The expenses were covered by PES funds. In earlier times, such an event might have precipitated a family member's migration to raise medical funds.

PES funds – together with community members' *tequios*, funds from other government agencies, and donations from a downstream industrial water user – have also supported local construction projects building cabins, kitchens, a local museum, and a bottling kitchen. These projects provided employment directly, which reduced migration pressure. They also led to a rustic but comfortable infrastructure for tourism, including lodging, kitchens, trails, and guide services.

Ecotourism now generates sporadic wages to community members working as managers, guides, cooks, and cleaning staff, and generates US$4000 to US$6000 a year above expenses.[5] Profits are currently used for infrastructure improvements but will eventually go to community coffers:

> The idea is to conserve our children in our own pueblo, so they don't have to be in danger over there [in the US]. I'm betting that this will work. When I started to work in ecotourism, I dropped the idea of emigrating myself!
>
> (Pablo, 60-year-old community leader)

In 2000, Pablo had been poised to follow his daughters to go find work in the US, but the village assembly elected him to an important post in village government, and he could not leave. Instead, he fulfilled his responsibilities to the collective and over the next several years helped to build the community's productive conservation strategy. The incident illustrates the paradox at the heart of migration and environment in Santa Cruz; at the same time that migration creates conservation opportunities, it threatens the community's ability to manage those opportunities.

Productive conservation and cultural survival projects all put local village government at the centre of land management and conservation and so they require a great deal of physical, intellectual, and administrative labour to carry forward. This labour occurs in the context of a village government structure which is sorely challenged by migration.

More constraint: community controls on migration

Residents recognize the costs that migration imposes on the community. The absent cannot participate in production cooperatives (Mutersbaugh 1999: 46) or perform *tequios*, and so the time and physical labour of building and maintaining roads, powerlines, the health clinic, and other public works falls on residents. Cargos pose another area where residents must work without compensation more frequently than if their neighbours were present to share the burden (Mutersbaugh 2002). Village governance requires 101 unpaid administrative posts (Table 7.1) among a population of 550 inhabitants and 190 male rights-holding commoners. The major cargos are unpaid, remove male heads of households from important household productive activities, and require the support of the entire family – especially women – to make it possible to serve. Women fill some of those cargos, and some people hold multiple cargos at a time, but even so migration stresses the village's ability to staff these self-governance positions. The community rule granting a rest of one year for shorter cargos and three years following the three-year *comisariado* cargos is not respected. 'Some work [serving cargos] for three or five years before they get a break. Others serve all the time,' village authorities told me.

Table 7.1 Cargos needed for community governance

No. of cargos	Area of community governance
6	*Comisariado de Bienes Comunales*: These cargo-holders are responsible for matters regarding the community's 12,000 ha collective private property. They serve three-year terms.
6	*Consejo de Vigilancia*: An oversight committee providing checks on the *comisariado*
20	*Agencia de Policia*: Civil authorities linking the community to municipal and state authorities. Includes village mayor, support staff, the *policia* who enforce local laws and provide security at community festivals, and message runners
6	CORENCHI: Secretary, technical staff, and delegates to a regional organization of communities engaged in conservation, land management, and sustainable development projects
12	Ecotourism committee.
6	Community store committee: provides governance, oversight, and organizes *tequios*.
6	Road committee: provides governance, oversight, and organizes *tequios*.
6	Clinic committee: provides governance, oversight, and organizes *tequios*.
6	Chapel committee: provides governance, oversight, and organizes *tequios*.
25	Preschool, primary and junior high school committees

Source: Interview with communal authorities.

Residents remember the poverty of the coffee crisis and the intense *tequios* needed to build the powerline, the road, and the health clinic. They recall hard labour carrying heavy loads along steep forest paths while migrants avoided these responsibilities, presumably earning good wages and enjoying consumer goods that village residents could not access. For residents, it is not fair for migrants to simply return home and freely drive their new cars on a road they didn't help construct and plug their new stereos and appliances into an electrical grid they didn't help build.

> Migrants bring some income to the community. They pay people to farm for them and to build their houses.... But the clinic, electricity, the road, maintaining the border with neighbouring communities ... all that was tequio! The chapel was built with bags of cement carried on people's back. With rebar on top! It's not okay for the youth to refuse cargos these days. If we had had that idea, where would we be now?
>
> (Lalo, 56-year-old non-migrant)

At the same time, current residents recognize that migration can be vital for the family economy. Residents have likely migrated in the past and may do so in the future. They have family members who have been, are, or will be migrants. Remittances can resolve medical crises, finance home construction, and are a crucial part of household income for many cargo-holders. Thus, although migration can be an *individual* abandonment of community identity and obligation, it can also be a means to permit a *family* to meet community obligations. Lalo's experience exemplifies this tension.

> I would lose my personality if I left. It means a lot to live in your community and to not lose your position [of being a commoner] ... [But my son migrated] and he left out of need. There was no money and he left to support the family.... He sent us remittances [when I was serving the cargo of secretary of communal resources]. He saved us from hardship.

For many cargo holders, it would be difficult to serve the community without the help of migrants; remittances help feed their families while they forgo productive activities in order to serve the community. To mediate these tensions, the commoners of Santa Cruz Tepetotutla developed rules to control their migrants' behaviour. By 1995, the village had already established an internal rule linking usufruct rights to *tequio* participation, and this was perceived as a control on migration (Mutersbaugh 1997, 1999). The community could also jail or fine members who missed *tequios, cargos,* or community assemblies, and returning migrants were generally welcomed home with a cargo. By 2001, the community could impose a kind of civic death on migrants who did not comply with communal obligations, especially cargos; exile was the punishment for failing to serve (Mutersbaugh 2002).

These rules evolved into a written constitution (*reglamento comunitario*) adopted in assembly in 2003. Migrants must request permission from the assembly to leave, and they must appoint a representative to comply with their obligations while they are absent. The community then grants a three-year window to migrants during which time their appointed representative complies with the migrant's *cargo* and *tequio* obligations without charge or sanction to the migrant. Once the three-year window has passed, the representative is relieved of duty and a fine imposed on the migrant. Migrant heads of household with families established in Santa Cruz must pay a fine of 5000 pesos (roughly US$500) per year. For migrants who leave as youths without having established a family in the village, the fine is 1000 pesos per year starting at age 18. The assembly may revoke the three-year window for villagers who leave without permission, and for abandoning a cargo, migrants face an additional fine of 5000 pesos.

Migrants normally leave a family member as a representative responsible for covering *tequios*, and they face a 100 peso fine for *tequios* the representative could not cover. The migrant's representative might also get named to minor communal cargos such as *topil* in the church or school committees. Women especially suffer the absence of male heads-of-household who migrate. They experience deeper poverty, usually abandoning the hard labour of hillside slash-and-burn-and-fallow *milpa* agriculture but maintaining work on coffee, backyard gardens, minor livestock, and household productive activities.

> When I returned to the village [in 2001] I paid my missed assemblies and tequios. My wife had attended for me, but sometimes she couldn't go because she was caring for the kids, including our sick boy.
>
> (Ernesto, comunero of Santa Cruz)

> [Ernesto's absence] was really hard.... He left nothing behind for us except some coffee to sell. We were very poor! At least we had some chickens. We ate those. I suffered! There was no telephone to find out where he was, but finally a cousin arrived and told us he had arrived OK. Later, a letter came too.
>
> (Flora, Ernesto's wife)

Remittances provide relief for migrants' families, but collection requires travel to Oaxaca City or Tuxtepec. Until the road arrived in 2004, this included hiking multiple hours through the rainforest to reach the nearest road.

The 'Reglamento' as community discipline

Santa Cruz's rules have the goal of encouraging migrants to conform to community expectations of citizenship. The fines are so commoners don't go to the US only to 'fall into vice'. As Pablo explains:

> There is no room for slackers in Santa Cruz ... migration is about the 'dream of the dollar', it is about earning money. But many migrants lose

themselves among their friends. They are absent [from the village] for years and years, and there they are drinking beers while we are here carrying posts for the powerline – the guy who carried the post for electric power, here he is with no TV! The rules are so people don't fall into vice, so that they support their families. Otherwise, over there they'll be drinking their beers while here we suffer.

The three-year window gives migrants time to earn the money they need to meet their families' economic goals. After four or five years of absence, migrants are failing to respect the community. 'They say, "Nothing will happen to me, let those fools do the tequios!" But it's thanks to us fools you could arrive to the village in your car,' Pablo explained.

Migrants are seen to have responsibilities to make up for the investments in time and money that residents will have made in community maintenance while migrants are absent. The fines are a symbolic acknowledgement of the labour that residents invested in maintaining the community. But these fines also add up, creating a barrier to entry. However, if a migrant comes humbly before the assembly and asks to be charged less because things didn't go well for him, that fine could be reduced and paid over time. Negotiation is a possibility under some circumstances.

> Some migrants come home with nothing. They didn't achieve a thing. It's a problem when they arrive – they waste the assembly's time. Deportees don't bring back anything – a little backpack is all.
> (Carlos, 45-years old, member of community government)

> As soon as they get out of jail the community gives them a 5000 peso per year fine. That's 50,000 for ten years! 'How is a deportee going to pay that?' I think my sons would return if the cost wasn't so high
> (Andres, 73-years-old, comunero)

Jose, for example, was deported from the US in 2008 at age 26. He had been absent from the community since the age of 18. He lacked the funds and motivation to rejoin the community at that time, but changed his mind in 2010 because he wanted to be with his parents. He raised the 10,000 pesos fine by working on construction in Oaxaca. Several of Andres' adult sons, meanwhile, live in Oaxaca City, having never paid to re-establish their village membership after returning from the US.

The rules governing migration are designed to discipline community members. They reinforce a very strong communitarian ethic and filter out those who do not wish to comply with it. Pedro, for example, migrated from Santa Cruz as a teenager, returned, refused to pay fines or participate in *tequios*, and unsuccessfully sued the communal authorities when they tried to suspend his rights. Villagers contrast this behaviour with that of a 'good' migrant, who sent money home from his job in Pennsylvania to buy a steer to feed the elderly as an apology for missing cargos while he was away. After a decade of fighting with Pedro, the community exiled him. 'We don't want free-riders in Santa Cruz,' Pablo told me.

Conclusions

In Santa Cruz Tepetotutla, migration, environment, and community intertwine to produce a more hopeful outcome than in many cases. This case illustrates three main lessons. First, migration here has not been driven by environmental change. The most intense period of migration corresponded not to climate change or any biological crop failure, but rather to an economic crop failure brought on by a drastic decline in coffee prices. Environmental change may play some role in future migration dynamics, however. Commoners fear that coffee harvest failures due to changing pest ecologies could again drive migration. They are also concerned about changes to the local climate which make the staple corn and bean harvests less reliable than in the past. So far, however, the environment–migration story has had more to do with a forest-transition-like narrative than an environmental collapse narrative. Migration is also sensitive to the demographics of local family size, opportunities elsewhere in Mexico compared with those in the US, and US immigration enforcement policies.

Second, community rules, expectations, and labour demands actively shape migration and return. A major spike in migration accompanied a particularly intense period of communal labour demand (*tequios*).[6] Currently, residents' ability to leave, and migrants' ability to return is constrained by an explicit community strategy designed to discourage migration, to reaffirm communitarian values, and to reinforce individual responsibilities to support community institutions; as Mutersbaugh (2002) argues, Santa Cruz demonstrates that communities can exert agency over migration. Furthermore, because of this community strategy, migration has strengthened village cohesion in this case. Community rules were explicitly designed to discipline return migrants and to keep out the ones who won't support a rather strict communal regime; non-communitarian members have been purged. To confront the challenge of migration, collective coercion conserves the community. Third, migration creates opportunities for conservation. The community has both social cohesion and a less-pressured community territory in which to pursue conservation and to develop conservation as a productive, community-enhancing activity.

Santa Cruz's experience suggests a potential path for productive conservation as a biocultural conservation strategy in key areas. Santa Cruz is a rich community in terms of biological resources, cultural cohesion, and village institutions. Much of that richness has so far been protected through the collective labour of villagers, supported by a series of NGOs mobilizing national and multilateral funding opportunities.

Acknowledgements

Funding for this research was provided by National Science foundation grant #1127534, a Fulbright-Garcia Robles fellowship, and the University of Redlands. I am extremely grateful to the communal authorities of Santa Cruz, Biologist Fernando Mondragón, and Geoconservación, AC for facilitating my various visits to the community, and to Tad Mutersbaugh who commented on an advanced draft of this manuscript.

Notes

1 In Spanish, these vegetation types include bosque de pino, bosque de pino-encino, matorral de ericáceas, bosque tétrico, encinar húmedo, bosque mesófilo de lauráceas, bosque mesófilo de montaña, bosque de Oreomunea y selva alta perennifolia de montaña.
2 These numbers are higher than a census of residents made by the nurses in the local health clinic. In 2013, they counted 450 individuals in the village, 226 males and 224 females. I suspect the village authorities count people who may not be present but are members of families that are active in village life, such as dependent children attending school outside of the community. In 2001, Mutersbaugh (2002) estimated a population of 120 comuneros and 750 residents. In 2003, an NGO working in the region counted 644 residents and 172 comuneros, and a 0.9 per cent annual reduction in population due to migration (Anta Fonseca and Mondragón Galicia 2006). Official census data are reported in Figure 7.1.
3 With deportation and other involuntary returns, the small population of US-born children in Santa Cruz is likely to increase. What kinds of transnational lives will these US-citizen, village-raised Chinantec young adults construct 10 or 15 years from now?
4 The NGOs working in this region over the past 25 years included Centro de Apoyo al Movimiento Campesino y Popular Oaxaqueño, AC (CAMPO), the National University's Integrated Use of Natural Resources Program (Programa de Aprovechamiento Integral de los Recursos Naturales, PAIR), Estudios Rurales y Asesoría Campesina, AC (ERA), and Geoconservación AC. Organizations providing some of the funding for work in the region included Program for Conservation and Forest Management (PROCYMAF), the National Commission for Protected Areas (Comisión Nacional de Áreas Naturales Protegidas CONANP), United Nations Development Program, and the National Commission for the Development of Indigenous Peoples (Comisión Nacional para el Desarrollo de los Pueblos Indígenas, CDI).
5 Ecotourism has a committee of 12. Each year it receives about five groups of 20 each who stay for two nights and three days and perhaps 10 groups of three or four who stay for two or three nights. They charge 350 pesos a day for food and lodging and a guide, and clear about 40,000 to 60,000 pesos a year after costs.
6 Hellman (2009) also observes that community practices can push migration. In the case she describes, the weight of patri-local marriage practices in a northern Puebla indigenous community drives women to leave; they prefer to migrate than to live under the domination of their mother-in-law while their husbands are away.

References

Anta Fonseca, S. and F. Mondragón Galicia. 2006. El Ordenamiento Territorial y los estatutos comunales: El caso de Santa Cruz Tepetotutla, Usila, Oaxaca. In: Anta Fonseca, S.A.V. Arreola Muñoz, M.A. González Ortiz, and J. Acosta González (eds),

Ordenamiento territorial comunitario: un debate de la sociedad civil hacia la construcción de políticas públicas, pp. 191–208. Mexico City, Mexico: Instituto Nacional de Ecología.

Bernard, H.R. 2017. *Research Methods in Anthropology: Qualitative and Quantitative Approaches*. Lanham, MD: Altamira Press.

Bray, D., E. Duran, and O. Molina. 2012. Beyond harvests in the commons: multi-scale governance and turbulence in indigenous/community conserved areas in Oaxaca, Mexico. *International Journal of the Commons* 6(2): 151–178. Available at www.the-commonsjournal.org/articles/10.18352/ijc.328/.

Hellman, J.A. 2009. *The World of Mexican Migrants: The Rock and the Hard Place*. New York: The New Press.

INEGI (Instituto Nacional de Estadísticas y Geografía). 1970: 28 de enero de 1970: localidades por entidad federativa y municipio con algunas características de s población y vivienda. Available at http://internet.contenidos.inegi.org.mx/contenidos/productos/prod_serv/contenidos/espanol/bvingi/productos/censos/poblacion/1970/iter/IX_hdo_oax/702825413514I.pdf.

INEGI (Instituto Nacional de Estadísticas y Geografía). 1973. IX Censo general de Población.

INEGI (Instituto Nacional de Estadísticas y Geografía). 1990. XI Censo General de Población y Vivienda 1990. Available at www3.inegi.org.mx/sistemas/scitel/Default?ev=1.

INEGI (Instituto Nacional de Estadísticas y Geografía). 2000. Conteo de Población y Vivienda 1995. XI Censo General de Población y Vivienda 1990. Available at www3.inegi.org.mx/sistemas/scitel/Default?ev=1.

INEGI (Instituto Nacional de Estadísticas y Geografía). 2010. II Conteo de Población y Vivienda 2005. XII Censo General de Población y Vivienda.

INEGI (Instituto Nacional de Estadísticas y Geografía). 2018. Censo de Población y Vivienda.

Jaffee, D. 2014. *Brewing Justice: Fair Trade Coffee, Sustainability, and Survival*. Berkeley, CA: University of California Press.

Mutersbaugh, T. 1997. Rural industrialization as development strategy: cooperation and conflict in co-op, commune and household in Oaxaca, Mexico. In: *Yearbook. Conference of Latin Americanist Geographers*, 23(1997): 91–105.

Mutersbaugh, T. 1999. Bread or chainsaws? Paths to mobilizing household labor for cooperative rural development in a Oaxacan village (Mexico). *Economic Geography* 75(1): 43–58.

Mutersbaugh, T. 2002. Migration, common property, and communal labor: cultural politics and agency in a Mexican village. *Political Geography* 21(4): 473–494.

Van der Wal, H. 1998. *Chinantec Shifting Cultivation and Secondary Vegetation: A Case Study on Secondary Vegetation resulting from Indigenous Shifting Cultivation in the Chinantla, Mexico*. Wageningen (Países Bajos): BOS Foundation.

8 Migration, community, and land use in San Juan Evangelista Analco

Fermín Sosa Pérez and James P. Robson

Summary

In this chapter, we investigate change following migration in the Zapotec community of San Juan Evangelista Analco, exploring how shifts in demographics and culture are reconfiguring two central tenets of community life. First, in the context of an expanded social field, migration has prompted the community to reconsider its terms of membership, and adapt an age-old system of communal service expectations that migrants struggle to adhere to. Second, Analco provides an example of a migrant-sending community that is considering how best to use its territorial commons within a context of agricultural abandonment and forest regeneration.

Methods

This case draws on ethnographic research conducted over different periods by Sosa Pérez and Robson. In the case of Sosa Pérez, who is a citizen and *comunero* (commoner) of Analco, the work draws on direct observations and participation in community institutions and assemblies over a 10-year period (2008–2018), and informal interviews during this same period with municipal and communal authorities, village residents, and migrants and their families in Mexican and US destination centres. Sosa Pérez also played a lead role in Analco's Land Planning process in 2015. In the case of Robson, the work presented here draws on household survey data, interviews, and a territorial mapping exercise conducted during the period 2007–2009, interviews with village authorities and residents in 2014 and 2015, and interviews with migrants, migrant leaders, and migrant organizations in Oaxaca City, Mexico City, Los Angeles, and Las Vegas during the period 2014–2016.

Setting

The Zapotec community and municipality of San Juan Evangelista Analco (hereafter referred to as Analco) (Figure 8.1) is located 87 km north and a two-hour drive from Oaxaca City, in the Sierra Norte (northern highlands) of Oaxaca.

Figure 8.1 View of the village of San Juan Evangelista Analco.
Source: photo credit: Jim Robson.

The area was first permanently settled in 1450, and given the Zapotec name *Lachi-aduni* ('Lachi' meaning 'hill', 'aduni' meaning 'standing'). In 1486, members of the *mexica* ethnic group invaded the village, giving it its current name of 'Analco' ('to the side of water' or 'by water' in *náhuatl*). In 1825, Analco was awarded municipal status. In 1910 and 1911, many men left to fight in the Mexican Revolution, leaving the community's territory open to incursions from neighbouring communities, principally San Juan Atepec. While Analco recovered some lands, its territorial conflicts with Atepec continued into the late 1950s. In 1966, the community was granted official title to a portion of its customary territory. The community now collectively owns 1658 ha,[1] including: dry tropical forests at 1200 to 1800 m.a.s.l., through to the village site, the main area of agricultural fields, and oak forests at 1800 to 2300 m.a.s.l., and pine-oak and pine forests from 2300 to 3000 m.a.s.l (Lara 2007; Lara and Manzano 2005; Robson 2010).

Like many communities in the region, Analco remained relatively isolated until the mid-twentieth century. Construction of Federal Highway 175 brought with it considerable change. The village's first potable water system was installed in 1964, with electricity arriving a few years later in 1968. While a primary school was established in Analco as far back as the 1930s, only boys attended.[2]

In 1965, the current primary school building was opened, with a tele-secondary school established in 1982. In 1990, the first health post was opened (with an attendant nurse), upgraded in 2002 to a Community Health Centre with a resident doctor, nurse and ambulance. In 1994, the first village-wide drainage and sewerage system was installed, along with a public telephone line.

According to government census data, Analco was home to 404 inhabitants in 2010, living in a total of 126 households, with a quarter of residents over the age of 65. About two-thirds of the population self-identifies as Catholic, and the remainder as Evangelical Protestant.[3] Analco is still best described as a *campesino* community, with farming and work in the home identified as the main occupations by four-fifths of residents (Table 8.1).

Men in the village who are not farmers earn an income as builders, bakers, labourers, local traders, or teachers. A handful work as professionals in regional urban centres (Ixtlán de Juárez or Oaxaca City) while maintaining a home in the village. Most women still self-identify as *amas de casa* (housewives) even though their daily duties may include farming, the collection of firewood or other activities in the countryside. A small but increasing number of women work in professional careers or as casual workers in the local service sector. A number of families run small businesses in the village, including general stores, bakeries, carpentry workshops, and taco stalls. Such businesses require start-up capital, and a number of local business owners are returned migrants. A few commoners have *yuntas* (teams of oxen) that are rented out to help families plough their fields ready for seeding. Average household income is low, with 82 per cent of families in 2013 receiving the equivalent of one minimum salary from their productive activities. Additional sources of household income include migrant remittances and government social welfare programmes.

Migration dynamics

The first waves of notable migration from Analco took place during the early part of the twentieth century. From 1910–1920, adult men left to participate in

Table 8.1 Principal occupations among residents in San Juan Evangelista Analco

Occupation	No. of residents	%
Home	174	43.7
Farmer	141	35.4
Employed (off-farm)	10	2.4
Professional	9	2.2
Builder	2	0.4
Student	36	9.0
Local business owner/trader/vendor	23	5.8
Unemployed	3	0.6
Other	2	0.4

Source: SSO (2014).

the Mexican Revolution, with many others living in exile when the village and its territory was temporarily taken over by neighbouring communities (between 1912 and 1918[4]). Once the community was re-established, Analqueños embarked on new migration streams, in the 1930s and 1940s, to work seasonally in plantation agriculture in and around Loma Bonita (close to the border with Veracruz state). While most returned to Analco, some families settled in the area. Towards the end of this same period, some families left Analco for a growing Oaxaca City. In the 1940s and 1950s, a number of adult men joined temporary, guest-worker labour streams to the US under the *Bracero* Program (see Chapter 3). In the 1960s, there was a marked increase in the number of community members pursuing wage labour or education migration to regional and national urban centres. While some settled in Oaxaca City, the majority went to the Mexico City area, attracted by higher wages.[5] Many migrants (and their families) settled permanently in the capital, some stayed for an extended period of time (15–25 years) before returning to Analco in the 1990s and early 2000s, and some settled in Mexico City before moving on to the US once networks there became established in the 1980s and 1990s.

Undocumented wage labour migration to the US emerged in the late 1970s. Most Analqueños headed to Los Angeles, with smaller numbers settling in New York, Miami and North Carolina. In the mid-1990s, some families living in Los Angeles moved to Las Vegas, Nevada. US migration streams intensified in the late 1980s and throughout the 1990s – the result of migrant networks, limited paid work in Analco, and, for some, the IRCA 'amnesty' of 1986 (see Chapter 3 for more on this).[6]

Despite the ebb and flow of migration streams over time, household survey data from 2008 indicates the extent to which migration has defined household and village demographics. At that time, 43 per cent of family members were living outside of Analco, with 43 per cent of these individuals in the US and 57 per cent in other parts of Mexico (Robson 2010). Only 7 per cent of the households surveyed had no direct experience with migration. Most respondents stated that migration was a response to economic needs. As one male resident explained: 'Some of us are fortunate in terms of education and work opportunities but for the rest that want to stay here [in the village], what are they going to do? From ten, only two will stay'. Whatever the reasons for leaving, migration has been aided by strong social networks, with 2008 survey data showing that 72 per cent of migrants had family or friends to help them at their destination centre (Robson 2010).

Many Analqueños who left for a Mexican urban centre in the 1960s and 1970s (sometimes with family in tow) did so with little intention of moving back to Analco, save perhaps to spend their retirement there. This contrasts with initial waves of US-bound migration in the 1980s and 1990s, with most migrants planning sojourns of 2–5 years. This manifested in temporary, circular migration patterns, many new house-builds in Analco, and a desire among migrants to maintain strong ties with the 'home' village.

Circular migration was made possible by limited border enforcement throughout the 1980s and much of the 1990s. Over time, however, movements north became more complicated, dangerous and expensive,[7] with the number migrating to the US declining sharply from the mid-2000s onwards as a result of economic recession (in 2008 and 2009), increased enforcement at the US–Mexico border, and security risks associated with travel through the northern states of Mexico.[8] Circular migration is no longer feasible for those without papers, and has given way to a semi-permanent[9] migration dynamic. In 2015, Analqueños in Los Angeles had spent between one and 35 years living there, with an average hiatus of 17 years (and counting). Long-term absenteeism is reflected in changing remittance trends. Only a small number (15 per cent) of migrant-sending households surveyed in 2008 lived entirely off of remittances. In contrast, for a majority (58 per cent) of these households, little or no financial support was provided by migrant members (Robson 2010). As one mother of four explained: 'The money [that my two daughters living in the US] sent us was very important ... we have seen a big change [in how we live] now they can no longer help us'.

Governance impacts

> In economic terms, migration has improved the village because families now eat and dress better but the problem is that there are no people here and the village is becoming deserted.
>
> (Female resident, Analco)

Analco's population peaked in the 1970s at just over 950 residents before falling steadily as out-migration intensified and family planning initiatives resulted in negative growth-rates (Figure 8.2). Since the turn of this century, the community's resident population has levelled out at around 400, a fall of approximately 55 per cent from its peak three to four decades prior. From 1970 through to 2010, the village age–sex structure transitioned from a (broad base) expansive pyramid indicating high birth rates and relatively rapid growth through to a (narrow base) constrictive pyramid showing much lower percentages of children as well as a clearly aging population (Figure 8.3).[10] This included a notable slimming in productive age groups (residents aged between 20 and 45), affecting male and female populations to similar degrees.

These demographic changes have had a marked impact on local governance institutions and structures. In 2008, Analco had a resident comunero (commoner) population of 104[12] compared with over 300 comuneros in the late 1970s – a decline of close to 60 per cent. In addition, of the 104 comuneros resident in 2008, village authorities noted that approximately 82 could be considered fully 'active' (between 18 and 65 years of age) and expected to comply with the full range of cargo and tequio obligations. Fewer than half (43 per cent) of Analco's resident comuneros in 2008 were under the age of 50 and only nine were under the age of 30 (Robson 2010).

As detailed in Robson (2010) and Robson and Berkes (2011a), these changes have driven an increased communal service workload for village residents. Since

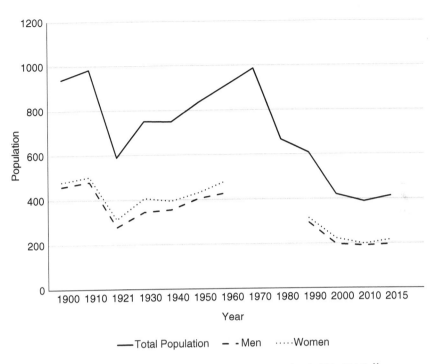

Figure 8.2 Population change in San Juan Evangelista Analco (1900–2015).[11]

Note
1921 (rather than 1920) is used on the x-axis as it is the year recorded by INEGI, in recognition of the census that decade being carried out a year late.

Robson has been working in the community (2007–present), it is not uncommon to find men in the village holding down an official cargo and another committee position simultaneously, while those free of obligations are unlikely to enjoy more than one or two terms' 'rest' before being given a new position to perform. These pressures have led to a number of 'forced' changes to governance structures. These include the disappearance of some lower-level municipal cargos, discontinuation of the scaled system of assigning cargos with progressively greater responsibility, a weakening of rules around age of retirement from active service, and a decline in the number of projects requiring tequio (Robson and Berkes 2011a). In addition, it has become increasingly difficult to find qualified people for the most important positions within the community (Robson and Wiest 2014), which makes it harder to ensure that municipal and communal governance adheres to customary standards. This has become a matter of concern among local people, worried that the community will lose its municipal status if trends continue.

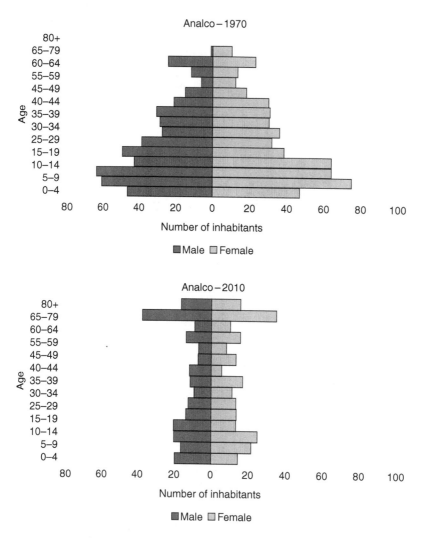

Figure 8.3 Population pyramids for San Juan Evangelista Analco (1970 and 2010).

Debating the terms of community membership

Community-level responses to the stresses placed on communal governance institutions fall into two main categories: reactive (coping) mechanisms (such as those noted above); and, more proactive, adaptive strategies designed to reduce future vulnerability to demographic change by managing the flow and/or timing of migration, or finding ways for absent members to subsidize community development or governance (see Robson and Berkes 2011a). In recent years,

Analco has responded to its new demographic reality by looking to legislate the rights and obligations of non-resident (migrant) members. Compared with some other communities in the region (such as Santa Cruz Tepetotutla, see Chapter 7), this move has been late in coming. While migration was an important livelihood strategy in Analco as far back as the 1960s and 1970s, and migration rates rose sharply in the 1980s, it was only in the early 2000s, as border enforcement increased and migrants began to acquire more stable jobs and family obligations in their destinations, that the negative impacts of migration on community life became an issue for debate in the community assembly. Up until then, the relationship between residents and non-residents had been reasonably good, with regular communication and cooperation between village authorities and migrant organizations in Mexico City, Oaxaca City, and Los Angeles.

The trend towards long-term absenteeism (especially among US-based migrants), and a much-depleted pool of collective village labour, encouraged more village residents to openly resent the burden placed on their shoulders to cover municipal and communal governance obligations. Many felt that migrant support did not compare with the work that they carried out to keep the village functioning. Migrants pushed back, arguing that their contributions over an extended period of time be deemed sufficient for them to maintain their status as full community members, and thus the right to return, to use communal firewood, water, and grazing resources, and to maintain usufruct over houses and farmland. As tensions rose, they highlighted how migrant–village relations and obligations were being perceived differently by factions emergent within a broad community membership – from those who envisaged a relationship loosely defined by a shared moral commitment to the collective, to relations more explicitly tied to adherence (or non-adherence) to collective work and communal service demands.

On each side of this divide, there is a sense that generational changes have played an important role. Migrant leaders in Mexico City told Robson in 2014 that younger adult village residents didn't appreciate or

> know the history of migration and its organizations, of both the efforts of and challenges faced by migrants … our people [in Analco] are struggling, we know full well how difficult it is for them there … [but] we also face difficult moments.

At the same time, village residents (as well as some older migrants) believed that the attitudes of migrants had shifted over the course of time. In the 1970s and 1980s, many who migrated were adult men and women who had been actively involved in community life (i.e. performing cargos and tequios, making decisions in the Assembly). This instilled a firm commitment to those 'back home', and manifested itself in the establishment of migrant organizations in Mexican and US destination centres. However, as social networks were established, more of those leaving Analco were adolescents and young adults yet to be immersed in the communalist ideology and institutions of the community.

The result was a greater focus on their own lives and increasing resistance to village requests for support.

It is within this context that the Assembly in Analco began to discuss, on a regular basis, the idea of legally enforcing migrants to meet their cargo obligations, although no concrete action was taken until the late 2000s. In 2009 and 2010, Mexico's National Forestry Commission (CONAFOR) requested that Analco's communal statute be updated, and this provided an opportunity for the community to rethink its comunero (commoner) rights and obligations, which would extend to comuneros who had been absent for many years. Thus began a complicated period of negotiation, with the Assembly called on countless occasions to analyse and debate the issue from the perspectives of two antagonistic and seemingly intractable positions. While most village residents insisted that the same obligations be made of all community members (irrespective of where they lived), most migrants (and even a few village residents) advocated for a mechanism of differentiated rights and obligations.

Multiple group identities had emerged within Analco's community sphere. There were the resident villagers, aggrieved to be so few in number – left to carry the burden of governance to the detriment of themselves, their families, and the local economy – but who remain committed to sustaining their community in terms of territory, tradition, and culture. There were the disparate groups of citizens no longer living in the home village, who shared a sense of commitment to their community of origin, but who held different ideas in terms of what continued membership in the community ought to require. Caught in the middle, there were the village residents who shouldered the burden of population loss, but also had family members who were migrants and thus sympathetic to their situation and viewpoint. Robson's conversations with migrants living in Oaxaca City, Mexico City, and the US pointed to the large number who want to maintain rights as community members, do not want to lose their identity as Analqueños, want to support the community as best they can, and yet feel a duty to prioritize their individual and family needs and wellbeing (Robson 2010, in press). In essence, their lived reality weakens their actionable commitment to the village collective back in Oaxaca.

With a majority-held belief that there can be only one category of comunero or comunera, with no room for stratification into first- and second-order community members, the Assembly enacted changes in its communal statute so it could name migrants to perform village cargos. Those named had the choice to live in the community and perform the cargo in person, or pay for a substitute to carry out the cargo they had been assigned to do. However, push-back from migrant groups (especially those in Mexico City) made it difficult for the Assembly to enforce these new stipulations. While new clauses in the communal statute set out what migrant comuneros had to do in order to maintain their land rights, the reality is that from 2010 through to 2015, the new laws were rarely enacted. For migrants, this resistance constituted their response to a hardening of attitudes among those in the village. Migrant leaders in Los Angeles[13] and Mexico City complained how they had 'less of a voice than before', while those in the village were 'more critical [of them] than had been the case previously'. No longer was there a sense that everybody was pulling in the same direction.

In 2015, a new land use planning process began, prompted by a raft of territorial projects and initiatives in the community, including its first Forest Management Program (2012–2022). This required a further updating of the Communal Statute in 2016 and 2017, with changes focused on two main areas: the provision of rules governing a new conservation area, timber production, and forest restoration; and the adaptation of existing rules and the crafting of new agreements to regulate these emergent practices and to improve territorial use and management. Following their limited involvement in the 2009–2010 updates, migrants were more active in discussions this time around. But as negotiations got underway, it was clear that the previous divisions were still in place. Village residents saw an opportunity to revisit the issue of governance obligations, and tackle specific issues pertaining to territorial resource use and access. This had become a bone of contention in the village because of the practice among migrant comuneros to acquire and transfer usufruct rights to plots of land in the community, regardless of whether they had contributed to village governance obligations. For migrants, it was an opportunity to revisit the question of migrant rights and responsibilities, and they came prepared – proposing that migrants meet their individual obligations by contributing collectively to a set number of cargos per administrative period. This was rejected outright by the Assembly, who reiterated their position that local governance demands an equal contribution from all rights-holders.

Currently, the community's membership finds itself in deadlock, with the impasse set to continue as different truths, realities, and interests circulate and gain or lose currency among member sub-groups. For active migrants, the danger is that frustrations will boil over and some will choose to break ties with the community. Migrants in Mexico City are beginning to ask themselves, 'do we walk away, is it right that we are being criticized and pressured in this way … what's the objective, do we integrate or do we separate?' As one migrant leader explained, 'if people in Analco don't want our support, well the organization has no meaning', adding that the community was reaching 'a critical or delicate moment in terms of its relationship with migrant members'.

Changes in territorial use and management

Analco's lands are located wholly on the leeward side of the Sierra Madre de Oaxaca mountain range, and are home to tracts of temperate pine-oak forest, dry oak-pine forest, and dry tropical forest (Lara and Manzano 2005). This customary territory is divided into three main land use zones – urban (where the main village is sited), agricultural and grazing lands, and communal use lands (under forest or natural vegetation cover). In Analco, it is a tradition that resident males over the age of 18 are granted comunero (commoner) status.

This gives them the right to plots in the village to have their own home, usufruct rights to land where they can cultivate or graze livestock, as well as the right to access and harvest resources (firewood, NTFPs, timber for domestic use) from the communal use areas. These rights, and associated access, use, and management rules are enshrined in the village's communal statute.

In the 1970s, when Analco was at its peak in terms of resident population (close to 1000 inhabitants), the area of land designated to agriculture and grazing was extensive, covering a large part of the community's territory. Evidence of this is provided by the artefacts that dot the landscape – from the terracing that farmers experimented with in the 1970s, to stone *eras* (circular work places where harvests would be stored and distributed) and *zacatero* trees (modified through inosculation to provide a dry place above ground to store zacate or post-harvest maize stalks). They help to identify former fields, now long-abandoned and covered in brush and secondary forest.

Between 1970 and 2015, migration and a subsequent process of agricultural abandonment led to changes in the areas officially designated by the community to agriculture and grazing versus lands set aside for communal use (Table 8.2).

Declines in the numbers of people farming had their clearest impact in agricultural zones located farthest away from the village (Robson 2010; Robson and Berkes 2011b). With the passage of time, the loss of individual usufruct rights to these plots or parcels of land and the fading memory of the migrants who once 'owned' them, led to their reclassification back to communal use lands. Yet the data in Table 8.2 tell no more than half the story, since they only account for lands that were formally reclassified. They do not consider the many plots and grazing areas that have been left unused for many years (and covered in brush or successional forest species) but to which absent 'owners' still lay claim. If one considers all of the land that has been either formally or de facto abandoned, then the change from open to vegetated/forested areas is considerably greater.

This becomes apparent upon review of the community's land use plans for 2005 and 2015, which illustrates the rate of change in the area under forest cover and for the different forest types found in Analco's territory (Table 8.3).

In 2005, it was estimated that 905 hectares (or 55 per cent of Analco's territory) were forested (Lara and Mazano 2005). By 2015, this had increased to 1094 hectares (or 66 per cent of Analco's territory).[14] While these data capture

Table 8.2 Change in area by land use (1970 to 2015)

Land use zone	Area (ha) in 1970	% of total area in 1970	Area (ha) in 2015	% of total area in 2015
Urban	40	2.45	42	2.58
Parcelled for agriculture and grazing	1325.68	81.30	1135.68	69.64
Communal use	265	16.25	453	27.78
Total area	1630.68	100	1630.68	100

Source: Sosa Pérez *et al.* (2017).

Table 8.3 Percentage change in area of different forest types (2005–2015)

Forest type	Area (ha) in 2005	Area (ha) in 2015	% change
Temperate humid pine-oak forest	104	115	+11
Temperate humid oak-pine forest	40	72	+80
Temperate pine-oak forest	50	97	+94
Temperate oak forest	280	300	+7
Temperate dry pine-oak forest	187	293	+57
Temperate dry oak-pine forest	26	41	+57
Dry tropical forest	218	176	−19
Total area	905	1094	+21

Sources: Lara and Manzano (2005); Sosa Pérez *et al.* (2017)

the rate of change for a recent 10-year period, they follow a trend that began as far back as the 1960s or early 1970s when out-migration from Analco first took hold and a pattern of forest resurgence following agricultural abandonment emerged.

Exploring new directions in territorial use and management

Changes in land cover over time have influenced how the community zones and makes use of its territory and its forest resources. Analysis of the land use plans for 2005 and 2015 (Table 8.4, Figure 8.4) show how some of these changes are being instituted, specifically in the areas designated for forest production, forest conservation, and soil restoration.

The expansion of commercial timber production has been a key recent development. Filemon Manzano, a commoner of Analco and professional forester, explained how forest sanitation work in the mid-2000s highlighted some of the problems (i.e. outbreaks of mountain pine beetle) that are associated with a 'minimal use' forest policy, as well as the economic benefits that could be generated through commercial timber exploitation. This experience led Filemon and others to propose 'the idea of a forest management plan' to the community. While some in the community were receptive, considerable push-back was also

Table 8.4 Number of hectares designated for commercial timber production, domestic forest use, forest conservation, and soil restoration in 2005 and 2015

Forest use	2005	2015	% change
Commercial timber production	60.5	87.7	+44.9
Domestic forest use	304.5	342.6	+12.5
Forest conservation	130.9	227.03	+73.4
Soil restoration	41.6	47	+13

Sources: Lara and Manzano (2005); Sosa Pérez *et al.* (2017)

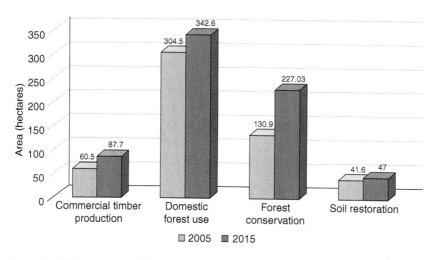

Figure 8.4 Change in area designated for commercial timber production, domestic forest use, forest conservation, and soil restoration (from 2005 to 2015).

encountered – both from older residents concerned about the environmental impact of felling trees in a community that had long resisted commercial forestry, and from migrants in Mexico City who espoused a strong conservationist ethic.[15] As Filemon recalls, 'there were a lots and lots of doubts to answer'.

Indeed, it took several years of internal debate in the Assembly before the community agreed to implement formal forest management (for an initial 10-year period, 2012–2022) and a community-based forestry enterprise. The goal is that forestry can generate regular employment for 5–10 local people, with youth employment a priority. The monies generated by the forestry enterprise are limited so rather than being shared among Analco's resident comuneros, they are being invested in social and communitarian projects. The annual volume being cut is small (between 800 m³ and 900 m³), reflective of how little commercially-viable pine forest the community has access to. In this regard, current forestry operations owe a debt to forest resurgence in recent decades, with an estimated 15–25 per cent of the area designated for logging accounted for by secondary pine forest established on corn fields abandoned as far back as the 1960s (Sosa Perez, personal communication; Lara 2007; Robson 2010).

The example of commercial forestry forms part of a broader shift in Analco by which village demographics, land use change, and new territorial dynamics are driving the emergence of new production and consumption patterns. The overall effect, according to Sosa Pérez, has been to alter local perceptions of territorial identity, which are qualitatively different today than they were in the 1960s or 1970s – marking a period during which the community's territory has been increasingly used and valued for off-farm and non-subsistence activities, including conservation and eco-tourism.[16]

Such change is also reflected in the way that community members come to experience and subsequently relate to their customary lands. This was illustrated to Robson when he showed a photo, taken in 2008 of a hillside east of the village (see Figure 8.5), to a group of migrants who had left Analco for the US in the early 1980s.

They were shocked by the change they saw: 'it's very closed, with a lot of vegetation ... that's not how it was'. It prompted one to reminisce about the hustle and bustle of village life during harvest time in November and December,

> in the mornings, the animals would arrive in the village carrying all the product ... and in those times we worked collectively, in groups ... and afterwards, after finishing the harvest, we would all get together in the fields to eat,

Figure 8.5 Forest resurgence, hillside to the east of the village.

Source: photo credit: Jim Robson.

adding how the decline in farming was mirrored by the neglect of village orchards,

> the noise coming from the houses, of the nogales [walnuts] being washed before being laid out to dry ... it was such a strange and unique sound ... it's something that won't be heard now, the kids growing up there will not experience that.

Today, this same hillside forms part of the recreational area that tourists can use to go mountain-biking or hiking, while also incorporating a small part of the zone designated for commercial forestry.

Conclusions

Since the 1970s, a culture of migration has become firmly established in Analco and sufficiently pervasive to drive far-reaching change in the community's social and territorial landscape. This case highlights two areas of village life that are being reconfigured because of change following migration, and people's responses to such change.

First, the unsustainable governance burden placed on village residents forces the community to demand more from its migrants. This throws multiple groups, with often divergent views, into debate and conflict, and questions how member rights and responsibilities are understood and operationalized. The Analco case highlights the internal conflicts encountered when a village policy to coerce migrants into meeting communal service obligations is drafted many years after migration streams begin, migration dynamics have since changed, and migrants have been providing the home village with other forms of support. These findings align with previous observations about the inherent conflict between resident commoners and migrants in an Indigenous Mexican context (Klooster 2013).

Second, migration takes people off the land, driving ecological change at the landscape level, and encourages communities to consider how best to make use of their communal resources within a context of demographic and cultural change. Analco's move into commercial forestry, on the one hand, and non-consumptive uses such as ecotourism and conservation, on the other, are indicative of new landscapes of territorial use and perception that are emergent across the region (Robson and Klooster, in press).

Notes

1 In 1966, the community's area was reported as 2111.20 hectares. In 2003, however, the federal government's Programa de Certificación de Derechos Ejidales y Titulación de Solares (PROCEDE) recalculated the territorial area using more precise techniques, and revised this estimate down to 1658.68 ha. The community's own land planning process in 2005 calculated it at 1630 ha, and it is this figure that is used most often by the community in territorial management processes and plans.

2 Parents did not view schooling at that time as being necessary for girls in the village.

3 The rise of evangelical Protestantism in Latin America is well documented, where it has been known to divide communities into religious factions. In Analco, village residents have generally been able to hold the interests of the community over and above their religious loyalties. Tensions do exist, however, and become apparent during the annual patron saint festivities, which have their roots in Catholic traditions.

4 Analco was prone to incursion because of its allegiance to the ideals of the Mexican revolutionary Francisco I. Madero – a stance not shared by others in the region – and an already established territorial conflict with the neighbouring community of San Juan Atepec (Sosa Alavéz 2002). In 1918, Analqueño leadership, bolstered by the return of local men from fighting in the Revolution, was successful in repelling invaders and recovering a portion, although not all, of the community's former lands and territory. This period of upheaval is highlighted by village population change – from 983 inhabitants in 1910 to 590 inhabitants in 1921. Many of those who had fled during the previous decade didn't return but rather remained living in the regional communities or other places in Oaxaca where they had sought refuge.

5 Interviews with migrant leaders in 2014 confirmed that young women were among the first to migrate to Mexico City, predominantly to work in middle to upper-class houses in the San Angel area of the city. Once these women had secured regular work, men from Analco followed, often finding work as gardeners in the same houses.

6 Robson (2010) estimates that approximately 75 per cent of first-generation migrants in the US are undocumented.

7 Interview and survey data show that *coyotes* (people smugglers) charged between US$200 and US$500 dollars per migrant per crossing north in the 1970s and 1980s, around US$1000 per crossing by the early 1990s, US$3000–US$4000 per crossing during the period 2007–2009, and an exorbitant US$8000 plus per crossing in the period 2014–2016.

8 In addition to the role played by US immigration policy, increased security at the border over the past decade is tied to US and Mexican efforts to weaken the drug cartels of Sinaloa and Chihuahua.

9 Semi-permanent in the sense that those without papers in the US are always at risk of deportation or enforced return to Mexico.

10 The number of children under the age of 15 has decreased dramatically since 1970, a result of both the reduction in adult population (of reproductive age) and family size (from an average of 8–10 children in the 1960s to an average of 3–4 today).

11 Male and female population numbers are unavailable for the 1970 and 1980 census data.

12 However, at the December 2007 general assembly, which is a time of the year when most resident *comuneros* are present in the village, only 94 were in attendance.

13 While the Assembly discussions involved representatives from the migrant organizations in the Valley of Mexico (Mexico City and surroundings) and Oaxaca City, migrants in the US were not similarly represented.

14 The total forested area may be underestimated in these plans. A 2016 report by CONAFOR reports 1274.7 hectares (or 77 per cent) of Analco's territory being under forest cover (CONAFOR 2016). The discrepancy probably lies in how much of the land in the early stages of forest transition (brush and other successional vegetation) gets captured as forest or not.

15 Contrasting views around forest use is evident in the signs that can be viewed as you drive down to the village from Highway 175. It was migrants in Mexico City who sponsored the signs erected in the late 2000s that state categorically that there is 'no hunting, no forestry' permitted in Analco. While Filemon and others have respected these signs, and they remain, they hardly reflect current realities and practices, with more recent signs put up in nearby forests that explain about the community's forest

management plan, logging volumes, and the economic and social benefits derived from the extraction and sale of timber resources.

16 For example, over the past 15 years, the community has invested heavily in building and running rustic tourist cabins, a tourist restaurant, and offering guided tours as well as recreational activities, such as hiking and mountain-biking, on their customary lands.

References

CONAFOR. 2016. Desarrollo local con conservación de biodiversidad en San Juan Evangelista Analco, Oaxaca. Proyecto de Biodiversidad en Bosques de Producción y Mercados Certificados, Casos de éxito 10. Mexico City, Mexico: CONAFOR/UNDP/ GEF.

Klooster, D. 2013. The impact of trans-national migration on commons management among Mexican indigenous communities. *Journal of Latin American Geography* 12(1): 57–86.

Lara, Y. 2007. *Plan de manejo de la biodiversidad: Comunidad de San Juan Evangelista Analco, Oaxaca.* Prepared by CERTIFOR/ERA, AC, for internal community use.

Lara, Y. and F. Manzano. 2005. *Ordenamiento comunitario del territorio: Comunidad de San Juan Evangelista Analco.* Prepared by ERA, AC, for internal community use.

Robson, J.P. 2010. *The Impact of Rural to Urban Migration on Forest Commons in Oaxaca, Mexico.* Unpublished PhD Thesis, University of Manitoba. Winnipeg, Canada.

Robson, J.P. In press. Indigenous communities, migrant organizations, and the ephemeral nature of translocality. *Latin American Research Review.*

Robson, J.P. and F. Berkes. 2011a. How does out-migration affect community institutions? A study of two indigenous municipalities in Oaxaca, Mexico. *Human Ecology* 39(2): 179–190.

Robson, J.P. and F. Berkes. 2011b. Exploring some of the myths of land use change: Can rural to urban migration drive declines in biodiversity? *Global Environmental Change* 21(3): 844–854.

Robson, J.P. and R. Wiest. 2014. Transnational migration, customary governance and the future of community: A case study from Oaxaca, Mexico. *Latin American Perspectives* 41(3): 103–117.

Robson, J.P. and D. Klooster. In press. Migration and a new landscape of forest use and conservation. *Environmental Conservation.*

SSO. 2014. San Juan Evangelista Analco Household Census, Oax, 2013. Servicios de Salud de Oaxaca (SSO), Jurisdiccion Sanitaria No. 6 'Sierra', Coordinacion de Servicios de Salud.

Sosa Alavéz, L. 2002. *San Juan Evangelista Analco: Su historia, tradiciones, y leyendas,* p. 209. Mexico City, Mexico: Universidad Autónoma Metropolitana.

Sosa Pérez, F., M. Sánchez, and F. Manzano. 2017. Ordenamiento Territorial Comunitario de San Juan Evangelista Analco, para promover el manejo adaptativo, el resguardo local y la gobernanza de la biodiversidad. INDAYU, AC. For internal community use.

9 Adaptive governance or cultural transformation?

The monetization of *usos y costumbres* in Santiago Comaltepec

James P. Robson

Summary

This final case study chapter looks at the response to declining numbers of villagers available to serve cargos and tequios made by the Chinantecs of Santiago Comaltepec. To reduce their reliance on unpaid collective work and communal service, they have replaced some municipal tequios with paid labour and are providing a salary for municipal cargos in the home village. This has made the community a more attractive proposition to young people, and may provide a foundation for a better economic future. But it also signifies a move away from the strict communalist ethos of service upon which village governance and community membership has long been based.

Methods

This chapter draws on two separate periods of ethnographic fieldwork: doctoral research conducted during the period 2007–2009, and postdoctoral research conducted in 2014 and 2015.

Setting

The Chinantec community (and municipality) of Santiago Comaltepec (hereafter referred to as 'Comal') was formally established in 1603. Its name originates from the Chinantec words *comalli* (or 'ridge') and *tepetl* (or 'hill'), while 'Santiago' refers to the community's patron saint, the Apostle James.

The head village of Santiago Comaltepec (Figure 9.1) is located at an altitude of 2005 m.a.s.l., a three-hour drive north of Oaxaca City.

Federal Highway 175 (which connects Oaxaca City to Tuxtepec, on the Veracruz border) bisects a large portion of Comal's territory. Built at the end of the 1950s, the highway was the catalyst for Comal to formally establish two further permanent settlements as municipal agencies: La Esperanza (at 1600 m.a.s.l.) in the 1960s and San Martin Soyolapam (at 168 m.a.s.l) in the early 1980s (Figures 9.2 and 9.3). While Santiago Comaltepec acts as the municipal seat, these two villages help the community to maintain a presence throughout its extensive communal territory.

Figure 9.1 Head village and municipal seat of Santiago Comaltepec.
Source: photo credit: Jim Robson.

Figure 9.2 Village and municipal agency of La Esperanza.
Source: photo credit: Jim Robson.

Figure 9.3 Village and municipal agency of San Martin Soyolapam.
Source: photo credit: Jim Robson.

In 2010, the head village was home to 710 inhabitants (194 households), La Esperanza was home to 128 inhabitants (35 households), and Soyolapam home to 97 inhabitants (26 households) (INEGI 2010). A further 18 Comaltepecanos were living at spots alongside Highway 175. The 2010 resident population of 953 represented a 51 per cent decline from the 1876 inhabitants who lived in the community in 1970 (Figure 9.4). Much of that loss can be attributed to out-migration, with US streams – mainly to Los Angeles, California – starting at the end of the 1970s, and intensifying throughout the 1980s and 1990s (Robson 2010). In the case of La Esperanza, the sharp decline experienced in the 1980s and early 1990s was largely due to the global crash in coffee prices, which impacted producers across Oaxaca.

The community's territory covers 18,300 ha, making it one of the largest in this part of northern Oaxaca. Because its lands span an altitudinal gradient of nearly 3000 m across the leeward (dry) and windward (humid) sides of the Sierra Madre de Oaxaca, Comal is home to a diverse forest, including 5000 ha of largely unbroken cloud forest, significant areas of tropical evergreen forest, and a production forest where pine and oak are logged (Martin 1993; Robson 2008, 2010). Variation in precipitation, temperature, and vegetation along altitudinal

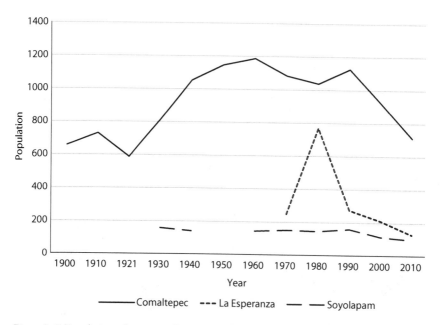

Figure 9.4 Population change in Santiago Comaltepec, La Esperanza, and San Martin Soyolapam (1900–2010).

Note
1921 (rather than 1920) is used on the x-axis as it is the year recorded by INEGI, in recognition of the census that decade being carried out a year late.

gradients is reflected in the local classification system of territorial zones (Martin 1993) (Table 9.1).

Resource practices are equally as diverse. Those living in 'temperate-humid country' practise long fallow *milpa* cultivation and tend small-scale shade coffee and agro-forestry systems. In the hot and humid lowlands, people take advantage of climatic and topographical conditions to grow tropical fruits, raise livestock,

Table 9.1 Territorial zones, and correlation to rainfall, temperature, elevation and vegetation type

Territorial zone	Rainfall (mm/yr)	Temp. range (c)	Elevation range (m)	Main forest type
Hot and humid (gʷóo'ᴸᴴ gineᴸ)	3200–3700	21–25	100–1000	Tropical Evergreen
Temperate humid (gʷóo'ᴸᴴ 'ojmᴴ)	2700–3200	16–20	1000–2200	Montane Cloud
Cold (gʷóo'ᴸᴴ gʷᴸ)	2000–2700	9–14	2200–3200	Pine-oak
Temperate and dry (gʷóo'ᴸᴴ kiᴸ)	1300–2000	15–18	1600–2200	Oak-pine
Hot and dry (gʷóo'ᴸᴴ giᴹ)	800–1300	16–21	1000–1600	Tropical dry

Source: Robson (2010), adapted from Martin (1993).

and produce corn for both subsistence and commercial sale (López López 2005; Robson 2010). High rainfall allows for up to two harvests of corn per year in these zones. The leeward (western) side of the range is less extensive, drier, and where most Comaltepecanos live. Surrounding lands are used heavily for agriculture, with local forests exploited for edible plants, mushrooms and firewood, among other products (López López 2005; Robson 2010). Rain over a four- to six-month period guarantees one annual corn crop. So-called 'cold country' divides the humid and dry sides of the range, rising to Cerro Humo Chico at 3250 m.a.s.l. This zone holds reserves of pine forests that yield large quantities of commercially-valuable timber – logged by a community forest enterprise that feed a community-owned sawmill (Robson 2010).

Migration dynamics, cargo demands, and village return

This section provides insights into recent migration dynamics, migration goals, and the possibilities for return. It draws heavily on interviews with community residents of different ages, including a number who have spent time living outside their home village.

Don Jorge (pseudonym) and his wife have seven children, three sons that live in the head village of Santiago Comaltepec, and one son and three daughters who live outside the community, including two in Los Angeles. Of the three boys who live in Comal, the eldest, Benito, spent a decade (1995 to 2005) moving between LA and Comal,[1] before the trip north became too costly and dangerous. He notes how 'people aren't leaving like they were'. This has changed a dynamic in the community where, for a long time, 'heading to the US was what you did'. The current reality has given

> young people [here] pause for thought ... they now say 'well, if I don't want to stay here, what do I do [if migration is no longer an option]?' Some think 'perhaps I can make a go of it here'.

Others, such as his youngest brother and sister, are choosing to continue with their studies, which means leaving Comal, perhaps indefinitely ('most will meet someone, settle down, and won't return').

Benito's middle brother, Juan, spent nine years living in LA, returning with his family following the 2008–2009 economic downturn. He says that if he were a youngster today he wouldn't make the trip, 'once it gets above US$3000 [for the coyote] you really have to think about whether it's worth going'. He was working two jobs in LA, on just a few hours' sleep a day, so that he could earn the money to build a house in the community. He is married with three young children and always wanted the option of a possible return. But this means 'having something to come back to', which isn't possible for everyone,

> I know guys who have been there [in LA] for 20 years and really have nothing to show for it ... they are without papers, they live a difficult

existence, and have nothing in Comal ... no house to go back to, and they haven't kept up with their obligations so the community won't welcome them back.

He says his two sisters are a case in point. One 'works hard and she and her husband have built a house for themselves in Comal and intend to come back'. Their 16-year old son (born in the US) recently visited Comal to see if he liked it here. In contrast, his other sister has been less astute,

> she doesn't work and so with just one income they struggle to save any money to invest in Comal ... they would like to come back but have no place to move into, no house in Comal ... no future here.

I ask Benito whether it is possible to make a living in the village and he says

> yes, there is work here and it provides a little bit of money and three meals a day. If that's good enough, then one can live happily [in Comal], but if you want different things then you need to look elsewhere.

He adds how tricky it can be to make ends meet during the periods when you have a cargo to perform. Juan, for example, was given two cargos to do in quick succession upon his return to Comal in 2010: municipal policeman (for a year) and then police commander (for a further year). He said that the cargos don't bother him, 'it's part of being a Comaltepecano', but the problem comes 'when they are full-time [posts], you aren't making any money but you still have household expenses to pay for'. With three young children in school,

> it works out at about $1000 pesos a year for the inscriptions and on top of that, you have [the cost of] uniforms, books ... but the biggest expenses are the basics ... you know, food and clothing for the family.

He says that

> you find a way ... your wife helps and finds some work to bring in a little bit of money ... we sold bread to raise cash, and used the money we had saved up in the US. All of that helps you to survive.

Nestor is in his early 40s, and married with four children. He came back to Comal in the late 2000s, after 14 years living elsewhere in the Sierra Norte. He believes that Comaltepecanos hold a strong attachment to their village and can regret their decision to migrate, 'many leave without really knowing what they plan to do, they go because others have gone before them. They know they can earn some money but don't necessarily know what for, they don't have a plan'. Yet return to Comal is not straightforward. Many of the migrants in LA left as single men or women before meeting someone (often a fellow Comaltepecano) and starting a family. Nestor says that

> the kids keep them from moving back ... they are in school with friends who aren't from Comaltepec, some don't speak Chinantec very well, many won't have visited the community, so the idea of moving back with the family ... it's just not feasible.

His friends in LA tell him '"I want to return [to Comal] brother but I can't" ... they feel sad that they can't go back'.[2] There are exceptions. Nestor mentions Beto, who spent many years in LA, where he learnt carpentry and became highly skilled. He had lots of work, steady employment, but also

> that longing to be back in Comaltepec. He and his wife had two children aged 7 and 9 and they decided to leave it all behind and come back before their children got too old and told them 'no way am I going to live there!'.

Nestor says that 'if they had left it just a few more years it would have been too late and they would still be in LA, sad because they are away from Comal'. He says that their children have adapted well, with the eldest son working with Beto in the carpentry workshop he runs in the head village.

It is because of these different experiences that Nestor tells youngsters in Comal, 'find out what life is like in LA and ask yourself, "why am I going?"' He says that 'it's not enough [for them] to say, "I'm going because my aunt and uncle live there"'. Youngsters 'need to know why they are going. If it's about improving their situation in the village then, sure, go but return with something to invest ... a business idea or a productive activity that can help [them] reintegrate well'.

The monetization of municipal cargos and infrastructure work

Throughout the 1980s, 1990s, and most of the 2000s, Comal experienced first-hand the impact that a declining and aging resident population had on the collective burden of meeting cargo and tequio obligations. Over the past decade, a new context has emerged. Driven by limited possibilities for wage labour migration, especially to the US, more people are choosing to stay in the community – prompting leadership to explore ways to make village life more attractive (and viable).

In 2004, using newly-available funds provided by the state government to support municipal projects, Comaltepec began to provide a small stipend to some municipal cargo-holders. This became 'official' practice in 2011 and, since 2013, has applied to all 15 municipal cargos in the head village and municipal seat of Santiago Comaltepec. The amount provided varies, with payments in 2014 ranging from $6000 pesos a month (US$400–450[3]) for the Municipal President to $1000 pesos a month (US$65–70) for a topil. Adoption of a stipend model has required significant funding. An estimated $500,000 pesos (US$35,000) was needed in 2014 to cover monthly payments for all 15 cargos.

According to Maria Delfina, a Comaltepecana and Professor at the regional Universidad de la Sierra Juarez, the policy is 'having a significant impact' in reducing the burden of local governance in the head village. Her husband, Norberto, agrees, noting 'there are more young people living in Comal now ... there are more investments and politically things have changed with these adjustments [to customary governance]'. He notes that in addition to providing a stipend to municipal office-holders, the municipal budget has also been used to replace municipal tequios with contracted wage labour, which has become a source of 'employment for young people and returned migrants'.

As of 2014, the stipend had only been provided to municipal cargo-holders and not those serving in the Comisariado de Bienes Comunales (CBC) (Commissioner of Common Property) or other committees. This has created tensions within the community, with those who meet service obligations in other areas of village life wanting their contributions to be similarly compensated. As Nestor explains:

> It's snowballing ... if you provide support to some but not to others, well then you have inequality and people aren't happy, especially in a community where everything is meant to be equal. What happens if you complete your six years of cargo service[4] between the church committee and the Comisariado and you don't earn anything? Six years of service without any financial remuneration ... it's a problem when you compare [yourself] to someone who has three of their six years doing 'paid' municipal cargos. How is that fair?

While people are okay, even content, to be named for municipal postings in the head village, service in the Comisariado[5] can be viewed with a sense of dread.

Some community members also worry about the implications of these changes for the ethos of traditional governance. As Eusebio, from La Esperanza, explains, 'now you have paid cargos, now they hardly call tequios ... it doesn't compare with how things were, it's not *usos y costumbres* anymore, it's something else ... no one's complying [with service obligations] because everyone's getting paid!'. He believes that members are no longer 'serving the community' once a salary is drawn. Nestor concurs,

> [I'm] not in agreement that they [the cargos] become paid positions because where does that take us? As time passes, the idea of doing these things for free will become absurd to people ... they will talk fondly of the time when people did jobs for nothing!

He feels that some are too quick to dismiss cargos as antiquated, forgetting how the system enables great freedom in other areas of village life,

[I'm] a free man because I comply, I do my service ... [so] you get to feel really good about yourself because you meet your obligations and you have your rights ... people don't value that, they forget that their children can run free here ... [I can say] 'that's your waterfall son, those are your forests, look at what we have here'.

He believes that people need to remind themselves of the positives,

when I'm not serving a cargo I can enjoy everything that this territory has to offer ... I can go from tierra caliente all the way to the tropical lowlands, my kids can learn about and enjoy being in nature ... this is what membership of the community gives you.

Others appreciate both sides of the argument. Don Jorge's daughter, Jazmine, had recently returned to the community, having completed a degree in agrobiology at a university in Saltillo, Coahuila. Upon her return, she could feel the 'tension in Comal about payments for cargos ... that [for some comuneros] it's too much of a departure from the traditional system, and unfair on those who have gone through the cargo system without receiving any money'.[6] But she also saw how village governance 'is definitely under less strain than before'.

Indeed, the benefits of paid municipal cargos and contract labour have led more community members 'to question the value of the system in general', much to the chagrin of people such as Eusebio and Nestor. While Eusebio acknowledged that the system 'had to change ... if you don't have enough people to carry out cargos and do tequios then you can't carry on in the same way', he warned that there was '[always] a consequence to change ... [and Comal] can expect to see impacts on community cohesion and identity'. Beyond the ideological ramifications, the practicalities of maintaining such a policy was questioned: 'what happens when there are no longer the funds to pay [for] the stipend?' Nestor asked. He added how the Assembly 'has discussed on multiple occasions the idea of raising taxes in order to increase the municipal funds needed', which he saw as unworkable. It would, he said, leave the village authorities with no alternative but to 'use money that is meant for other things'.

Limited funds are the main reason why stipends and paid tequios have only been seen in the municipal seat of Santiago Comaltepec. In contrast, cargoholders in La Esperanza and San Martin Soyolapam – localities with smaller resident populations and so more affected by shortfalls in collective labour – receive no compensation for the civic and communal service they provide. With few active citizens (under the age of 60), the job of covering local cargo and tequio demands remains a key challenge in both localities. It has left Daniel, the municipal agency secretary in Soyolapam, feeling conflicted about the traditional governance system – 'it allows us to live in union, it's beautiful, focused around social organization and convivencia, which is really important for such a small village ... [but] it involves real sacrifice [to function properly]'.

When he returned from LA in the late 2000s, he knew 'the cargos would be frequent and a burden for the family, and I prepared myself by saving money so we could support ourselves while I was serving'. But his savings are limited and will soon be used up, which is why he and others in Soyolapam are demanding that they receive the same level of support as their counterparts in the head village.

As Zetino, the Municipal Agent in Soyolapam, noted, the burden of performing cargos and tequios remains *the* reason why people in his village leave and are discouraged from coming back. While some migrants have returned in recent years, Soyolapam's citizens still struggle to cope and no one believes that the system (as it is currently set up) can be sustained over the long term.[7]

Towards a successful future

One evening, during a visit to Comal in late 2014, I went for an *atole* and quesadilla at a local eatery in the head village. Chatting with the owner, he asked me about the research, and noted that while migration had been intense for a long time, rates had fallen in recent years, people had started to come back, and he believed that the community was 'more vibrant than in years past'. This presented village authorities with the challenge 'to think about how we maintain that' and derive benefits from the fact that more people were choosing to stay and hopefully make a life for themselves in the community. When I asked the restaurant owner what young people could do in Comal, he said it was uncertain, because

> while our ancestors found a way to live here on next to no money, just from what they could produce farming and hunting ... well, people now, they're used to having money, they want money, and so it's difficult for them here.

As Nestor noted, the community must 'provide people with options that give them a reason to stay, to stop them from thinking that migration is the only path'. Otherwise he worried that Comal would come to resemble (neighbouring) Macuiltianguis, 'where you go and it's so quiet, no one is around or those who are depend on the money that migrants send them'.

A number of Comaltepecanos and other serranos (people from the Sierra Norte) interviewed for this research can be considered 'expert insiders' – they have served important cargos in their community but also work in the region for government and non-governmental agencies on formal environmental management or rural development projects. This gives them a particular vantage point from which to perceive and assess the changes instituted to date and reflect upon next steps. For Norberto, an ex-Comisariado in Comal and former employee of the National Forestry Commission (CONAFOR), the fact that more young people were staying offered an opportunity. In the head village alone, there were '50 or 60 chavos [those in their late teens or in their early 20s] who haven't left, and it seems they aren't going to because [migrating to the US] has become so complicated'. If they stay, 'they are going to need jobs' and

Comal has looked to develop or design initiatives and projects to create employment locally. One example is its forestry enterprise, which in 2014 was employing 40–50 people, up from 15–20 employees seven or eight years prior. 'Investment in a new community sawmill having increased production', while paid work in forest sanitation – 'that was previously accomplished by tequio' – had generated further sources of income.

Comal enjoys a competitive advantage compared with many communities in the region. As Felicito, an acquaintance from the Chinantec community of Maninaltepec who also worked for CONAFOR, explains, Comal has 'a big territory, lots of forest, and is its own municipality … to be a municipality with a sizeable population provides a chance [to develop economically]'. Israel, a Comaltepecano and another former Comisariado, who now works for an NGO in Oaxaca City, was of the opinion that the community's 'natural capital [means that] we can benefit from that while keeping conservation at the heart of what we do'. Filemon Manzano, a professional forester from the nearby community of Analco, said that you cannot ignore the multiple sources of income that Comal's lands and forests can generate,

> you have PES that brings in $2 million pesos, $800,000 pesos for the [mobile phone] antennae located on its territory … perhaps as much as $4 million pesos a year when you take into account its forestry operations. That is a lot of money with which to invest in community infrastructure and projects.

Yet Israel also believed that the community would only realize its potential if it provides its membership with greater freedom in how they organize themselves. He sees the cargo system as a just one, helping to 'keep the community together, and if we are unified there are many things we can do', but also said it would falter if unable to accommodate individuals' changing needs: 'young people don't want to simply farm and do their cargos … they aspire to other things'. Similarly, Norberto noted how Comal had a lot of highly educated people 'who have gone off and studied and are back wanting to work in their community … [but] these are people who expect to be earning $20,000 pesos a month'. As the community thinks about how to benefit from a stabilizing population, it is challenged to create spaces and opportunities that can match these kinds of expectations.

Israel also felt it was important that the community do a much better job of bringing migrant members into the fold, 'to create a functioning mechanism that connects properly with those living outside'. He had seen how limited migrant–village ties – Comal currently has no functioning migrant management boards in Mexico or the US – led to problems as people returned, 'if more come back, what are they going to do? It's important that they are ready to contribute … but that won't happen if you shut them out, that is just counter-productive'. The need for greater inclusion in decision-making extended to young people in the community, with problems arising when the sons and daughters of those in the assembly are never involved. These are the people that the community will depend on over the next ten years or so ... [and if they aren't involved] it's going to end with agreements being broken because they don't know the context, the history, the reasons that inform past decisions ... they will come in and push their own ideas without having the knowledge of what took place before.

Conclusions

Claims of 'tequio is done' and 'governance has changed for good' highlight the extent to which traditional structures are modifying in Comaltepec in response to a changing (indeed, changed) rural reality. In trying to choose a viable communal future, it is unclear where Comal's monetization of municipal cargos and tequios fits on the spectrum of adaptive governance (see Folke *et al.* 2005; Stockholm Resilience Centre, n.d.) – whereby actors can choose to reorganize a system in response to changing conditions and surprises, or recombine adaptability with innovation and novelty to transform a system into a new regime. In the Oaxacan context, moves towards the latter would potentially constitute a form of 'cultural transformation', where the outlook, values, beliefs, and behaviours of Indigenous collectivities undergo some form of irreversible change. The case of Comaltepec is a reminder that the study of responses to migration is an opportunity to track how community cultures develop over time, and how new practices and ideas are exchanged within a group until they potentially (re)define 'how things get done around here'.

The case also highlights how the response options open to communities are necessarily conditioned by the resources they have access to. As Comaltepec strives to provide meaningful work for its membership, and especially its young people, natural and territorial resources take on an importance far beyond that of community identity. Rather, they can determine whether a community has a viable foundation upon which local economies and sustainable rural futures can be built. Comaltepec has a distinct advantage because of the size and diversity of its territory, combined with its municipal status. The possibilities for communities that are not municipal seats, or are home to small resident populations, or lack access to forests of high conservation or commercial value, will be more restricted.

Notes

1 In 1995, he left straight after finishing school, paying US$400 to make the crossing. He returned to Comaltepec in 1998, heading north again in 1999 (paying US$1200). He spent a year in the US, returning to Comal in 2000. He went one more time in 2005, paying US$1800 and again stayed for a year.
2 Changing domestic situations in the US also affect the ability of migrants to help the home village. As Nestor notes, '[their support] is something but it's not what the community is asking for [to pay for cargos] because that's not possible for most of them'.
3 US$ figures are estimates, based on historic Mexican peso–US dollar exchange rates.

4 In the case of Comaltepec, 'retirement' from cargos is achieved after six years of service are provided. This contrasts with some other communities in the region, where retirement is tied to one's age rather than history or length of service.

5 As of 2014, the exception is the President of the CBC who receives $220 pesos a day (as a small stipend) from the community forestry enterprise during the six-months of the year when logging takes place.

6 An illustration of this comes from Eusebio, who notes '[I did] nine years of cargos without any kind of compensation … to the contrary, I received complaints and abuse!' This can be contrasted to the situation in 2014 where two topiles in the head village were not only getting paid by the migrants they were substituting for, but also received the stipend they were due as municipal cargo-holders.

7 Zetino cited his role as mayordomo in 2008 for the village's patron saint festivities as an example of the financial burden of performing cargos. He explained how this '[involves] looking after the church, purchasing candles on a regular basis, and providing food for everybody who comes'. He reared 60 chickens for the fiesta, noting that the mayordomo in 2014 was killing two pigs for the event. 'It's a major burden, it's meant to be an honour but I think most of us, when we get elected, we kind of go "oh no!"'. Traditionally, you only act as mayordomo once in your life, so you think 'well at least I'm getting it out of the way', but Zetino notes that if comunero numbers remain low or drop further, 'there's definitely a chance I'll have to do it for a second time'.

References

Folke, C., T. Hahn, P. Olsson, and J. Norberg. 2005. Adaptive governance of social-ecological systems. *Annual Review of Environment and Resources* 30: 441–473.

INEGI. 2010. *Censo de Población y Vivienda 2010. Principales resultados por localidad* (ITER) Available at www3.inegi.org.mx/sistemas/iter/default.aspx?ev=5.

López López, W. 2005. *La etnobotánica de la comunidad de Santiago Comaltepec.* Unpublished report. Santiago Comaltepec, Oaxaca, Mexico.

Martin, G.J. 1993. Ecological classification amongst the Chinantec and Mixe of Oaxaca, Mexico. *Etnoecologia* 1: 17–33.

Robson, J.P. 2008. *Plan de Manejo de la Biodiversidad: Comunidad de Santiago Comaltepec, Oaxaca.* Unpublished report for internal community use.

Robson, J.P. 2010. *The Impact of Rural to Urban Migration on Forest Commons in Oaxaca, Mexico.* Unpublished PhD Thesis, University of Manitoba. Winnipeg, Canada.

Stockholm Resilience Centre. No date. Adaptive governance. Online at: www.stock holmresilience.org/research/research-streames/stewardship/adaptive-governance-.html.

Part III
Synthesis and conclusions

10 The changing landscapes of Indigenous Oaxaca

James P. Robson and Dan Klooster

Introduction

Oaxaca is known for the high level of social organization among its Indigenous communities, the extent of lands that are held and managed communally, and forest landscapes that are biologically diverse (Bray 2013; Chapela 2005; Duran *et al.* 2012). A goal of our research over the past decade has been to consider how change following migration affects these key regional realities and characteristics. Thus, our work responds to calls for an enhanced understanding of migrant–environment linkages in migrant-sending regions (Hecht *et al.* 2015; Hunter, Luna, and Norton 2015; Meyerson *et al.* 2007; Neumann and Hilderink 2015).

In this chapter,[1] we use key findings from our empirical research in the Sierra Norte (northern highlands) of Oaxaca to unpack the complex set of relationships connecting migration with community, territory and biodiversity. We show how agricultural crisis and the de-territorialization of rural livelihood can transform the places that migrants leave (and potentially return to), including the collectives that manage them. We show how a change of direction for forest- and farm-based livelihoods enables new forms of people–environment interactions to emerge, with implications for both biodiversity and local rural economies. Finally, we make the case that Indigenous communities in Oaxaca, functioning within a changed landscape of territorial use and conservation, are challenged to deliver livelihood opportunities that match agriculture's foundational contribution to village life and culture.

Our findings come from work conducted in five Indigenous communities (Figure 10.1) – the Zapotec of Santa María Yavesía and San Juan Evangelista Analco, and the Chinantec of Santiago Comaltepec,[2] Santa Cruz Tepetotutla, and San Miguel Maninaltepec.

While they represent different ethnicities, population sizes, territorial configurations, and forest types, these communities all share similar histories and a way of life based around territory, collective work, communal governance, and ritual celebrations (Martínez Luna 2010; Robson *et al.* 2018). Household surveys, semi-structured interviews with land users and communal authorities, and territorial mapping exercises, all helped to identify the impacts of migration

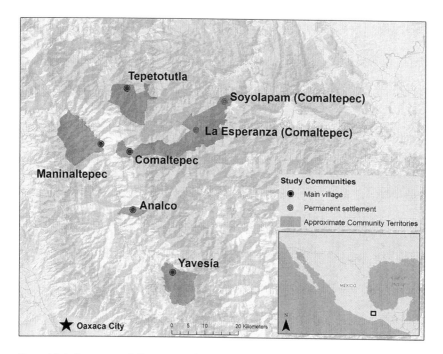

Figure 10.1 Location of Zapotec and Chinantec study communities, Sierra Norte of Oaxaca.

Source: map produced by Lisa Benvenuti, Center for Spatial Studies – University of Redlands.

on self-governance, farming, forest use, and other forms of local environmental practice and knowledge. Field data were collected in Analco and Comaltepec during the period 2007–2010, and in Analco, Comaltepec, Yavesía, Maninalte-pec, and Tepetotutla during the period 2013–2016.

Empirical insights

Changes in resource practice and territorial mobility

Over a 40-year period, a significant number of households in the Sierra Norte have turned their back or reduced their reliance on agriculture in favour of off-farm activities. In the head village of Santiago Comaltepec, for example, approximately one-quarter of households had stopped farming altogether as of 2008. The average area under cultivation per farming household has decreased, with households in Analco and Comaltepec working less than half the area in 2009 they were in 1995. As a farmer from La Esperanza put it in succinct terms, 'people no longer work in the countryside … there are fewer [of us] every year'. Across the study communities, households traditionally depend upon the labour of family members to get their fields ploughed, sown and harvested. With household size dwindling because of migration and reduced fertility rates, there has been a subsequent fall in the relative importance of agriculture, even if most adult resident males still consider farming to be their primary productive occupation.

The widespread abandonment of fields and pasture has coincided with declines in the territorial mobility of community members. This has been particularly apparent in the more extensive territories of Comaltepec and Maninaltepec, where families customarily participated in agricultural transhumance, involving the seasonal movement of people between a main, permanent settlement and temporary settlements at different altitudes on the wetter and drier sides of the Sierra. In recent decades, there has been a steady reduction in the numbers dividing their time between such zones, with many seasonal settlements abandoned altogether. In Santa Cruz, Analco, and Yavesía, the majority of farmers now carry out land-based activities much closer to their homes than in the past, abandoning more distant cultivation zones at higher or lower elevations. In Analco, Comaltepec, and Yavesía, most *milpa* production (traditional corn-bean-squash agriculture found across Mesoamerica) now takes place within a 20 to 50-minute walk of the home village. Figure 10.2 shows the pattern of

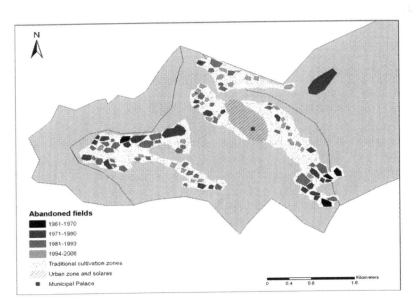

Figure 10.2 Pattern of agricultural abandonment around head village of Santiago Comaltepec (1961–2008).

Source: Robson (2010).

abandonment for traditional cultivation zones accessed by residents in the head village of Comaltepec. Those fields farthest from the village were generally those abandoned first.

In Analco, farmers are no longer working lands on the community's higher slopes (above 2300 m.a.s.l.) or in the drier zone to the west of the village (1700–1900 m.a.sl.). Considered a transition zone where dry pine-oak forest gives way to tropical dry forest, mixed with cactus shrub (matorral), this area provides excellent climatic and soil conditions for particular drought-resistant varieties of bean and corn. Forty years ago, large hillsides areas in this region were under heavy cultivation. In 2008, just one family had a ranch in the area.

The contraction of farming zones has resulted in declines in long-standing resource practices (Table 10.1). While these declines can be partly explained by fewer people farming – i.e. fewer people to opportunistically harvest wild foods and other raw materials as they travel to and from their plots or pasture areas – they are also attributable to the fall in average family size, a preference for modern materials in new house builds, a switch from firewood to gas as a primary fuel source, as well as the advanced age (and reduced mobility) of many community members (see Robson 2010; Robson and Berkes 2011 for detailed analyses). While grazing goats, sheep, and bovine cattle remain important for a minority of households in the communities compared here, in no instance have labour shortages led to a drastic increase in the number of animals managed. Only in San Martin Soyolapam (the tropical lowland locality of Santiago Comaltepec) has deforestation for pasture been a significant component of land cover change (Robson 2008, 2009).

Alternative forest uses have appeared

Table 10.1 also indicates a change in how communities prioritize use of their communal lands, with forestry, conservation and ecotourism activities having increased or newly emerged in several cases. Land use planning in our study communities, as is the case in other parts of the Sierra Norte (Pazos-Almada and Bray 2018), is placing greater emphasis than before on non-extractive and non-agricultural uses, supported by the explicit protection of high conservation-value forest lands (Lara and Manzano 2005; Robson 2008; Sosa, Sánchez, and Manzano 2017). We find Santa Cruz, Comaltepec, Analco, and Yavesía all investing in physical infrastructure (rental cabins, trout farms, restaurants, etc.) designed to attract tourists and associated revenue streams. Formal conservation has sometimes been tied to the existence of government-promoted payment for environmental services (PES) schemes, with Tepetotutla (see Chapter 7), Comaltepec (Chapter 9), and Maninaltepec targeting PES as a way to address employment, infrastructure, and health service shortfalls and to discourage youth from migrating. In some communities, there has been a shift from subsistence to commercial forest use. Comaltepec (see Chapter 9) and Maninaltepec have long-established logging operations which provide work for community members and funds for community projects. In Analco (see Chapter 8), secondary

Table 10.1 Observed and reported changes in resource practice (1995–2015)

Resource practice	Analco	Santiago Comaltepec	La Esperanza	San Martin Soyolapam	Yavesía	Santa Cruz Tepetotutla	San Miguel Maninaltepec
Milpa agriculture	Decline	Decline	Decline	Decline	Decline	Decline	Decline
Mono-cropping	Increase	Increase	No discernible change	No discernible change	Increase	No discernible change	Yes, in some cases
Home gardens and orchards	Decline	Decline	Decline	No discernible change	Decline	Increase – to reduce reliance on coffee	No data
Animal husbandry	Decline	Decline	Decline	Increase	Decline	Decline	No discernible change
Gathering of wild plants and fungi	Decline	Decline	Decline	Decline	Decline	No data	No data
Hunting	Decline	Decline	No discernible change	No discernible change	Decline	Decline (restricted by communal law)	No discernible change
Harvest of medicinal plants	Decline	Decline	Decline	Decline	Decline	No data	No data
Harvest of ornamental plants	Decline	Decline	Decline	Decline	Decline	No data	No data
Domestic forestry and firewood collection	Decline	Decline	Decline	Decline	Decline	No discernible change.	Decline (low)
Commercial forestry	New practice	Reported decline (2008), then increase (2014)	n/a	n/a	No change	n/a	Continues with ups and downs
Ecotourism	New practice	Reported decline (2008) followed by increase (2014)	Increase	No discernible change	New practice	New practice	Not present
Formal conservation	New practice	New practice	New practice	New practice	New practice	New practice.	New practice

Sources: adapted from Robson (2010) and Robson and Klooster (in press).

pine forests on abandoned agricultural fields have helped the community to establish, for the first time, a commercial forestry operation.

Environmental knowledge systems are changing

Interviewees noted that migration and agricultural decline have contributed to the erosion of knowledge that one needs to farm and forage, by taking people off the land and reducing the numbers who move across multiple territorial zones. Intergenerational knowledge transmission (see Hunn 2008) has been affected. Most community members now remain in school until at least 16 years of age, thus taking them away from regular work in the fields. While active farmers continue to produce environmental knowledge through the application of long-standing practices, as well as experimenting with new activities, few share these experiences with their children (Robson 2010). As one Comaltepec farmer noted: 'My sons do not go up into the mountains ... they don't know them'. Across all study communities, elders lamented that few young people appear interested in continuing traditional resource practices and activities, driven they say by changes in highland culture – heavily influenced by new media – and declines in work ethic (Robson *et al.* 2018).

At the same time, new forms of environmental knowledge have emerged. For example, as non-consumptive forest use (i.e. ecotourism, conservation) becomes more important to communities, local people not only use but begin to associate with and perceive of their territories in new and different ways (see Analco, Chapter 8). Younger community members (those under 35 years of age), in particular, are more likely to generate and hold knowledge through mapping boundaries, doing conservation zoning, developing ecotourism activities, and creating forest management plans, than knowledge gained through hunting, harvesting and planting (Robson 2010; Robson *et al.* 2018). Finally, it should be noted that the loss of 'traditional' environmental knowledge-holders may be tempered by migrants who resettle in the home village and take up farming again. This is most evident in Santa Cruz and in Comaltepec, where a number of families have returned over the past decade, and have begun to cultivate previously abandoned plots.

Territorial governance and collective work

Our published work (Curiel, Hernández-Díaz, and Worthen 2015; Klooster 2013; Robson *et al.* 2018), as well as the community case studies featured in this book, show how migration challenges the social institutions that structure territorial governance. As a resident of Analco explained:

> We suffer from a lack of people ... there are no citizens, no people to carry out cargos ... those that are here are older people, there are few youngsters, and it is the same group of citizens that have to do all the work.
>
> (Resident of Analco, 2008, cited previously in Robson 2010)

Migration can produce marked declines in local citizen:cargo ratios (Klooster 2013; Robson 2010), with lower ratios equating to a reduced pool of active resident labour and an increased collective workload for remaining villagers. In addition, in some communities, new or expanded land uses (e.g. forestry, eco-tourism) have led to the establishment of new committees and an increase in the overall number of cargos – thus exacerbating the burden of collective work and communal service obligations.

Such labour deficits are felt most acutely in communities (Analco, Yavesía) and localities (La Esperanza and San Martin Soyolapam) with small village populations (see Chapters 6, 8, and 9).

Fewer people means a reduced pool of well-qualified candidates for cargos, impacting communities' ability to adequately staff village governance authorities, including the *Comisariado de Bienes Comunales* (Office of the Common Property Commissioner) and *Consejo de Vigilancia* (Surveillance and Oversight Council) (see Robson and Wiest 2014). Communities are also choosing to forgo less urgent collective tasks and dedicate their tequio requests to the most urgent activities, which now take longer due to the shortage of labour (Robson *et al.* 2018). This impacts the work that communities can carry out within their territories, including the maintenance of forest roads and boundaries, and reforestation work. Because of a reduced territorial presence in areas where people no longer farm, graze animals, hunt or gather, the authorities of several communities acknowledged how difficult it can be to monitor extensive and densely forested territorial commons.

Impacts on biodiversity

Agricultural abandonment over a period of decades has led to significant forest regeneration, as confirmed by our interviews, walking tours with local land users (Figures 10.3 and 10.4), and our direct landscape observations compared with historic aerial photographs and satellite imagery we took with us to the field (see also Robson and Berkes 2011).

In Comaltepec and Analco, ecological and land use data were collected through forest transects in tropical dry, dry oak, mixed pine-oak, and cloud forests, and territorial walking tours[3] conducted across areas of current and former farmed lands to map areas of agricultural abandonment and new forest growth. Interviews were used to confirm similar retrenchment patterns in Maninaltepec and Tepetotutla, where new stands of pine have colonized former fields in temperate-cold and temperate-dry zones, while fewer areas of cloud forest are opened up for long-fallow agriculture or thinned out to establish small-scale coffee and banana plantations on the windward side of the range.

What might these forest transitions mean for biodiversity at a landscape scale? We respond to this question by looking at observed and potential impacts on: ecological succession and disturbance; edge effects and patch size; and, agroforestry systems and home gardens.

Figure 10.3 Walking tour with local land user in area of new forest growth above head village of Santiago Comaltepec.

Source: photo credit: Jim Robson.

Ecological succession and disturbance

Historically, patterns of disturbance in the Sierra Norte have helped to create a mosaic of primary and secondary forest, characterized by relatively small perimeter/forest patch area ratios (Robson and Berkes 2011). In Comaltepec, for example, while extensive areas have been cleared in and around the road-side hamlet of Metates (for coffee groves) and the village of San Martin Soyolapam (for cattle ranching), in most other zones disturbance has been more localized and small-scale, helping to keep sizeable tracts of primary forest intact, interspersed by secondary forests at varying successional stages. Across the Sierra Norte, low to moderate population densities, as well as periodic shifts in the economic activities of land users, have allowed for the recovery of secondary forest over multi-decade periods, especially on the windward side of the range where long-fallow shifting cultivation is widely practised. As Martin's (1993) work in the Chinantla and Mixe regions show, such processes

Figure 10.4 Walking tour with local land user in grazing and forest areas close to San Martin Soyolapam.

Source: photo credit: Jim Robson.

tend to produce a diverse patchwork of secondary vegetation types along altitudinal gradients.

There are clear biodiversity benefits from having a diverse mix of primary and secondary forests (Chazdon 2014). This is most apparent from the perspective of overall tree diversity, since the trees found in secondary forests are virtually absent in old growth and primary forests (Castillo and Blanco-Macías 2007).[4] As such, while large areas of primary forest exhibit much higher species richness (with several canopy layers), limited extensions of secondary forest play an important role in increasing overall diversity. In addition to their biodiversity value, secondary forests play important roles in watershed protection and help buffer mature forest fragments from edge effects, and increase the degree of connectivity between them. For example, in both Analco and Comaltepec, secondary forests constitute the key source of firewood and other non-timber forest products (NTFPs) for local resource users, thus protecting primary forest from exploitation.

With widespread agricultural abandonment, this long-standing disturbance regime is altered, with fewer opportunities for forest clearing and recovery, with the patterns and intensities of secondary succession thrown into flux.

Edge effects and patch size

Edges may induce changes in the abundance and distribution of species, which in turn produce changes in species interactions, such as predation, herbivory, pollination and seed dispersal (López-Barrera *et al.* 2007). Edges can modify forest structure, tree regeneration and mortality (Harper *et al.* 2005). Nevertheless, studies in Mexico (Davidson-Hunt 2003; López-Barrera *et al.* 2007; Turner, Davidson-Hunt, and O'Flaherty 2003) indicate that edge effects on biodiversity are not immediately obvious. In the Sierra Norte, the reduction in cultivated areas has led to changes in the mosaic of forest patches, generally leading to fewer but larger patches. This alters edge effects, which in northern Oaxaca can have a weak but positive effect on tree diversity (Rey-Benayas *et al.* 2007), especially on the windward side of the range where shifting cultivation allows many species to disperse and flourish, including both pioneers and late-successional species. In areas of cloud forest, for example, increased patchiness can represent opportunities for forest regeneration and forest fragment expansion, as many species (ferns, bryophytes, for example) have flower displays that are more attractive than in the forest interior (López-Barrera *et al.* 2007). Similar effects occur at the edges of riparian vegetation strips, where birds are observed to deposit a large number and diversity of seeds (farmer interviews in Analco and La Esperanza). Habitat generalists, in particular, are well placed to exploit the opportunities presented by low to moderate rates of forest fragmentation. In both study communities, the evidence provided by local land users suggests that the traditional mix of forested and open areas has provides conditions to which multiple species respond (Robson 2009). Many birds (*faisan*, among others), butterflies, and forest mammals (white-tailed deer, wild boar, *tejon*, racoon, among others) are frequent visitors to areas where grains, and wild and domesticated fruits are grown (Robson, unpublished field observations and interviews, 2007–2008; Robson 2009, 2010).

With agricultural abandonment, forest patches (along an altitudinal gradient) have begun to increase in size and connectivity to form larger and larger patches (consistent with Watson 2002), which reduces the edge contrast between forested and semi-open and open areas. Although a lack of data limits our ability to determine the biodiversity impact of such change, anecdotally, local farmers reported seeing fewer birds, butterflies, and mammals as open areas reduce in number, size, and extent (Robson 2009, 2010). A transition to a heavily forested landscape, with minimal levels of disturbance, combined with the loss of landscape features associated with cropland and pasture, could represent a decline in overall diversity (see Martinez *et al.* 2004; Navarro *et al.* 2004).

Impact on agro-forestry systems and home gardens

Through varied crop selection – a result of farmer experimentation and a response to environmental variation – communities in the Sierra Norte are traditionally home to high levels of agro-biodiversity[5] (Boege 2008; Robson

2010) and maize races in particular (Gonzalez 2001; Soleri *et al.* 2006). With agricultural abandonment taking place across the region, and farmers beginning to favour mono-crops[6] over *milpa* and traditional multi-species cropping systems, this looks set to change.

As noted, the majority of fields still farmed tend to be clustered around settlements, concentrated across just a few altitudinal zones, and can be simpler in their crop makeup and structure than in decades past. In Analco and Comaltepec, Robson (2010) found that the contraction of farmed zones went hand in hand with changes to the type and diversity of crops being grown. On higher slopes above the head village of Santiago Comaltepec and the community of Analco, potato, and black and mottled corn varieties, are now largely absent from local dinner tables because so few farmers still maintain plots at the kind of elevations (>2300 m.a.s.l.) (and cooler and wetter conditions) that such crops and varieties require. Similarly, wheat and barley, as well as some bean and maize varieties, are no longer maintained because farmers are abandoning the drier, warmer lands (<1800 m.a.s.l.) where they were traditionally grown. On the humid side of the Sierra Norte, depressed coffee prices and labour shortages have forced many family producers to abandon their *cafetales* (coffee groves) (Hite *et al.* 2017). As coffee groves reduce in number, so too have the associated agro-forestry systems used to produce avocado, banana, mamey, and vanilla, among other crops. In southern Mexico, research has shown how these agro-forestry systems 'mimic'[7] the structure of natural forest ecosystems (Challenger 1998; Moguel and Toledo 1999), supporting an impressive diversity of trees, birds, bats and beetles (Bandiera *et al.* 2005; Pineda *et al.* 2005).

In addition to plots outside their villages, households in the Sierra Norte have customarily planted and maintained in their yards and adjacent gardens (solares), different edible, medicinal, and ornamental plants, including local crop varieties that are no longer cultivated in other parts of the community (Martin 1993; Robson 2010). In Analco, these home gardens are very important for maintaining local varieties of mottled, purple, yellow and white corn. In Santa Cruz Tepetotutla, and in Comaltepec's localities of La Esperanza and San Martin Soyolapam, they function as *in situ* seed banks for tepejilote palm (Chamaedorea tepejilote), corn (local varieties), avocado (native variety), tomato (native varieties), papaya, coffee, grapefruit, tamarind, vanilla (local varieties), mango, chilli, banana, plantain, cocoa, and coconut, among other tropical fruits. Maintaining such a diversity of cultivars provides the additional benefit of increasing the resilience of local farming systems to changing climatic, demographic and economic conditions (Gonzalez 2001).

In Comaltepec and Analco, data pointed to a decline in the number of households maintaining home gardens. Few families said they had the time, resources, or need to maintain them, thus reflecting the wider decline in farming activities. The disappearance of home gardens negatively impact on agro-biodiversity because of the way these gardens are embedded in and complement other aspects of the larger land use system (Eyzaguirre and Linares 2004). In Oaxaca, for example, agro-biodiversity is maintained and enriched by plant and seed exchange (Aguilar-Støen *et al.* 2008), and it is the home garden that plays an essential role in enabling such practices.

Summary

While patterns of agricultural abandonment fit the general theory of 'forest transition' (Rudel, Schneider and Uriate 2007) previously reported across Latin America, including Mexico (Klooster 2003; Rudel *et al.* 2005), it is unclear what impact such transitions may have on biodiversity beyond an obvious increase in forest cover. Although a substantial research literature exists relating to deforestation processes (Fahrig 2003), edge effects (Ries *et al.* 2004), forest dynamics and succession (Shugart 1998), among other principles and processes of landscape ecology (Turner *et al.* 2001), the precise ways by which human activity affects forest biodiversity remain poorly defined. This is particularly relevant in global regions where traditional farming landscapes have been strongly associated with biodiversity conservation (Dorresteijn *et al.* 2015; Liu *et al.* 2013; Palang *et al.* 2006; Ranganathan *et al.* 2008; Takeuchi 2010).

In the Sierra Norte, traditional land use has driven secondary succession with impacts on forest composition, structure and regeneration through practices such as long fallow rotational agriculture, ground fires, lopping of hardwoods for fuel wood, pine for timber, and sporadic cattle grazing. Progress in landscape ecology (Forman 2014; Turner 2005; Wiens and Moss 2005) and its application to conservation management (Gutzwiller 2002; Borgerhoff Mulder and Coppolillo 2005) has highlighted the importance of assessing threats to these processes at both a forest patch and forest landscape scale (Newton 2007). When disturbance is low to moderate in intensity, it can produce a level of spatial heterogeneity within landscapes that permits the coexistence of a high number of species (Tilman 1982). Pioneering work by Del Castillo and Blanco-Macías (2007) has shown how species diversity in southern Mexico displays maximum values at intermediate disturbance intensities. Although our work has not produced the empirical quantitative data to measure changes in biodiversity, qualitative evidence and general field observations do allow us to hypothesize that the shift to off-farm activities in northern Oaxaca, will: (i) interrupt processes of ecological succession and disturbance in the agricultural–forest mosaic; (ii) reduce edge effects and cause changes in patch size; and, (iii) drive declines in agro-forestry systems and home gardens.

As the ratios between different vegetation categories are thrown into flux, especially in zones closer to permanent settlements, such modifications can result in localized declines in biodiversity, despite (or because of) extensive forest resurgence (see Robson and Berkes 2011). Such outcomes would necessarily challenge the assumption that the depopulation of rural areas automatically provides a boon for the provision of ecosystem services and biodiversity. Given such informed speculation, it is apparent that more work is needed to better understand how a modifying landscape mosaic impacts ecological integrity in regions where biodiversity and culture are so clearly intertwined (Naveh 1995; Nazarea 2006).

Changing landscapes and community trajectories

In Indigenous Oaxaca, we find that migration partially depopulates communities, reduces the collective labour pool that underpins customary resource management, drives agricultural abandonment and a contraction in territorial use, and creates emergent opportunities through forest recovery and resurgence. While traditional agricultural and pastoral activities are declining, the agricultural frontier is contracting but not disappearing, and new forestry, conservation, and ecotourism activities are appearing and on the increase.

In this way, the 'community' of today is no longer the 'community' of yesteryear, when communal lands were used, understood, and related to by all (Martínez Luna 2010). The venues for environmental knowledge to be produced and tested are being reduced, with intimate understandings of soils, local climate crops, or wild species (Gonzalez 2001; Hunn 2008; Martin 1993) being of limited daily relevance to broad sections of contemporary community memberships. At the same time, while 'knowing the land' by planting, hunting, gathering, and herding may be on the decline, 'knowing the land' by mapping of boundaries and sacred landscapes, conservation zoning, and creating forest management plans has increased. The establishment of new land uses (whether ecotourism, commercial forestry, or formal conservation) sees communities produce local professionals, including foresters, who, together with community members engaged in logging (Figure 10.5) and conservation activities, 'know the land' differently compared with their fathers and grandfathers.

Emergent economies based in part on non-consumptive resource use will alter people's daily links to land and territory, both in terms of resource practice and because villagers may no longer be required to spend much time out on the land, or be present across multiple territorial zones. This presents communities with a particular challenge. Namely, as fewer people maintain an active presence throughout the landscape, capacities to monitor and defend forest commons are necessarily impacted, making communities vulnerable to the interests of external actors – whether these are neighbouring communities, protectionist conservation organizations, or large-scale mining and forestry operators. This has become a concern for communities with small populations, such as Analco and Yavesía, as well as those with extensive forest lands easily accessible to outsiders, such as Comaltepec (Robson 2010; Robson *et al.* 2018).[8]

As communities embark on building sustainable futures, they must also find a way to develop significant benefit streams from such shifts in land use, which will need to account for the decline in the agricultural component of rural livelihoods (Kaimowitz and Sheil 2007). In highland Oaxaca, it is farming as much as forestry that makes a foundational contribution to village life, economy, and territory, and in exploring alternatives, it remains unclear

Figure 10.5 Commercial logging in San Juan Evangelista Analco.
Source: photo credit: Jim Robson.

whether the resources and capitals accrued from ecotourism, biodiversity conservation, payment for environmental services, even logging in many places, are sufficient to support more than a small number of local families (Robson and Klooster, in press). Also, in a context where wage labour migration has fallen away but student migration has increased, communities, and the agencies that support them, must strive to develop a culture of land-based work that is attractive to young people and can meet their aspirations (Plieninger *et al.* 2006; Davidson-Hunt *et al.* 2016).

In summary, changing patterns of livelihood and territorial use, increases in forest cover, changes in wild and agro-biodiversity, and smaller village populations (with the challenges to self-governance that this poses), provide communities with new trajectories and possibilities to consider.

The choices open to them are partly determined by the natural resources that they can access. For example, those without tracts of high conservation value forest will be limited in terms of the biodiversity conservation or PES (Payment for Environmental Services) opportunities they can tap into. In Chapter 8, we saw how Analco's small territory (1659 hectares) is located wholly on the leeward side of the Sierra Madre range, lacking areas of cloud forest and tropical rainforest. Thus, Analco is limited in terms of non-consumptive forest uses. Rather, it is taking advantage of forest resurgence following migration to make its first forays into commercial logging. In contrast, Santa Cruz Tepetotutla (Chapter 7) is home to an extensive, extremely biodiverse rainforest territory that, in conjunction with a reduced and stabilized agricultural frontier, provides a comparative advantage by which PES and eco- and scientific-tourism opportunities can be exploited. To date, such moves have helped the community to reinforce internal conservation goals and generate economic alternatives to migration. Other communities may have uncertain territorial futures. Yavesía (Chapter 6), whose communal territory contains important areas of old growth pine and conifer supports a current policy of strict forest protection, yet a lack of economic opportunities locally and the ongoing loss of young people is leading some in the community to reassess the value of commercial forestry, despite previous conflicts around logging.

Lastly, we must consider changing migration dynamics, which can reverse what may seem like established trends. Mexican migration to the US has declined to a relative trickle because of stricter US immigration policies, increased border enforcement, US recession, and insecurity on the Mexican side of the border. The final years of the Obama administration saw a spike in the number of returnees (whether escaping economic hardship or deportation) to rural Mexico. In northern Oaxaca, we have seen parts of community territories, long-abandoned, being tilled and planted again. While the numbers returning or deciding to stay have been insufficient to reverse the overall effects of population loss or forest resurgence that we describe in this book, the planned immigration policies of the current US administration could see the repatriation of hundreds of thousands of undocumented migrants back to Mexico, and the prospect of large numbers of Indigenous migrants returning to their villages.

This is a further reminder of the importance of ongoing, longitudinal research that observes, tracks, and analyses the meaning of such changes as they unfold over time.

Conclusions

Change following migration is producing a new landscape of territorial use and conservation in Indigenous Oaxaca. As rural areas depopulate, local people's reliance on and use of land and forest for livelihood is transformed. This not only restructures different elements of community life but may drive a redefinition of territoriality and unexpected or unforeseen impacts on biodiversity. Yet rather than trigger the erosion of 'know the land' as a central pillar of

Indigenous *comunalidad*, migration opens up spaces for forest recovery and use, and creates new opportunities and trajectories for communities to consider. The Oaxacan experience shows that communities can remain viable, especially those with the resource and forest base to take advantage of emergent land use opportunities. Nevertheless, they remain challenged as memberships become stretched across borders and are less and less rooted in the agricultural and forest traditions of the past.

Such challenges will not be restricted to a few remote villages in Mexico. Rather, we anticipate that empirical insights from Oaxaca will resonate for communities in other contexts, which are also being impacted by a series of processes – rapid urbanization, simplified agricultural systems, a decline in local resource use traditions, and deforestation–reforestation outcomes – sweeping across Latin America and beyond (Aide *et al.* 2013; Boillat *et al.* 2017; Hecht 2014).

Notes

1 Some text in Chapter 10 is reproduced in an article by Robson and Klooster, 'Migration and a New Landscape of Forest Use and Conservation', forthcoming in the journal *Environmental Conservation*. Reproduced with acknowledgement.
2 Santiago Comaltepec is the only study community with multiple localities (the head village of Comaltepec, and two smaller settlements of La Esperanza and San Martin Soyolapam). Our analysis takes accounts of this.
3 Local land users would participate in these walking tours, providing a history of land use (year of, and reason for abandonment) as well as current status. These field-based observations of change in land use were supplemented by qualitative analysis of aerial photographs and LANDSAT imagery (INEGI databases) for the period 1990–2015.
4 Our intent is not to downplay the importance of old-growth or primary forests, which are critical suppliers of environmental services; locally and regionally in terms of regulating hydrological resources, and globally as a carbon sink, both in terms of tree biomass and soil organic matter. Old-growth forests also harbour the highest abundance of epiphytes, and other groups of organisms, such as large mammals and frugivorous birds (a group particularly susceptible to forest disturbance, see Giraudo *et al.* 2008). The role of old-growth forest in trapping cloud water is also higher than that of young forests. Adjacent old-growth forest acts as an important source of colonists to the developing secondary forest, thereby facilitating the transition from pine to broadleaf in temperate and tropical montane forests. Indeed, forest succession very much depends on a source pool of old-growth forest, as many species typical of early stages cannot succeed under their own canopy (Wirth *et al.* 2009).
5 The International Institute for Environment and Development (IIED, www.diversefoodsystems.org/keycon.html) defines agricultural biodiversity as the

> variety and variability of animals, plants, and microorganisms that are important to food and agriculture. It comprises genetic resources (varieties, breeds, etc.), species used directly or indirectly for food and agriculture (including crops, livestock, forestry and fisheries), fodder, fibre, fuel and pharmaceuticals, species that support production (soil biota, pollinators, predators, etc.) and those in the wider environment that support agro-ecosystems (agricultural, pastoral, forest and aquatic).

Agricultural biodiversity takes into account not only genetic, species and agro-ecosystem diversity but also cultural diversity, which influences human interactions at all levels. The definition thus includes domesticated, semi-domesticated, manipulated or 'wild' species, with no clear-cut demarcation between natural and managed plant and animal populations.

6 Non-organic, monoculture farming is considered one of the most damaging forms of agriculture as it drains the soil of nutrients and depletes the biodiversity of the general area (by taking potential food source and habitat away from birds, insects, and some mammals).

7 Farmers do not clear-cut, or use commercial pesticides or chemical fertilizers, but rather use careful hand culturing to leave the land intact, with little visible erosion. This *método rustico* (see Challenger 1998) allows for forest structure to remain largely unchanged, with minimal canopy interference. Field observations in and around Vista Hermosa and Puerto Eligio (Comaltepec) identified small-scale agro-forestry systems with up to 20 native tree species, which provide shade, maintain humidity and improve soil fertility. These shade coffee and multi-crop agro-forestry systems can exhibit high levels of beta-diversity and floristic heterogeneity (Bandiera *et al.* 2005) – considered to be of particular importance for tree conservation. In northern Oaxaca, they provide an important food source to many native birds and butterflies, including the *faisan*, or Crested Guan (*Penelope purpurascen*), which local farmers note is particularly fond of coffee husks.

8 Migrants have had limited direct effect on environmental governance issues in their communities of origin in the Sierra Norte. This contrasts with multiple cases in Latin America where migrants actively drive farming and forest activities, and other land use change (Hecht *et al.* 2015; Taylor *et al.* 2016).

References

Aguilar-Støen, M., S.R. Moe, and S.L. Camargo-Ricalde. 2008. Home gardens sustain crop diversity and improve farm resilience in Candelaria Loxicha, Oaxaca, Mexico. *Human Ecology* 37(1): 55–77.

Aide, T.M., M.L. Clark, H.R. Grau, D. López-Carr, M.A. Levy, D. Redo, M. Bonilla-Moheno, G. Riner, M.J. Andrade-Núñez, and M. Muñiz. 2013. Deforestation and reforestation of Latin America and the Caribbean (2001–2010). *Biotropica* 45(2): 262–271.

Bandiera, F.P., C. Martorell, J.A. Meave, and J. Caballero. 2005. Floristic heterogeneity in rustic coffee plantations, and its role in the conservation of plant diversity: a case study of the Chinantec region of Oaxaca, Mexico. *Biodiversity and Conservation* 14(5): 1225–1240.

Boege, E. 2008. *El patrimonio biocultural de los pueblos indígenas de México: Hacia la conservación in situ de la biodiversidad y agro-diversidad en los territorios indígenas*. Mexico City, Mexico: Instituto Nacional de Antropología e Historia, Comisión Nacional para el Desarrollo de los Pueblos Indígenas.

Boillat, S., F.M. Scarpa, J.P. Robson, I. Gasparri, T.M. Aide, A.P. Dutra Aguiar, L.O. Anderson *et al.* 2017. Land system science in Latin America: challenges and perspectives. *Current Opinion in Environmental Sustainability* 26: 37–46.

Borgerhoff Mulder, M. and P. Coppolillo. 2005. *Conservation: Linking Ecology, Economics and Culture*. Princeton, NJ: Princeton University Press.

Bray, D.B. 2013. When the state supplies the commons: origins, changes, and design of Mexico's common property regime. *Journal of Latin American Geography* (2013): 33–55.

Castillo, R.F. and A. del Blanco-Macías. 2007. Secondary succession under a slash-and-burn regime in a tropical montane cloud forest: soil and vegetation characteristics. In: Newton, A.C. (ed.), *Biodiversity Loss and Conservation in Fragmented Forest Landscapes:*

The Forests of Montane Mexico and Temperate South America. Wallingford, Oxford, UK: CABI.

Challenger, A. 1998. *Utilización y conservación de los ecosistemas terrestres de México: Pasado, presente y future*. Mexico City, Mexico: Comisión Nacional para el Conocimiento y Uso de la Biodiversidad/Instituto de Biología/Universidad Nacional Autónoma de México/Sierra Madre.

Chapela, F. 2005. Indigenous community forest management in the Sierra Juarez, Oaxaca. In: Barton Bray, D., L. Merino Perez, and D. Barry (eds), *The Community Forests of Mexico: Managing for Sustainable Landscapes*. Austin, TX: University of Texas Press.

Chazdon, R.L. 2014. *Second Growth: The Promise of Tropical Forest Regeneration in an Age of Deforestation*. Chicago, IL: University of Chicago Press.

Curiel, C., J. Hernández-Díaz, and H. Worthen. 2015. *Los dilemas de la politica del reconocimiento en México*. Mexico City, Mexico: Juan Pablos Editor.

Davidson-Hunt, I.J., H. Asselin, F. Berkes, K. Brown, C.J. Idrobo, M. Jones, P. McConney, M. O'Flaherty, J.P. Robson, and M. Rodriguez. 2016. The use of biodiversity for responding to globalised change. In: Davidson-Hunt, I.J., H. Suich, S.S. Meijer, and N. Olsen (eds), *People in Nature: Valuing the Diversity of Interrelationships between People and Nature*. Gland, Switzerland: IUCN. September 2016.

Del Castillo, R.F. and Blanco-Macías, A., 2007. Secondary succession under a slash-and-burn regime in a tropical montane cloud forest: soil and vegetation characteristics. *Biodiversity Loss and Conservation in Fragmented Forest Landscapes. The Forests of Montane Mexico and Temperate South America*, pp. 158–180. CABI, Wallingford, Oxfordshire, UK.

Dorresteijn, I., J. Loos, J. Hanspach, and J. Fischer. 2015. Socioecological drivers facilitating biodiversity conservation in traditional farming landscapes. *Ecosystem Health and Sustainability* 1(9): 1–9.

Duran, E., J.P. Robson, M. Briones-Salas, D.B. Bray, and F. Berkes. 2012. Mexico: Wildlife conservation on community conserved lands in Oaxaca. *Protected Landscapes and Wild Biodiversity* 71. Gland, Switzerland: IUCN.

Eyzaguirre, P.B. and O.F. Linares. 2004. Introduction. In: Eyzaguirre, P.B. and O.F. Linares (eds), *Home Gardens and Agrobiodiversity*. Washington, DC: Smithsonian Books.

Fahrig, L. 2003. Effects of habitat fragmentation on biodiversity. *Annual Review of Ecology Evolution and Systematics* 34: 487–515.

Forman, R.T., 2014. *Land Mosaics: The Ecology of Landscapes and Regions*, p. 217. Washington, DC: Island Press.

Giraudo, A.R., S.D. Matteucci, J. Alonso, J. Herrera, and R.R. Abramson. 2008. Comparing bird assemblages in large and small fragments of the Atlantic Forest hotspots. *Biodiversity and Conservation* 17(5): 1251–1265.

González, R.J. 2001. *Zapotec Science: Farming and Food in the Northern Sierra of Oaxaca*. Austin, Texas: University of Texas Press.

Gutzwiller, K.J. 2002. Conservation in human-dominated landscapes. In: Gutzwiller, K.J. (ed.), *Applying Landscape Ecology in Biological Conservation*. New York: Springer Books.

Harper, K.A., S.E. Macdonald, P.J. Burton, J. Chen, K.D. Brosofske, S.C. Saunders, E.S. Euskirchen, D.A.R. Roberts, M.S. Jaiteh, and P.A. Esseen. 2005. Edge influence on forest structure and composition in fragmented landscapes. *Conservation Biology* 19(3): 768–782.

Hecht, S.B. 2014. Forests lost and found in tropical Latin America: the woodland 'green revolution'. *Journal of Peasant Studies* 41(5): 877–909.

Hecht, S.B., A.L. Yang, B.S. Basnett, C. Padoch, and N.L. Peluso. 2015. *People in Motion, Forests in Transition: Trends in Migration, Urbanization, and Remittances and their Effects on Tropical Forests.* Vol. 142. Bogor, Indonesia: Centre for International Forestry Research (CIFOR).

Hite, E.B., D.B. Bray, E. Duran, and A. Rincón-Gutiérrez. 2017. From forests and fields to coffee and back again: Historic transformations of a traditional coffee agroecosystem in Oaxaca, Mexico. *Society & Natural Resources* 30(5): 613–626.

Hunter, L.M., J.K. Luna, and R.M. Norton. 2015. Environmental dimensions of migration. *Annual Review of Sociology* 41: 377–397.

Hunn, E.S. 2008. *A Zapotec Natural History.* Tucson, AZ: University of Arizona Press.

Kaimowitz, D. and D. Sheil. 2007. Conserving what and for whom? Why conservation should help meet basic human needs in the tropics. *Biotropica* 39(5): 567–574.

Klooster, D. 2003. Forest transitions in Mexico: institutions and forests in a globalized countryside. *The Professional Geographer* 55(2): 227–237.

Klooster, D.J. 2005. Producing social nature in the Mexican countryside. *Cultural Geographies* 12: 321–344.

Klooster, D.J. 2013. The impact of transnational migration on commons management among Mexican indigenous communities. *Journal of Latin American Geography* 12(1): 57–86.

Lara, Y. and F. Manzano. 2005. *Ordenamiento comunitario del territorio: Comunidad de San Juan Evangelista Analco.* Prepared by ERA, AC, for internal community use.

Liu, Y., M. Duan, and Z. Yu. 2013. Agricultural landscapes and biodiversity in China. *Agriculture, Ecosystems and Environment* 166: 46–54.

López-Barrera, F., J.J. Armesto, G. Williams-Linera, C. Smith-Ramírez, and R.H. Manson. 2007. Fragmentation and edge effects on plant-animal interactions, ecological processes and biodiversity. In: Newton, A.C. (ed.), *Biodiversity Loss and Conservation in Fragmented Forest Landscapes: The Forests of Montane Mexico and Temperate South America.* Wallingford, Oxford, UK: CABI.

Martin, G.J. 1993. Ecological classification amongst the Chinantec and Mixe of Oaxaca, Mexico. *Etnoecologia* 1: 17–33.

Martinez, A.L., J.L. Busquets, A.D. Warren, and I.V. Fernandez. 2004. Lepidopteros: papilionoideos and hesperioidios. In: García-Mendoza, A.J., M. De Jesús Ordóñez, and M. Briones-Salas (eds). 2004. *Biodiversidad de Oaxaca.* Mexico City, Mexico: Instituto de Biología de la UNAM, Fondo Oaxaqueño para la Conservación de la Naturaleza, and the World Wildlife Fund.

Martínez Luna, J. 2010. *Eso que llaman comunalidad.* Oaxaca City, Mexico: CONACULTA-CAMPO-Fundación Harp Helú-Secretaria de Cultura-Oaxaca.

Meyerson, F. AB., L. Merino Pérez, and J. Durand. 2007. Migration and environment in the context of globalization. *Frontiers in Ecology* 5(4): 182–190.

Moguel, P. and V.M. Toledo. 1999. Biodiversity conservation in traditional coffee systems of Mexico. *Conservation Biology* 13(1): 11–21.

Navarro, A.G., E.A. Garcia-Trejo, A. Townsend Petersen, and V. Rodrigues-Contreras. 2004. Aves. In: García-Mendoza, A.J., M. De Jesús Ordóñez, and M. Briones-Salas (eds). *Biodiversidad de Oaxaca.* Mexico City, Mexico: Instituto de Biología de la UNAM, Fondo Oaxaqueño para la Conservación de la Naturaleza, and the World Wildlife Fund.

Naveh, Z. 1995. Interactions of landscapes and cultures. *Landscape and Urban Planning* 32: 43 54.

Nazarea, V.D. 2006. Local knowledge and memory in biodiversity conservation. *Annual Reviews of Anthropology* 35: 317–335.

Neumann, K. and H. Hilderink. 2015. Opportunities and challenges for investigating the environment-migration nexus. *Human Ecology* 43(2): 309–322.

Newton, A.C. (ed.). 2007. *Biodiversity Loss and Conservation in Fragmented Forest Landscapes: The Forests of Montane Mexico and Temperate South America*. Oxford, UK: CABI.

Palang, H., A. Printsmann, E.K. Gyuro, M. Urbanc, E. Skowronek, and W. Woloszyn. 2006. The forgotten rural landscapes of Central and Eastern Europe. *Landscape Ecology* 21: 347–357.

Pazos-Almada, B. and D.B. Bray. 2018. Community-based land sparing: territorial land-use zoning and forest management in the Sierra Norte of Oaxaca, Mexico. *Land Use Policy* 78: 219–226.

Pineda, E., C. Moreno, F. Escobar, and G. Halffter. 2005. Frog, bat, and dung beetle diversity in the cloud forest and coffee agroecosystems of Veracruz. *Conservation Biology* 19(2): 400–410.

Plieninger, T., F. Höchtl, and T. Spek. 2006. Traditional land-use and nature conservation in European rural landscapes. *Environmental Science & Policy* 9(4): 317–321.

Ranganathan, J., R.J.R. Daniels, M.D.S. Chandran, P.R. Ehrlich, and G.C. Daily. 2008. Sustaining biodiversity in ancient tropical countryside. *Proceedings of the National Academy of Sciences* 105: 17852–17854.

Rey-Benayas, J.M., L. Cayuela, M. González-Espinosa, C. Echeverría, R.H. Manson, G. Williams Linera, R.F. Castillo, N. del Ramírez-Marcial, M.A. Muñiz-Castro, M.A. Blanco Macías, A. Lara, and A.C. Newton. 2007. Plant diversity in highly fragmented forest landscapes in Mexico and Chile: implications for conservation. In: Newton, A.C. (ed.), *Biodiversity Loss and Conservation in Fragmented Forest Landscapes: The Forests of Montane Mexico and Temperate South America*. Oxford, UK: CABI.

Ries, L., R.J.J. Fletcher, J. Battin, and T.D. Sisk. 2004. Ecological responses to habitat edges: mechanisms, models and variability explained. *Annual Review of Ecology, Evolution and Systematics* 35: 491–522.

Robson, J.P. 2008. *Plan de Manejo de la Biodiversidad: Comunidad de Santiago Comaltepec, Oaxaca*. Unpublished report for internal community use.

Robson, J.P. 2009. Out-migration and commons management: social and ecological change in a high biodiversity region of Oaxaca, Mexico. *International Journal of Biodiversity Science and Management* 5(1): 21–34.

Robson, J.P. 2010. *The Impact of Rural to Urban Migration on Forest Commons in Oaxaca, Mexico*. Unpublished PhD Thesis, University of Manitoba. Winnipeg, Canada.

Robson, J.P. and F. Berkes. 2011. Exploring some of the myths of land use change: can rural to urban migration drive declines in biodiversity? *Global Environmental Change* 21(3): 844–854.

Robson, J.P. and D. Klooster. In press. Migration and a new landscape of forest use and conservation. *Environmental Conservation*.

Robson, J.P. and R. Wiest. 2014. Transnational migration, customary governance and the future of community: A case study from Oaxaca, Mexico. *Latin American Perspectives* 41(3): 103–117.

Robson, J.P., D.J. Klooster, H. Worthen, and J. Hernandez-Diaz. 2018. Migration and agrarian transformation in Indigenous Mexico. *Journal of Agrarian Change* 18(2): 299–323.

Rudel, T.K., O.T. Coomes, E. Moran, A. Achard, A. Angelsen, J. Xu, and E. Lambin. 2005. Forest transitions: towards a global understanding of land use change. *Global Environmental Change* 15(1): 23–31.

Rudel, T.K., L. Schneider, and M. Uriate. 2007. Forest transitions: an introduction. *Land Use Policy* 27(2): 95–97.

Shugart, H.H. 1998. *A Theory of Forest Dynamics: The Ecological Implications of Forest Succession Models.* Caldwell, NJ: Blackburn Press.

Soleri, D., D.A. Cleveland, and F.A. Cuevas. 2006. Transgenic crops and crop varietal diversity: the case of maize in Mexico. *AIBS Bulletin* 56(6): 503–513.

Sosa Perez, F., M. Sánchez, and F. Manzano. 2017. Ordenamiento Territorial Comunitario de San Juan Evangelista Analco, para promover el manejo adaptativo, el resguardo local y la gobernanza de la biodiversidad. YUTZINA S.C. For internal community use.

Takeuchi, K. 2010. Rebuilding the relationship between people and nature: the Satoyama Initiative. *Ecological Research* 25: 891–897.

Taylor, M.J., M. Aguilar-Støen, E. Castellanos, M.J. Moran-Taylor, and K. Gerkin. 2016. International migration, land use change and the environment in Ixcán, Guatemala. *Land Use Policy* 54(2016): 290–301.

Tilman, D. 1982. *Resource Competition and Community Structure.* Princeton, NJ: Princeton University Press.

Turner, M.G. 2005. Landscape ecology: what is the state of the science? *Annual Review of Ecology, Evolution, and Systematics,* 36: 319–344.

Turner, M.G., R.H. Gardner, and R.V. O'Neill. 2001. *Landscape Ecology in Theory and Practice: Pattern and Process.* New York: Springer Books.

Turner, N.J., I.J. Davidson-Hunt, and M. O'Flaherty. 2003. Living on the edge: ecological and cultural edges as sources of diversity for social—ecological resilience. *Human Ecology* 31(3): 439–461.

Watson, D.M. 2002. A conceptual framework for studying species composition in fragments, islands and other patchy ecosystems. *Journal of Biogeography* 29: 823–834.

Weins, J. and M. Moss (eds). 2005. *Issues and Perspectives in Landscape Ecology.* Cambridge, UK: Cambridge University Press.

Wirth, C., G. Gleixner, and M. Heimann (eds). 2009. *Old-Growth Forests: Function, Fate and Value.* Berlin: Springer Books.

11 Migrant organizing, village governance, and the ephemeral nature of translocality

Jorge Hernández-Díaz and James P. Robson

Introduction

> We have several projects to promote traditional music and dance and to rescue our Indigenous language, in addition to providing material and economic support to the community ... we want to do what we can for our pueblo.
>
> (Migrant leader from Analco, Oaxaca City, 2008)

Decades of internal and US-bound migration streams have had a profound impact on village life and governance in Oaxaca (Cohen and Sirkeci 2011; Hernández-Díaz 2013; Robson *et al.* 2018; VanWey *et al.* 2005). Migration has drawn people away from their home villages, reducing the resources available for local development, including the collective resident labour that underpins customary forms of civic and communal governance (Klooster 2013; Mutersbaugh 2002; Robson and Berkes 2011). Although Oaxacan wage labour migration has fallen dramatically in recent years (Cohen 2016; Passel, Cohn, and Gonzalez-Barrera 2012), village populations have not rebounded (Bada and Formann 2016) and local governance remains under pressure, especially in communities with small resident populations (Hernandez-Diaz 2013; Robson *et al.* 2018).

A major hope for affected communities is said to reside in the translocal institutions and connections (Fox and Rivera-Salgado 2004; Fox and Bada 2008; Greiner and Sakdapolrak 2013) by which 'community' is recreated by migrants in faraway places (Grieshop 2006; Stiffler 2007) (Chapter 3, this book). Through the construction of a translocal community sphere, migrants have the potential to function as 'agents of development' (Glick Schiller and Faist 2010) in their communities of origin, both through tangible means – sending monies and (sometimes) labour to meet village governance obligations or finance community projects and infrastructure improvements – and in more symbolic forms, as community norms and ceremony become embedded across an expanded social field (Stephen 2007; Martínez Luna 2013).

Although scholars have long debated the impact of migration on rural development in Mexico (Binford 2003; Cohen, Jones, and Conway 2005; De

Haas 2010), much of that work has focused on economic and social change forged through household-level remittances (McKenzie and Rapoport 2007; Rubenstein 1992; Taylor 1999). Yet these remittances, while significant in aggregate terms, can be small at the level of individual households, appear to be declining over time, and have limited village-level impact when used solely to meet basic family needs (see Chapters 4 and 8, this book; Delgado Wise *et al.* 2014). Such realities support a shift in focus from the household investments of individual migrants to the activities of the 'collective migrant' (after Moctezuma 2000); the groups of 'active' migrants who organize to affect change in their communities of origin (Fitzgerald 2008; Orozco and Rouse 2007).

While the establishment of hometown associations, and other types of migrant organization, is well documented (Chapters 3–6, this book; Escala-Rabadán 2014; Hirabayashi 1993; Lanly and Valenzuela 2004; Velasco Ortiz 1998), fewer studies have looked to demonstrate how these organizations impact their communities of origin over time (Levitt and Lamba-Nieves 2011). In a Mexican context, work has looked at how groups of organized migrants influence the accountability of public investment (and officials) in communities of origin (Burgess 2016; Fox and Bada 2008; Garcia Zamora 2005), shape village politics and inter-community conflicts (Duquette-Rury 2016; Gutierrez Najera 2009), and connect place of residence and 'home' (Waldinger, Popkin, and Magana 2008). Yet exploration of the efficacy and longevity of migrant organizations, while not new (see Delgado Wise *et al.* 2014; Perry *et al.* 2009), is limited.

This chapter[1] draws on research from study communities in the Mixteca and Sierra Norte regions of Oaxaca, and with migrants and migrant organizations in Oaxaca City, Mexico City, and US destination centres,[2] to assess the current state of migrant organizing and the potential for migrants to (continue to) contribute to village development and mitigate communal labour shortages – particularly within a context of long-term absenteeism and limited possibilities for village return (see Jones 2009, 2014; Mines, Nichols, and Runsten 2010; Passel, Cohn, and Gonzalez-Barrera 2012). We explore reasons for lulls in organizations' membership numbers, and how the migratory experience can fracture the ethos of collective work and communal service, leading to a weakening of migrant–community relations over time. We discuss whether the limited efficacy of present arrangements can be significantly improved and sustained, or whether migrant organizing is merely a temporary boost to village development, with support slowly eroded by the aging-out of organizational leadership.

Migrants' role in subsidizing village life and governance

In 2015, more than a quarter of Oaxaca's 12,000+ localities were home to fewer than 50 inhabitants (INEGI 2017). Across the Sierra Norte and the Mixteca, it is not uncommon to come across villages where the majority of houses stand empty:

Most of the people from Tindú are here [in California], more than 80 per cent. In the clinic in Tindú this year they gave me the names of 536 inhabitants and 205 homes in the village ... too few people and most of them elderly. I left Tindú in 1987. I was a teacher, and there were 17 of us ... now there's only one.

(Antonio, Migrant leader from Santa Maria Tindu, in Madera, CA, 2016)

The community case studies featured in this book (Chapters 4–9) show how demographic change following migration can be debilitating, weakening the structures of community governance and possibilities for village development. Communities have responded to shortfalls in collective resident labour in different ways. But in many cases, migrants have been approached to contribute to village development and infrastructure projects, and meet or subsidize the cost of communal service obligations.

In the area of village development, interviews with migrant leaders and village authorities from Analco, Yavesía, and Comaltepec (Robson 2010; Robson, in press) show that migrants tend to prioritize support (in descending order of importance) for: (i) village fiestas; (ii) religious infrastructure and ceremonies; (iii) public/community infrastructure improvements; (iv) school and health services; and, (v) community-level natural resource and territorial projects and activities. Migrants are also targeted for forms of support dependent upon where they are based. In Oaxaca City, for example, Analqueño migrants are less able to make financial contributions because of low salaries, but are asked to contribute labour (in the form of tequios) in the home village. In contrast, those living in Mexico City are more numerous and better paid, and approached more often to provide financial support for village development projects. In the case of both Analco and Comaltepec, US-based migrants are perceived to have the greatest earning potential and are typically the first to be asked to support larger projects in the home village, including patron saint festivities.

In the area of village governance, the situation around migrant support is more complex and arguably more pressing. While migrant investments have been important for maintaining and enhancing material assets in communities of origin, our case studies (Chapters 4–9) highlight how institutions of collective work and communal service remain under severe strain because of a dearth of village residents. In Santa Maria Tindú (see Chapter 5), so few people live in the home village that local governance positions are routinely filled by elderly residents who, under past circumstances, would be 'retired' from active service:

Tindú just has old people, and they shouldn't be having to do a cargo with the Municipal Agency but they are. My dad lives there and he's 86 years old, and two years ago he was still acting as the Treasurer of Bienes Comunales ... so even though he doesn't know how to read or write, he was named to do the cargo.

(Migrant from Santa Maria Tindu, in Madera, California, 2015)

Even in places where the situation is a little less drastic, village populations have contracted sufficiently that the stay-behinds struggle to cope with the burden of cargo and tequio demands (see Chapters 4, 6, 8, 9, this book). These systems have had to change in response. Fewer collective work days are now dedicated to less important or less urgent community projects in Analco, Yatzachi el Bajo (in the Zoogocho micro-region) and Yavesía. The reverse can be true for very important projects, with more days now needed to compensate for the shortage of labour. In Comaltepec (Chapter 9), authorities now direct municipal funds to turn tequio work into contract wage labour. Across study communities, some (lower-level) municipal cargos have been dispensed with. This has eased the burden overall but also reduces the support provided to remaining cargo-holders, and may impact a community's ability to maintain standards in local governance (Robson and Wiest 2014).

This lived reality has encouraged communities to do more to manage the negative impacts of migration. They have looked to achieve this by establishing rules, expectations, and obligations for non-resident (migrant) members to follow. Such adaptations can help communities to influence migration flows, including the length of time members remain absent, while providing a further opportunity for migrants to show their commitment to those resident in the home village. Communities have employed a range of different strategies – some strict, some more flexible – in determining what migrants must do in order to maintain village rights in absentia. In communities such as San Pablo Macuiltianguis, San Miguel Maninaltepec, and San Baltazar Yatzachi el Bajo, migrants are expected to return home to perform cargo duties or to hire someone to do this for them (Hernández-Díaz and Worthen 2018; Klooster 2013):

> It's been a while since they started to do this, to pay for cargos. Ever since migration started, and there weren't enough people to cover all the village cargos, those [migrants] who had their families here were obligated to do a cargo … and since the husband wasn't here and the women couldn't do them because they had children to look after, well they had no choice but to hire people. First, they [gave cargos] to the migrants whose families lived here but it's not like that now, now they are assigning cargos directly to the people who don't live here but have a house or something in the community. And even if they don't have a family member living in that house, even if they don't have any family member in the village, even if the house stands empty, they are obligated to serve the community from afar, so they have to look for someone to pay [to cover that obligation] … [if they do that] then there's no problem if they want to return.
>
> (Migrant from San Baltazar Yatzachi el Bajo, in Los Angeles, 2016)

This strategy typically requires citizens to return home to serve cargos and/or pay fines for being away. If they don't, they are said to have 'renounced the pueblo', and abdicated their village and resource rights:

Sure, everyone is obligated, there are some that, as I mentioned, don't want to contribute, or can't, or have simply decided that they don't want to continue with this [supporting the home village in this way] … it's very difficult, especially for those who don't have their papers, but as I said before, there are two, three [who have returned to serve as] municipal agents who are still there because they don't have the papers to get back [into the US] … so they've sacrificed a lot. There is a list of people who have quit the community, they are no longer part of it … they don't send any contributions, they don't serve any cargos, they aren't there physically or with investments. If they return to the village, they can stay or visit [for a short time], two or three months would be tolerated, they'll tolerate that, but after that … if we see them, let's say, bring firewood from the mountain, or start working the land … well that's no longer allowed, they are no longer one of us, they have not contributed to their people and their community, how can they be allowed to use our resources?

(Migrant from Santa Maria Tindu, in Madera, California, 2016)

Of the community case studies featured in this book, Tepetotutla (Chapter 7) has been the strictest in terms of the obligations and restrictions placed on non-resident members. Those who do not comply may face a form of 'civic death', and banishment from the village (Mutersbaugh 2002).

Enforcing such sanctions, however, is difficult. In San Bartolomé Zoogocho, US-based migrants who failed to meet their cargo obligations were once barred from returning to the village, but this rule proved unworkable and absent Zoogochenses can now make payments to maintain community membership:

With regards to cargos, those that aren't living here are not forced to come back to do them. Some come, but in general they're not made to. Rather they send someone [a family member], if that person wants to, or they pay [for some third party to do it] … we accept everything. Now it's not an obligation [to serve cargos in person] but before it was … now they don't take away your privileges [rights] if you decide not to come. It happened in the past … I don't remember who it was who didn't accept the mayordomia but, this was when they were stricter, and there was this case where they [the authorities] cut the water and took over the migrant's house. That wouldn't happen now because we are more open, more flexible, we understand now that it's not the same [there] as it is here, that they are struggling to survive out there, and now that we understand them [the migrants] better we don't force them.

(Village resident, Zoogocho, 2015)

Analco instituted obligations for migrants in 2010, although these have not been widely enforced and are currently being re-negotiated (see Chapter 8). The Analco case highlights the problems that result from a delay in implementing rules, and the lack of clarity around rules and rule changes that can emerge.

These are partly responsible for the current difficulties in migrant–village relations being experienced in the community.

Lastly, there are Indigenous collectives such as Yavesía that (thus far) have chosen not to enact laws stipulating migrant rights and responsibilities. Rather, they have left absentee members to be morally (not legally) obligated to meet community requests for support (see Chapter 6). In such cases, the ability of village authorities to impose sanctions to encourage migrant compliance is severely limited.

Participation in migrant organizing

Whatever strategy is adopted, the organizations that migrants establish in Mexican and US destination centres play a critical role. As described in Chapter 3, these organizations typically serve two main functions: to maintain a strong and united migrant community; and, to facilitate collective support for the home village through financial and cultural investments. They respond to community petitions for support (whether related to communal service shortfalls, infrastructure needs, or village festivities) and participate in other activities that can help migrant members to maintain a presence and status within local governance and political structures:

> What created these organizations [was] precisely because migrants remain citizens who do not forget about their community, their origins, their people, and know that it is through contributing and participating [in the life of the community] that the needs of the community, such as festivities and cargos, are met. So, they support that by collecting and sending money … that was the reason to organize, together with a petition from the [village] authorities at that time. And it's been in place for some time and I don't know if some other community organizes in this way but we feel that it strengthens us.
>
> (Municipal office-holder, Yalina)

As noted in Chapter 3, many organizations build institutional links with the community of origin through a Hometown Association, often called a *mesa directiva*, or management board, and which derives its formal legitimacy through recognition by customary authorities in the village of origin. Staffed by individuals from within the migrant community, these administrative bodies call assemblies of migrants to discuss, debate, and make collective decisions, oversee many of the organization's activities, and liaise with village authorities. In some cases, such as Tindu's migrant organizations in California and Oregon, the *mesa directiva* can become a leading player within a fully-integrated system of translocal community governance (Chapter 5).

However, in most cases, mesas directivas do not 'call the shots', but rather respond to requests from village authorities back in Oaxaca. Rarely considered an official *cargo* by the community of origin, serving on the *mesa* is nevertheless viewed positively 'back home' and provides notice that the incumbent remains 'active'. Beyond serving on one of these positions, migrants can show their 'commitment' by involving themselves in the activities of the migrant organization. This can include supporting local social events and fiestas, and fundraising for investments and projects in the home village. The more migrants who are involved in their organizations, the greater the social capital of the migrant collective and, potentially, the stronger the links forged with the community of origin.

Given this, the potential for migrants to support village development and governance is essentially determined by the number of migrants both willing *and* able to provide support and to do so over time. In this regard, migrants can fall into one of three broad categories – active, semi-active, or non-active (Robson, in press). *Active* migrants are those who pay their monthly or annual membership fee, fulfil *cargos* within the migrant organization when elected to do so, fundraise to support investments and festivities in the community of origin, and regularly attend (and vote in) member assemblies. In other words, they are the individuals willing to contribute most or all of the time to the majority of initiatives and investments. In contrast, *semi-active* migrants are those who tend to do what's needed, but no more, in order to protect their rights and interests as a community member. For communities that have not instituted strict rules around migrant obligations, migrants in the semi-active category will often pay their annual or monthly fees, sometimes but not always contribute money for specific community-level investments, attend some but not all organization meetings and assemblies, and often decline requests to serve positions on the mesa directiva. Migrants will thus consider whether their rights will be rescinded for non-compliance before deciding to invest time, money, or both, into migrant organizing activities.

The final category – *non-active* – refers to migrants who ignore or refuse requests for support from village authorities and eschew membership of their local migrant organization. In doing so, they essentially revoke their status and rights as community members.

The research shows that such categories are fluid, with movement between categories possible, indeed expected, as migrants' personal situations or perspectives change. Some communities do a better job than others of maintaining lists of who is active and who is not. Yatzachi el Bajo, for example, long maintained an up-to-date register of active migrants living in Los Angeles. Others, such as Analco, Yavesía and Yalina, have similar lists but they are not routinely revised, making it hard for village authorities to know who is active versus semi-active and thus track how participation in the organization's activities fluctuates over time. This can be a problem given the predilection of community assemblies to award cargos to non-active or semi-active migrants who maintain assets and investments in the home village.

Robson (in press) produced data on current (2015–2016) membership numbers (and status) for migrant organizations from Analco and Yavesía in both Mexican and US destination centres (Figures 11.1 and 11.2).

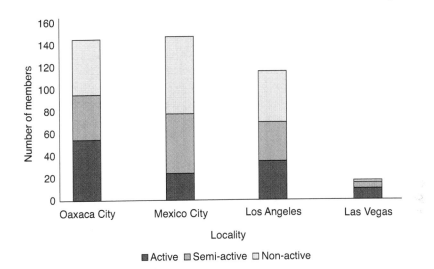

Figure 11.1 Status of first-generation migrants from San Juan Evangelista Analco living in US and Mexican destination centres (2015).

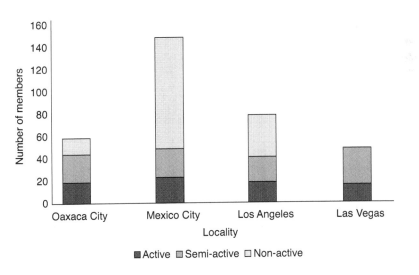

Figure 11.2 Status of first-generation migrants from Santa María Yavesía living in US and Mexican destination centres (2015).

He found that, in most locations, between one-sixth and one-third of first-generation migrants were maintaining an 'active' status. The proportion of active members was higher for Analco's than Yavesía's organizations, and (in the case of both study communities) higher among organizations in Oaxaca City than those in Mexico City or the US. For six of the eight organizations studied, the number of active migrants stands at around 20 individuals. In several cases, this number has remained consistent since the organization was established,[3] although as a proportion of the total number of migrants residing in that place, there has been a steady decline. For some migrants, a decision has been taken to have little or nothing to do with their local organization. In six of the eight organizations analysed, 'non-active' migrants outnumbered their 'semi-active' counterparts. Across this same sample, 'non-active' migrants constituted between 35 per cent and 70 per cent of the number of first-generation migrants living in that locality.

As an Analqueño in Los Angeles noted,

> there are a lot of non-active people here … the moment that they get settled they no longer have any interest in the village or its problems … it's just the way they think, and it's always going to be like that.

Migrant leaders stated that there was a higher proportion of non-active migrants in 2015 than in the 1980s, when most organizations were in their infancy and many first-generation migrants were men who had 'spent time in the community serving cargos, had material interests in the community, intended to go back, and the idea of cooperating was not a barrier … they knew what it was to serve their community'. Interviews with migrant leaders suggested that it was getting harder for organizations to recruit new members, with the migrants to have arrived in the last couple of decades seemingly less committed to the ideals of collective work and communal service than those who came before them. As one migrant from Analco explained, 'there came a time when migrants would arrive who didn't want to get involved … they arrived with a different attitude'. Ever since, the job of getting migrants fully involved 'has become a constant problem'.

'Active' migrants reported how a strong sense of moral duty and obligation underpinned their involvement, with a Yavesian in Los Angeles noting: 'it's easy not to be involved but if I did that I wouldn't feel good … I'd feel as if I was lacking as someone from my village … for me, I just want to help my people, my village'. For some, a moral argument for maintaining an active status combines with a desire to be buried in the village or to 'keep the door open' to possible future return (both contingent on maintaining good relations with village authorities). Yet many migrants, first through the decision to leave their home village and, second, through a decision to limit their contributions, can isolate themselves from traditional customs and structures. As one migrant from Analco pointed out, 'there are many who conform [to community expectations] but many who do not … the truth is that each of us thinks differently'. Among those willing to provide support, a sizeable number are not interested in meeting village governance obligations: 'there is a group that is happy to send their *cooperaciones* [monthly or annual monetary membership fee] but they don't want to do cargos … they are not interested in that'.

Several migrants acknowledged that unstable or limited economic opportunities in the US, especially for undocumented migrants, made it difficult for the collective to demand that all members contribute equally at all times. Not everyone agreed, however, with one migrant leader in Los Angeles arguing that the membership fee was 'the monthly equivalent of foregoing a coffee or two in Starbucks', and lamenting how his compatriots would 'cry for five or ten dollars, one hour's salary, while our people [in the home village] give up four or five hours of their time every Sunday for tequio'. The fact that many contribute so little was a source of frustration and gave some migrants reason to cooperate less than they would 'if everyone was pulling in the same direction'. As one explained, migrants would often take the view, 'well I'm not going to do anything while so-and-so doesn't do his cargos or cooperate, yet still has his rights and his name on the list [in the community of origin]'.

In Los Angeles, the issue of members not pulling their weight had prompted Analco's organization to restructure in the summer of 2016, to 'start afresh' with a committed group of fully active members bound by a clear set of membership obligations. Their list of registered members fell from 115 in April 2015 (35 active, 35 semi-active, and 45 non-active members) to 59 in July 2016 (59 active members[4]). This left 56 first-generation migrants off the list, who were now viewed as non-active by both the migrant organization and village authorities in Oaxaca.

Multiple factors can help to shape a migrant's level of involvement with their migrant organization. One key factor concerns the consequences of non-compliance:[5]

> We have to serve our community and support them when they are in need. [But] now that things like the mayordomía are optional, they can't force or fine me if I don't do it ... but there are still consequences, they'll still shame me here for refusing to serve my community. I participate in what I can ... what I want to do, I will do. But now it's more a question of faith.
> (Migrant from Santa María Tindú, in Madera, California, 2015)

As noted previously, Analco and Yavesía are among a number of communities that have either delayed their decision or chosen not to codify migrant obligations in local village statutes. In such cases, migrants effectively decide whether to meet calls to service or requests for support. As a migrant from Yavesía explains: 'when you leave there are no laws to say you have to keep helping out the home village ... that is up to you as an individual'. While any return to (live in) the home village may be met by fines and immediate *cargo* service for non-active migrants, their status as a community member is unlikely to have been rescinded completely. Migrants consider this when deciding to invest time and finances in migrant organizing.

While community rules set the context for migrant investments in village development or governance institutions, domestic realities also affect participation over time. For example, as migrants and their families put down roots in new places of residence, interest in hometown affairs may waver. The loss of Indigenous language, the purchase of homes in Mexico or the US, and reduced family ties back in Oaxaca, can all weaken ties. Our case studies point to how remittances have fallen as migrants have less money to send, fewer reasons to send money to Oaxaca, or more pressing demands in their places of residence. In many villages, the number of new house builds has decreased markedly. Among 'semi-active' migrants from Analco and Yavesía, a lack of funds and family needs were cited as reasons for not doing more. As a migrant in Los Angeles explained, 'things were better before ... everyone had more to give ... now there isn't as much work, household expenses are really high and it's diffi-cult to contribute funds'.

The ability (or inability) to visit the community of origin is an additional factor. In the 1980s and 1990s, it was common for migrants in the US to periodic-ally return to their places of origin. Some would come back for extended periods of time (1–2 years) before returning to the US as part of a circular migration dynamic. Others would make much shorter sojourns for Christmas or to partake in the village's patron saint festivities. While short visits are still made by migrants living in Mexican destination centres, they have become very difficult, if not impossible, for undocumented migrants in the US, for whom the costs associated with border crossings have skyrocketed over the past decade (Robson *et al.* 2018; Chapters 5 and 9, this book). As a migrant in Los Angeles explained, physical isolation means that many migrants 'no longer know their village, they don't know how things have changed', and are reliant on those with papers to visit Oaxaca and return with news.[6] This is much less of a problem for migrants in Oaxaca City, even Mexico City, who can visit in person or whose organizations can send delegations to attend important community assemblies and meetings.

Deterioration in migrant–village relations

The propensity of migrants to organize in support of their community of origin is also shaped by the nature of the relationship between groups of migrants and village authorities. Members of migrant organizations in Oaxaca City, Mexico City, Los Angeles, Las Vegas, and Chicago all complained of infrequent and limited communications, with many frustrated that municipal or communal office-holders would only contact them when financial support was needed (Robson, in press). As one noted, 'there is almost no communication ... only when they have a project that needs money and send a request asking for help'. As another explained,

> at all other times, it's like we don't exist ... they don't ask us how our health is, how the family is, work ... during the course of the year they don't speak to us ... nothing, they forget about us.

Migrants spoke of a lack of transparency with regards to the funds sent to support projects and activities in the village, which had created 'mistrust in how they [the authorities] use the money'. When asked if problems of poor communication and limited transparency were relatively new, migrant leaders said that they were long-standing issues. While the situation can improve under a particular administration, such improvements are generally temporary, reverting to type with a change of incumbents.

As organizations struggle to maintain the size of their active memberships, limited funds are being prioritized for a small number of often specific uses. Even when funds are readily available, many migrants are reluctant to support certain 'development' initiatives because of problems associated with previous investments, or the failure of earlier migrant-funded projects. As a Yavesian in Los Angeles explained, 'before there were more [active] members ... some 25 or 30 ... but the problem is that we would collect money from everybody, send it, but no one was ever sure what it was spent on'. Of those that remain, 'no one wants to give anything now, or at least not much'. For one migrant organization in Oaxaca City, the decision was recently taken to purchase all project materials themselves rather than send procurement funds to the village. Anger over a perceived misuse of funds had led some migrants to stop cooperating altogether.

Migrants also questioned the amount of money being used for particular activities. There was concern about too many resources being funnelled into village festivities:

> Personally, I don't like to support 100 per cent because they ask for a contribution of say $500, $400–$500 dollars per person and the money is sent and then spent on fireworks, it's something I'm not in agreement with because there are other more pressing needs in the community. I've participated, I've given my $50, $100, $200 maximum, but no more than a donation ... there are others who are okay with it, they enjoy the fiesta [in the village] but at the end of the day that money, for me, is 'money down the drain' because we have other priorities.
> (Migrant from San Martín Itunyoso, living in Madera, CA, 2015)

In one instance – Yavesía's migrant organization in Chicago – migrants had decided not to support such events, arguing that '[our] money could be better spent elsewhere'. In addition, they no longer respond to funding petitions from village authorities, but approach the community with their own project-funding ideas, which in 2015 were focused exclusively on improving local education services and infrastructure.

In addition to limiting the type and level of support that they provide to their community of origin, migrants can also direct more of their effort and energy to supporting each other in the diaspora. Such a shift is partially attributable to migrants feeling undervalued by villagers in Oaxaca. But it is also a consequence of long-term absenteeism, and the changing profiles and needs of first-generation migrants (and their families) in destination centres.

Some organizations face a difficult choice: shift focus away from the home village (and onto themselves) or disband because of an effective aging-out of their active memberships. Many of the migrants who established these organizations in the 1970s and 1980s are beginning to retire, and with a waning influence over the direction that migrant collectives take. As these migrants take a step back from 'active' service, it is unclear who will replace them. This question is most acute among organizations with small active memberships, few new arrivals, and where second-generation migrants may show little interest in the organization's activities – especially those that support a distant village few are ever likely to visit.

Migrant perspectives on traditional governance

> We left when we were young … but none of us imagined that we would stay away for so long and end up being responsible for supporting our village from afar.
>
> (Female migrant from Analco, living in Los Angeles)

Issues such as transparency and accountability, direct participation in decision-making, and power-sharing have been widely studied in the Oaxacan context (Carrasco 1961; Chance and Taylor 1985; Garibay 2007; Gijsbers 1996) but only in a limited way from the perspective of migration and changing community demographics (Curiel 2015; Worthen 2012). In the Sierra Norte and Mixteca, the practice of 'collective work' is engrained in community culture (Martínez Luna 2013; Robles and Cardoso Jiménez 2007), and based firmly upon the principles of reciprocity (Ahn and Ostrom 2008). However, such arrangements are hard to maintain, even rationalize, when so many members are not resident in the home village.

Through physical absence and time away from the home village, migrants enjoy a particular vantage point from which to consider traditional governance structures. In our interviews, we asked migrants in both Mexican and US destination centres for their views on such structures and the communalist ideology (Martínez Luna 2013; Mutersbaugh 2002; Robles and Cardoso Jiménez 2007) that underpins them. Frank exchanges among migrants in Los Angeles (Figure 11.3) and Las Vegas, for example, showed that the pressures of collective work and communal service was, for some, a reason for leaving their village or to remain absent. As one migrant from Analco explained, 'Why do you think we are here? [It is to avoid cargos] that many leave … of course it is a reason why people migrate'. Similarly, it encouraged some to avoid or shorten visits home, knowing that a series of cargos may await: 'I'm not going for long because I don't want [the authorities] to grab me to do cargos', limiting their stay to 'two or three weeks, maximum'. It is an attitude reported among migrants from other regions in Oaxaca, including the Mixteca (Castillo Balderas 2016; Velasco Ortiz 2004).

Some migrants were highly critical of such views, arguing that it was the work of 'an egotistical mentality … [because] to function as a community, to respect what *usos y costumbres* provides, at its core [is] the idea of contributing to the greater good'. And this meant, 'getting involved … [and] finding the best

Figure 11.3 Dissemination and discussion of research results with Analqueño migrants in Los Angeles, California, August 2016.

Source: photo credit: Jim Robson.

way to do that'. As a migrant from Analco living in Los Angeles explained, 'the objective of performing cargos is to bring people together and generate benefits for all'. He believed that it was a generational issue, noting how older migrants had 'a lot more solidarity (*sentido común*) ... [and] a respect for [community] rights and obligations'. As another noted, migrants were not forced to establish organizations in Mexican and US destination centres in the 1970s and 1980s. Rather, they came about because of a shared a sense of moral commitment and duty to those back in Oaxaca.

While migrants held differing opinions about the virtues of a governance system built upon institutions of collective work and communal service, discussions made clear how cargos and tequios are now viewed by most as a burden rather than an 'opportunity' to gain prestige by contributing to the common good. As an Analqueño living in Las Vegas explained, 'we no longer see it as a service to our community ... [in contrast] to the original idea behind *usos y costumbres*, it's no longer for *gusto* [pleasure or pride], it's for obligation'. It is this shift in perspective that feeds tensions between migrants and village residents, with the latter increasingly resentful of the former for not being around to help in the assembly or to cover cargo and tequio demands, while still expecting to retain usufruct rights to their family house and farm plots, and have access to the community territory when they return. It is a situation that lies at the heart of the current impasse between the two broad groups in Analco (see Chapter 8).

It is because village residents find it nigh on impossible to avoid compliance with communal service obligations, while migrants do not, that those living in

Analco and Yavesía, along with some active migrants, believe strongly that absentees have had it 'too easy for too long', and that it is 'right that [the authorities] become stricter ... [that they] create new rules for one simple reason, so that the pueblo can survive'. However, this view is not shared by most migrant Analqueños or Yavesians, who push-back against stricter legal obligations, arguing that it is unfair to 'change the rules' after migrants have been contributing (in other ways) for so long. Our work suggests that migrants are not averse to providing ongoing support but would like to see their contributions based on principles of solidarity – giving what they can, when they can, rather than being coerced into meeting (non-negotiable) collective work and communal service demands.

Proposals moving forward

Migrants in both Mexico and the US spoke of the need to streamline community governance, to get 'beyond tradition and allow for new ways [of doing things] to emerge'. This viewpoint resonated among some village residents who fear migrants will 'walk away' if the community fails to build flexibility into the way that its membership terms are structured. They worry that by forcing migrants to meet traditional governance obligations, many will be alienated and this will significantly reduce the level of support they already provide in other areas of village life. An idea floated by a migrant in Oaxaca City, and suggested by those in other places, was to '[jointly] develop an Agreement of Collaboration between those that live in the village and those living elsewhere', which would allow migrants to choose how best (based on their personal and family situations) to support their home village. This would essentially create a multi-tiered system of rights-holders, each with their own set of obligations to meet. The experience of Analco (see Chapter 8), however, highlights the difficulty in getting such a policy accepted.

A further proposal involves making changes to how the cargo system itself is structured. For some migrants, absence from the home village reinforces a belief that 'there are too many cargos, too many people in service ... [that] it doesn't make any sense what they [the community] are doing'. For migrants in Las Vegas, the coercive and onerous nature of *usos y costumbres* was a prime reason why 'youngsters [born in the village] no longer want to say they are from there ... they don't want a part of what that represents'. One idea, raised by Analqueños in both Los Angeles and Las Vegas was to evaluate and rank cargos as to their worth and remove any that presented redundancy:

> there are cargos that take up lots of time but don't produce anything ... but they are obligations that really affect the cargo-holder and his [or her] family ... one year serving as a community policeman is a real burden for those who live there, both physically and economically.

Again, while migrants may express such ideas, they can struggle to get their voices heard. This is partly due to a general resistance to change in their communities, 'it's really difficult that they [the community] will accept it because I know them, they are really stubborn ... one can't change the culture so easily!' But it also results from the short shrift generally given to migrant perspectives in the village assembly, where most migrants, especially long-term absentees, no longer hold '*voz y voto*' (voice and vote) and find themselves 'not listened to ... our opinions carry no weight'. Even those serving on a mesa directiva are not given the same right to speak as fully active citizens living in the village.

This acts as a powerful reminder that before migrants' ideas can be raised, debated, and potentially actioned, the nature of the relationship and channels of communication between migrant groups and village authorities (and the community assembly) require careful attention and nurturing. Migrant leaders in both Mexican and US destination centres felt that this was vital if village residents were to properly appreciate 'the moral support that people here [migrants] provide'. They advocated for municipal and communal representatives to travel on a regular basis to where migrants are, 'to speak with us ... [to understand the] reasons for any lack of commitment ... there are few of us and while we do what we can, they [the authorities] need to do their part'.[7] This was particularly important for US-based migrants, given that few can visit Oaxaca in person.

The problems that migrants experience in getting their voices heard also serves as a reminder that migrant organizations themselves could do a better job of pooling their resources and coordinating their actions. When Robson presented the results of his study to Los Angeles-based migrants from Yavesía and Analco, many were struck by the total number of 'active' migrants across Mexican and US destination centres, which was equal to or greater than the number of active citizens and comuneros living in the home village. To date, there has been little coordination between their respective mesas, and migrants clearly saw the potential to work together in order to streamline investments in the community, and create a more unified and powerful front when negotiating with village authorities.

Conclusions: the ephemerality of translocal community organization

In Indigenous Oaxaca, while migration weakens traditional arrangements by drawing labour away from civic and communal governance (Hernández-Diaz 2013; Mutersbaugh 2002; Robson and Berkes 2011), migrant organizing could help affected villages persist or flourish despite depopulation (Besserer 1999; Kearney and Besserer 2004; Klooster 2013). However, our work suggests that migrant organizing can be temporary and generational, framed by long-term absenteeism, an aging out of active members, strained relations between migrants and village authorities, and barriers to organizational renewal. For most migrants, a propensity to contribute is shaped by a sense of (moral) obligation, personal and family situations in places of residence, material ties to the home village, and the nature of migrants' (collective) relations with village authorities. Where the tie between migrant organization and village authorities is strained, migrants can be less willing to meet community requests for support. As border enforcement and family ties put an end to cyclical migration and frequent return visits, the limited time that migrants spend in the home village exacerbates this problem.

Such findings challenge the optimistic views that pervade the transnationalism literatures, which were summarized in Chapter 3. Rather, because migration not only expands but also de-territorializes the social field of Oaxacan communities (Stephen 2007), traditional governance among these Indigenous collectivities – based as it is on parity among members – becomes difficult to achieve, especially over time. We find that migrants often resist sharing collective work obligations with village residents. Tensions between residents, who disproportionately meet the burden of village governance, and migrants who want to limit the contributions they make, severely challenge governance regimes (Chapter 8, this book; Gutierrez Nájera 2009; Klooster 2013; Robson *et al.* 2018; Stephen 2007). Communities of origin may coerce migrants into meeting communal obligations, yet this runs the risk of alienating them and reducing the support they provide in other areas of village life. Because migrants perceive that they are often harshly treated by village authorities, and enjoy little to no influence in community-level decision-making, there is fertile ground for an 'us against them' attitude to take hold, and for continual conflicts to emerge (Waldinger, Popkin, and Magana 2008).

In this context, the traditions of migrant organizing may have reached a critical juncture; as translocal communities mature (after Smith 2006), changing migration and migrant dynamics limit the prospects for organizational renewal (Stephen 2007), and migrants question their role as agents of development 'back home' (after Glick Schiller and Faist 2010; Moctezuma 2000). For both internal and US-bound migration streams, long-term absenteeism has become the norm (see Jardón-Hernández 2016; Jones 2014) and this has recast the nature of migrant–village ties. It is a change that requires scholars to consider not only moments of intense connection across borders (Levitt and Lamba-Nieves 2011) but also to understand how translocal or trans-border communities recreate or repopulate over time. In the case of Indigenous Oaxaca, this may require communities to build greater flexibility into their terms of membership, improving the frequency and quality of communication between migrants and village authorities, while simultaneously streamlining their cargo and tequio systems.

Nevertheless, our observations lead us to expect that the links between migrants and their communities of origin will continue to decay over time, leaving residents to carry more and more of the burden of self-governance.

Notes

1 Some of the text in Chapter 11 is reproduced in an article by Robson, 'Indigenous communities, migrant organizations, and the ephemeral nature of translocality', forthcoming in the journal *Latin American Research Review*. As per the journal's open access

policy (https://larrlasa.org/about/), the 'authors of articles published remain the copyright holders and grant third parties the right to use, reproduce, and share the article according to the Creative Commons license agreement'. Robson grants Routledge the right to use material from his article in the current chapter.

2 Almost all interviews conducted in the US were with first-generation migrants – individuals born in the community of origin who left when they were children, adolescents or young adults to look for wage labour or pursue educational opportunities in Oaxaca City (and surrounds), Mexico City (and surrounds), and rural or urban areas in the United States.

3 Active Yavesians in Los Angeles jokingly called themselves *los mismos* (roughly 'the usual suspects'), referring to the fact that it is the same 15–20 individuals who do all the work.

4 In the two assemblies that followed this restructuring (July 2016 and August 2016), attendance was in the low 40s – suggestive that some among the 59 current members may struggle to maintain fully active status over time.

5 For migrants who have not been 'active' for an extended period of time, rights in the home village could be annulled, and/or their access to their homes and fields on communal lands denied by the assembly. For the small number of deported migrants that we have come across in our field work, these kinds of rules constitute a barrier for re-entry into village life. Some are able to comply and participate in the community. Those who don't must make their living in urban areas with limited participation in their communities.

6 These become key individuals engaged in efforts to span the 'here' and 'there' of translocal indigenous communities (see Waldinger 2008).

7 In the communities where we work, there have been very few in-person visits to the US by representatives of village authorities. Although 'virtual' (online) meetings could potentially be organized, none have taken place to date in any of our study communities.

References

Ahn, T.K. and E. Ostrom. 2008. Social capital and collective action. In: *The Handbook of Social Capital*, pp. 70–100. Oxford, UK. Oxford University Press.

Bada, X. and A. Feldmann. 2016. New challenges for migration studies in the western hemisphere. *Practicing Anthropology* 38(1): 33–34.

Besserer, F. 1999. Estudios transnacionales y ciudadanía transnacional. In: de Gail, M. (ed.), *En Fronteras fragmentadas*. Michoacán, México: El Colegio de Michoacán, Centro de Investigación y Desarrollo del Estado de Michoacán.

Binford, L. 2003. Migrant remittances and (under)development in Mexico. *Critique of Anthropology* 23(3): 305–336.

Burgess, K. 2016. Organized migrants and accountability from afar. *Latin American Research Review* 51(2): 150–173.

Carrasco, P. 1961. The civil–religious hierarchy in MesoAmerican communities: pre-Spanish background and colonial development. *American Anthropologist* 63: 486–497.

Castillo Balderas, E. 2016. *Vida comunitaria y conflictos políticos: Antagonismos y actores migrantes en San Miguel Tlacotepec, Oaxaca*. Unpublished Master's Thesis. Tijuana, Baja California: El Colegio de la Frontera Norte.

Chance, J.K. and W.B. Taylor. 1985. Cofradías and cargos: an historical perspective on the MesoAmerican civil–religious hierarchy. *American Ethnologist* 12(1): 1–26.

Cohen, J.H. 2016. Thinking, rethinking, and framing the discussion of migration. *Practicing Anthropology* 38(1): 40–41.

Cohen, J.H. and I. Sirkeci. 2011. *Cultures of Migration: The Global Nature of Contemporary Mobility*. Austin, TX: University of Texas Press.

Cohen, J.H., R. Jones, and D. Conway. 2005. Why remittances shouldn´t be blamed for rural under-development in Mexico: a collective response to Leigh Binford. *Critique of Anthropology* 25(1): 87–96.

Curiel, C., 2015. La amenaza de 'terminar con la costumbre': Migración y recreación de los sistemas normativos internos en la Mixteca. In: Curiel, C., J. Hernandez-Diaz, and H. Worthen (eds), *Los Dilemas de la Política del Reconocimiento en México*. Oaxaca, México: UABJO, Juan Pablos Editor.

De Hass, H. 2010. Migration and development: a theoretical perspective. *International Migration Review* 44(1): 227–264.

Delgado Wise, R., H. Márquez Covarrubias, and H. Rodríguez Ramírez. 2014. Organizaciones transnacionales de migrantes y desarrollo regional en Zacatecas. *Migraciones Internacionales* 2(4): 159–181.

Duquette-Rury, L. 2016. Migration transnational participation: how citizen inclusion and government engagement matter for local democratic development in Mexico. *American Sociological Review* 81(4): 771–799

Escala-Rabadán, L. 2014. Asociaciones de inmigrantes mexicanos en Estados Unidos: logros y desafíos en tiempos recientes. *Desacatos* 46 (Mayo 2014): 52–69.

Fox, J. and X. Bada. 2008. Migrant organization and hometown impacts in rural Mexico. *Journal of Agrarian Change* 3(2): 435–461.

Fox, J. and G. Rivera-Salgado. 2004. Building civil society among Indigenous migrants. In: Fox, J. and G. Rivera-Salgado (eds), *Indigenous Mexican Migrants in the United States*, pp. 1–65. La Jolla, California: Center for US–Mexican Studies.

García Zamora, R. 2005. *Migraciòn, remesas y desarrollo: los retos de las organizaciones migrantes mexicanas en Estados Unidos*. Unpublished doctoral thesis. Zacatecas, México: Universidad Autónoma de Zacatecas.

Garibay, C. 2007. *El dilema corporativo del comunalismo forestal*. CIESAS No. 23.

Glick Schiller, N. and T. Faist. 2010. *Migration, Development, and Transnationalization: A Critical Stance*. New York: Berghahn Books.

Greiner, C. and P. Sakdapolrak. 2013. Translocality: concepts, applications and emerging research perspectives. *Geography Compass* 7: 373–384.

Grieshop, J.I. 2006. The *envios* of San Pablo Huixtepec, Oaxaca: food, home, and transnationalism. *Human Organization* 65(4): 400–406.

Gutiérrez Nájera, L. 2009. Transnational migration, conflict and divergent ideologies of progress. *Urban Anthropology and Studies of Cultural Systems and World Economic Development* 38(2–4): 269–302.

Hernández-Diaz, J. 2013. Comunidad, migración y ciudadanía: Avatares de la organización indígena comunitaria. Mexico, Mexico City: Miguel Ángel Porrúa.

Hernández-Díaz, J. and H. Worthen. 2018. *Historia y relaciones de la vida transnacional: Migración de la Sierra Norte de Oaxaca*, Juan Pablos Editor. Mexico City, Mexico: Universidad Autónoma Benito Juárez de Oaxaca.

Hirabayashi, L.R. 1993. *Cultural Capital: Mountain Zapotec Migrant Associations in Mexico City*. Tucson, AZ: The University of Arizona Press.

INEGI 2017. *Catálogo único de claves de áreas geoestadísticas estatales, municipales y localidades*. Accessed May 13, 2017 at: www.inegi.org.mx/geo/contenidos/geoestadistica/CatalogoClaves.aspx.

Jardón-Hernández, A.E. 2016. *International Migration and Crisis: Transition toward a New Migratory Phase*. New York: Springer Books.

Jones, R.C. 2009. Migration permanence and village decline in Zacatecas: when you can't go home again. *The Professional Geographer* 61(3): 382–399.

Jones, R.C. 2014. The decline of international migration as an economic force in rural areas: a Mexican case study. *International Migration Review* 48(3): 728–761.

Kearney, M. and F. Besserer. 2004. Oaxacan municipal governance in transnational context. In: Fox, J. and G. Rivera-Salgado (eds), *Indigenous Mexican Migrants in the United States*, pp. 483–501. La Jolla, California: Center for US–Mexican Studies.

Klooster, D. 2013. The impact of transnational migration on commons management among Mexican Indigenous communities. *Journal of Latin American Geography* 12(1): 57–86.

Lanly, G. and B.M. Valenzuela. 2004. Introducción. In: Lanly, G. and B.M. Valenzuela (eds), *Clubes de migrantes oriundos mexicanos en Estados Unidos: La política transnacional de la nueva sociedad migrante*, pp. 11–37. Guanajuato, Mexico: Universidad de Guadalajara.

Levitt, P. and D. Lamba-Nieves. 2011. Social remittances revisited. *Journal of Ethnic and Migration Studies* 37(1): 1–22.

Martínez Luna, J. 2013. *Textos sobre el camino andando*. Coalición de Maestros y Promotores Indígenas de Oaxaca, AC (CMPIO)/Centro de Apoyo al Movimiento Popular Oaxaqueño, AC (CAMPO)/Coordinación Estatal de Escuelas de Educación Secundaria Comunitaria Indígena (CEEESCI)/Colegio Superior para la Educación).

McKenzie, D. and H. Rapoport. 2007. Network effects and the dynamics of migration and inequality: theory and evidence from Mexico. *Journal of Development Economics* 84(1): 1–24.

Mines, R., S. Nichols, and D. Runsten, D. 2010. *California's Indigenous Farmworkers*. Final Report of the Indigenous Farmworker Study (IFS) to the California Endowment.

Moctezuma, M. 2000. La organización de migrantes Zacatecanos en Estados Unidos. *Cuadernos Agrarios* 19–20, Mexico.

Mutersbaugh, T. 2002. Migration, common property, and communal labour: cultural politics and agency in a Mexican Village. *Political Geography* 21(4): 473–494.

Orozco, M. and R. Rouse. 2007. *Migrant Hometown Associations and Opportunities for Development: A Global Perspective*. Washington, DC: Migration Information Source.

Passel, J., D.V. Cohn, and A. Gonzalez-Barrera. 2012. *Net Migration from Mexico Falls to Zero – and Perhaps Less*. Washington, DC: Pew Hispanic Center, April.

Perry, E., N. Doshi, J. Hicken, and J. Ricardo Méndez García. 2009. Between here and there: ethnicity, civic participation and migration in San Miguel Tlacotepec. In: Cornelius, W.A., D. Fitzgerald, J. Hernández-Diaz, and S. Borger (eds), *Migration from the Mixteca: A Transnational Community in Oaxaca and California*. San Diego, CA: Center for Comparative Immigration Studies, University of California-San Diego.

Robles Hernández, S. and R. Cardoso Jiménez. 2007. *Floriberto Díaz escrito: Comunalidad, energía viva del pensamiento mixe Ayuujktsënää´yen-ayuujkwënmää´ny-ayuujk mëk´äjt*. Mexico City, Mexico: Universidad Nacional Autónoma de México.

Robson, J.P. 2010. *The Impact of Rural–Urban Migration on Forest Commons in Oaxaca, Mexico*. Unpublished PhD Thesis. University of Manitoba, Winnipeg, Canada.

Robson, J.P. In press. Indigenous communities, migrant organizations, and the ephemeral nature of translocality. *Latin American Research Review*.

Robson, J.P. and F. Berkes. 2011. How does out-migration affect community institutions? A study of two Indigenous municipalities in Oaxaca, Mexico. *Human Ecology* 39(2): 179–190.

Robson, J.P. and R. Wiest. 2014. Transnational migration, customary governance, and the future of community: a case study from Oaxaca, Mexico. *Latin American Perspectives* 41(3): 102–116.

Robson, J.P., D. Klooster, H. Worthen, and J. Hernandez-Diaz. 2018. Migration and agrarian transformation in Indigenous Mexico. *Journal of Agrarian Change* 18(2): 299–323.

Rubenstein, H. 1992. Migration, development, and remittances in rural Mexico. *International Migration* 30(2): 127–153.

Smith, R.C. 2006. *Mexican New York: Transnational Lives of New Immigrants*. Berkeley, CA: University of California Press.

Stephen, L. 2007. *Transborder Lives: Indigenous Oaxacans in Mexico, California, and Oregon*. Durham, NC: Duke University Press.

Stiffler, S. 2007. Neither here nor there: Mexican immigrant workers and the search for home. *American Ethnologist* 34(4): 674–688.

Taylor, E.J. 1999. The new economics of labour migration and the role of remittances in the migration process. *International Migration* 37(1): 63–88.

VanWey, L.K., C.M. Tucker, and E. Diaz-McConnell. 2005. Community organization, migration, and remittances in Oaxaca. *Latin American Research Review* 40(1): 83–107.

Velasco Ortiz, L.M. 1998. Identidad cultural y territorio: Una reflexión en torno a las comunidades transnacionales entre México y Estados Unidos. *Región y sociedad* (El Colegio de Sonora) 9(15): 105–130.

Velasco Ortiz, L.M. 2004. La costumbre de participar: Politización de las redes de migrantes y organizaciones de oaxaqueños en las Californias. In: de Lanly, G. and M. Valenzuela Basilica (eds), *Clubes de migrantes oriundos mexicanos en los Estados Unidos*, pp. 253–284. Zapopan, Jalisco: Universidad de Guadalajara, Centro Universitario de Ciencias Económico Administrativas.

Waldinger, R. 2013. Más allá del transnacionalismo: una perspectiva alternativa de la conexión de los inmigrantes con su país de origen. *Migraciones internacionales* 7(1): 189–220.

Waldinger, R., E. Popkin, and H.A. Magana. 2008. Conflict and contestation in the cross-border community: hometown associations reassessed. *Ethnic and Racial Studies* 31(5): 843–870.

Worthen, H. 2012. *The Presence of Absence: Indigenous Migration, a Ghost Town, and the Remaking of Gendered Communal Systems in Oaxaca, Mexico*. Unpublished PhD Thesis. Chapel Hill, NC: University of North Carolina.

12 Communities *shaping* migration

The migration–*community*–environment nexus

*Dan Klooster, James P. Robson, and
Jorge Hernández-Díaz*

Introduction

Out-migration might decrease the pressure of population on the environment, but what happens to the communities that manage the local environment when they are weakened by the absence of their members? In response to this crucial question, the goal of this book was to present and make sense of findings from over a decade of empirical research in Oaxaca – an Indigenous stronghold in southern Mexico and one of many rural regions in the world where biodiversity and culture are intimately connected (Gavin *et al.* 2015; Gorenflo *et al.* 2012).

This, the book's concluding chapter, summarizes the key lessons that this work generated. It is split into two main sections. In the first, we summarize the main observations derived from our ethnographic work in Oaxaca, which we group into the three themes of Community, Environment, and Migration. We look at each of these in turn – showing how communities, more than simply survive migration, can actively shape its impacts through their adaptations and cultural resilience. In the second section, we consider the relevance of these observations for migration–community–environment dynamics beyond Oaxaca's borders. We return to the question of demographic transitions (smaller families, better educational opportunities, etc.), and (associated) changes in the values of rural areas (declines in agriculture) to argue for their broader relevance given the transformative changes affecting such areas across Mexico, Latin America, and other global regions. We reflect upon the implications of aging rural populations, and the challenges that communities face to keep enough of their youth interested and invested in rural life.

Communities surviving migration

Our work has shown how 'community' is central to understanding migration-environment linkages in sending areas. In Chapter 1, we made the case that Indigenous communities globally are crucial actors for conservation and sustainable development (Boege 2008; Boillat *et al.* 2017; RRI 2017; Stevens *et al.* 2014), but that out-migration and associated changes are affecting the roles they can play as environmental managers and stewards. Our empirical research in

Oaxaca has provided us with insights to better understand the nature of such changes and their impact on community environmental governance, contributing important knowledge about migration–environment linkages in migrant-sending regions, an underreported field of study (Hecht *et al.* 2015; Hunter, Luna, and Norton 2015), and to show that such linkages can only be properly understood if the mediating roles of community and culture are considered.

Multiple case studies (Chapter 4–9) and a synthesis paper (Chapter 10) showed that migration, accompanied by the declining importance of agriculture in community livelihood, has driven deep-seated change among rural communities in the region, partially depopulating them, modifying and transforming resource practices, and eroding the ecological knowledge associated with traditional practices. Migration has physically separated those who migrate from the land upon which processes of labour and ritual practice are customarily based, thus challenging community capacities to self-govern forest and other territorial resources. In Oaxaca, most municipalities and communities govern themselves under a system of semi-autonomous social and political organization where the rules by which community membership is structured, and access to political power is secured, are distinct to those of Western liberal democracies. It is a system that encompasses a complex mix of institutional and moral relationships that help define the obligations, rights, identity, and sense of belonging of its subjects. It is only recently that research has begun to shed light on how these structures, institutions, and cultural norms are reorganizing in the context of a partially depopulated countryside (Robson 2010; Robson *et al.* 2018).

Migration weakens Indigenous land-managing communities in two ways. As individuals, families, and communities engage with national and international markets and geographies through migration, their relationships with customary practices and institutions can alter. Not only does migration affect the congruence between individual and collective rationality as migrants and would-be migrants make the choice to maintain or relinquish their community membership, it also depletes the pool of residents available for collective labour and participation in community governance. Our work, in this book and elsewhere, shows how the number of resident villagers for each unpaid governance position is decreasing over time, creating a growing burden on a shrinking, and aging, population of villagers (Robson *et al.* 2018). This can have serious implications for communities over time, especially those with small populations.

When one considers Indigenous governance systems in Oaxaca, predicated as they are on collective action and individual responsibilities to the collective, recent migration histories should place them in absolute crisis. Partial depopulation burdens the resident members of communities with excess governance responsibilities. Yet, despite the physical absence of so many of their members, communities endure. How is this possible?

It is possible because of the way that communities can and do adapt to these changes. Using the analytic categories of comunalidad, the concept by which life in rural Oaxaca is understood and operationalized (Maldonado 2011, 2013; see Chapter 2), our empirical work has shown that rather than driving an inevitable 'death of communalism' (after Otero 1999), change following migration prompts communities to find new ways to express themselves and to endure. Our work in Santa Cruz Tepetotutla, San Juan Evangelista Analco, and Santiago Comaltepec (see Chapters 7, 8, and 9) shows how the relationships that community members hold with territory and land continue but look different from the relationships that characterized how they 'knew the land' before migration took hold – when 'community' was partly defined by a territory that was used, understood, and related to by all (Martínez Luna 2010a, 2010b, 2013). Likewise, communities that are struggling to cope with the burden of village governance in a depopulated countryside are experimenting with adaptations that may break with customary principles of collective work and communal service (see Chapters 5, 8, and 9) but enable continued autonomy in the management of village affairs.

Oaxacan communities have long held a pervasive sense of what it means and what is required for an individual to be part of a territorial community. But long-standing norms, designed at a time when nearly all members lived and worked the land in the same 'home village', function less well when members are stretched across an expanded social field (after Stephen 2007), often living very different lives from one another. The reconfiguration of Indigenous governance following periods of intense migration is a complicated and potentially painful process, as community memberships grapple with such fundamental issues as cultural identity, understandings of individual responsibilities and rights, and change in the livelihood implications of territory. Tussles over migrant rights and obligations (Chapter 8) are evidence of a dialectic that can emerge between village residents and non-residents, with power struggles playing out across a re-spatialized geography of communal governance. In creating policies to better manage the debilitating impacts of migration, communities find themselves in a process of internal negotiation, in which they attempt to create forms of 'service' in which members can participate, and exercise citizenship, regardless of where they live (Aquino Moreschi 2012). As Froylán Martínez Rojas,[1] a Mixe who works for Mexico's National Protected Area Commission (CONANP) in the Sierra Norte and Mixteca regions of Oaxaca, explains, 'traditionally a community actor has been someone who lives in the village and participates in a complete way, meeting their obligations to the community ... but that isn't the reality today'. Consequently, communities are having to imagine internal normative structures that can provide meaning across member profiles – not just village residents versus non-residents but also returnees/deportees and youngsters, who may slip away if communities simply continue with traditional expectations of community membership rights and obligations instead of being open to 'other kinds of being' (Dietz 2010).

Despite these differences and distances, communities call on migrants to fulfil their duties to the community, and our work highlights the different strategies that communities adopt. A core strategy is a kind of coercive appeal to a community moral economy, in which communities develop formal rules to deny migrants access to communal resources if they do not comply with communal obligations. This is most clearly and draconically illustrated in Santa Cruz Tepetotutla, where migrants are expected to return after a set period of time and meet community obligations in person (Chapter 7). Strategies designed to 'keep migrants in line' and maintain traditional structures appear most successful in communities that instituted strict rules around village absence when migration first took hold (such as Tepetotutla), or that remain particularly attractive places to live (San Juan Tabaá or San Andrés Solaga in the Sector Zoogocho, Chapter 4) – such that fewer migrants risk non-compliance and a 'closed' door to a possible future return. For the residents and migrants forming the translocal community of Santa María Tindú (Chapter 5), participation in US-based migrant associations fulfils community obligations. This contrasts with communities such as Analco (Chapter 8) and Santa María Yavesía (Chapter 6), which also have strong migrant associations, but where the decision to recognize service in the US or Mexico City to migrant organizations is still under debate. These communities were late to institute rules governing migration and are less willing to enforce punishment for non-compliance. Yavesía has so far chosen a freedom of choice approach, in the hope that its members, both present and future, will make decisions that lead to continued participation and the enrichment of community life.

The monetization of community governance poses particular challenges. Softer versions of the coercive approach permit migrants to fulfil obligations to cargos and tequios through payments to substitute cargo holders. A more drastic form of monetizing community is evolving in Santiago Comaltepec (Chapter 9), where municipal funds are used to compensate office holders for cargos that were formerly unpaid, converting a kind of noble civic duty to something more like a job. This is contentious. For some community members, it fundamentally alters the social contract between members and their community. It used to be the case that participation in such institutions without remuneration was a way to demonstrate one's value and prestige as a community member. Doing unpaid tequios, serving cargos, and attending asambleas have long been considered non-negotiable in order for people to receive the rights and benefits of community membership. Comaltepec's strategy raises the central question: can one truly 'serve' one's community if one is paid a salary? Some community members think not, adamant that the introduction of paid cargos and the removal of tequio constitutes an irreversible deviation from traditional, communalist ideologies. Others are less beholden to past traditions, saying that such change is inevitable and necessary if collectives are to maintain control over civic and communal governance. It is this sense of pragmatism that is driving Analco (Chapter 8), and other communities and municipalities with small resident populations, to view fewer cargos and more paid cargos as the only way to continue under *usos y costumbres*.

Difficult as the challenge may be, communities have had little option but to re-evaluate how they do things, and to question whether a system that demands all right-holders to serve their community equally still holds in a contemporary context. Our work points to how village governance in Indigenous Oaxaca is undergoing significant change as communities strategize to protect what is important to them in a new rural context. The divergence of strategies makes it less clear whether such change constitutes a form of adaptive governance (after Folke *et al.* 2005) that opens the door for an alternate state or regime to emerge, and an indication that cultural transformation is unfolding (Tacoli 1998; Woods 2007). Only time will tell whether this is so. In all of our case studies, however, changes following migration have chipped away at long-standing norms and customs, and particularly the principles of reciprocity upon which collective work and community membership are based. Reciprocal ties are hard to maintain in the context of de-territorialized livelihoods and a geographically dispersed membership. Most migrants ask for a more balanced reciprocity that demands support from all but allows members to contribute in different ways based on their specific situations and capacities. If migrants continue to push this agenda, it can be expected that some communities will yield, and the emergence of a multi-tiered, multi-rights membership system would constitute a new social order in these places.

Regardless of future outcomes, migrants can and do play significant roles in these new phases of community-making. They frequently answer their communities' calls to contribute labour and money to community governance and development. In migrant communities in the US and Mexico, they also reconstruct, as best they can, what they have left behind. Their organizations – established to provide support to migrants in new places of residence as well as create formal political, economic, and social ties with hometowns (Hirabayashi 1993) – remain key components of translocal or transborder village life (Fox and Bada 2008; Fox and Rivera-Salgado 2004; Robson *et al.* 2018). The communities of the Sector Zoogocho (Chapter 4), the community of Santa María Tindú (Chapter 5), and the community of Santa María Yavesía (Chapter 6), illustrate how important these organizations can be for village development and cohesion.

However, while our work affirms the existence of strong bonds between migrants and their communities of origin – whether through hometown associations, community bands, dance organizations and the re-creation of ritual celebrations in migrant communities in Mexico and the US – we also find reason to doubt the permanence of these bonds (Chapter 11). Migrants point to communication challenges that reduce their ability to participate in the governance of a community far away. They are torn between solidarity with community members living in the village of origin, and the feeling that those community members don't understand the struggles of migrants, especially undocumented migrants in the US, arguing that they over-estimate the money that they earn, and simply expect too much. Meanwhile, perspectives diverge more and more over time as migrants become long-term absentees, establish families in the diaspora, and a younger generation expresses a reduced commitment to communitarian values. In other words, migrants support their communities of origin, but linkages are weakening.

We see migrant organizations in both Mexican and US destination centres experience changing attitudes and declining memberships (see Chapters 8 and

11), and a re-direction of resources away from collective remittances to the village of origin and towards the needs of the migrant community (Chapters 5 and 11). Over time, migrants can be less inclined to meet the customary labour obligations that underpin village life and identity, and even contributions to the cultural expression of '*la fiesta*' are now often questioned (Chapters 5 and 11). This is an important reminder that migrants can make choices that further extricate them from their communities, with the decision to meet community requests for support influenced by evolving migration dynamics (Jones 2009; Durand 2013) and the consequences of long-term absenteeism (Jones 2014; Robson and Wiest 2014). As such, while our work supports the contention that migration does not cut migrants off from their communities of origin, it also suggests the tenuous and ephemeral nature of these links as translocal communities mature (Levitt and Lamba-Nieves 2013; Robson, in press; Waldinger *et al.* 2008).

Migration-environment linkages

In rural Mexico, like many places in the world, the extent of communal land ownership provides communities with the ability to direct collective decision-making and members' resource use to dictate how fields and forests are used, by whom, and how benefits are to be distributed. Yet these commons-management functions occur within a context of environmental, demographic, and cultural change (Robson 2010; Klooster 2013). Our work shows how evolving community dynamics affect migration–environment linkages.

In migrant-sending regions including Oaxaca, out-migration reduces areas under cultivation, opening up spaces for forest recovery, and creating opportunities for new or expanded resource uses. Rural communities are seeing new land use opportunities emerge from this changing forest landscape, and some of these opportunities can be harnessed to enable more villagers to make a living from their territorial resources.

Forest resurgence following out-migration and agricultural decline fits the general theory of 'forest transition' reported for Mexico (Klooster 2003; Robson and Berkes 2011) and Latin America more generally (Aide *et al.* 2013; Rudel *et al.*, 2005). However, there is uncertainty about the type and particular characteristics of the transitions that will occur under differing socio-economic and environmental conditions (see Klooster 2003, 2005).

Land use changes might provide communities with an opportunity to benefit from payment for environmental services schemes, community conservation, ecotourism, and perhaps eventually REDD+ projects. But such possibilities will depend in part on the survival of commons-managing institutions and the communities in which they are embedded. The environmental implications of fewer people and less extensive land use, therefore, are mediated by the community institutions that survive – or not; the commons can survive migration only if the communities which manage them can survive migration.

The community experiences that we analysed highlight the possibilities and strategies open to commons managers impacted by migration. Spaces can emerge where institutional and organizational arrangements are challenged and reimagined (after Cleaver 2017; De Koning and Cleaver 2012). In the case of Oaxaca, we see long-standing commons regimes with the institutional flexibility (Daniels 2007), legitimacy across memberships (Armitage *et al.* 2012), and capacity to learn (Berkes 2017; Gavin *et al.* 2015) to remain viable within a context of migration and globalized change (Davidson-Hunt *et al.* 2016). Faced with changing demographic realities and new sets of livelihood options, many have found ways to adapt, rather than dismantle, existing commons governance structures, and maintain economies based on territorial use, rather than simply abandon land-based activities in favour of other livelihood options gained through migration.

With these changes, the uses of Indigenous rural territories are shifting, and territorial governance is reconfiguring around discussions of what rights are held by whom, and how landscapes are zoned and for what purposes they are administered. Our research reveals multiple cases where communities are trying to capture these new opportunities through community land zoning processes and plans (see Chapters 7 and 8, see also Pazos-Almada and Bray 2018), further evidence of the emergence of a new landscape of territorial use and conservation (Robson and Klooster in press). These conservation projects sometimes have productive, population-maintaining values through conservation work, forestry, ecotourism, and payment for environmental services.

Changing migration dynamics

The relationships between migration and environment that we observed in rural Oaxaca were not simple or direct. They highlighted how a better understanding of migration–environment linkages will require a better understanding of the dynamics inherent in the process of migration. From our work, a few things stand out. Environmental change was not the main driver of migration. Our informants explained migration as a search for better work and educational opportunities, or a response to a health crisis or the need for capital to build a house. On the other hand, crop failures were only rarely invoked as part of complex individual, family, and community decision-making processes. Demographic change, however, strongly affects migration. Smaller families mean fewer migrants. Border and migration policies also play important roles in shaping migration. Following increased border enforcement in the 2000s, the rising cost for smugglers and the increased danger have discouraged new migrants from leaving.

The latest government census data (for 2015) confirm what we have suspected – village populations are now entering a period of stability as low fertility rates combine with declining migration rates. Migration since 2010 seems to have entered a qualitatively different phase. Mexico is now in a kind of 'post-migration' era – 'post' in the sense that wage labour migration from Mexico to the US has fallen sharply since the mid-2000s, and such migration is no longer an expected rite-of-passage for Indigenous youth. A commonly-adopted strategy for meeting expenses related to building houses, providing family members with education, and meeting emergency health care costs is no longer open. Communities will face continued challenges as their populations age, youth leave for schooling elsewhere, and connections to migrant communities continue to decline.

Nevertheless, there is a possibility of large-scale deportations of undocumented immigrants with many years of experience living and working in the US. Most would probably be forced to make a go of it in Mexican cities, but some might find their best options in the rural areas of their sending communities, where community structures would again be forced to adapt.

Lessons learned for Mexico and beyond

Our work shows that, in areas of out-migration, environmental change is not necessarily the main driver of migration, nor does migration lead to environmental change in a straightforward, easily-traced way. Instead, we find that the migration–environment relationship is complicated by the broader context in which migration occurs, how migration *inter alia* affects community dynamics, and how community dynamics affect the environmental implications of migration, *inter alia*. Some of the environmental outcomes are quite hopeful, and have implications for sustainable rural development strategies.

Migration is part of broader rural transformations

Migration, of course, is both a driver and symptom of other processes unfolding across rural areas of the world. On the one hand, the world is less rural[2] today than it was in the past, and rural areas, while still significant, are declining in relative importance over time. For example, the three large developing regions, Africa, Asia, and Latin America, are experiencing a decline in what member countries officially define as the rural proportion of their national populations, at a rate of between 1–2 per cent per year for the period 1985–2015 (Currie-Alder *et al.* 2014). On the other hand, many countries maintain high numbers of rural localities and, despite increasing urbanization, 3.3 billion people on the planet still live in what are considered rural areas (UN 2017).

While their relative importance may be in flux, rural areas are transforming as people and places adjust to several processes impacting the global countryside at the same time: a rural demographic transition driven by declines in fertility rates and family size; the diversification of rural economies with reduced reliance on agriculture; greater dependence on distant places for trade and to acquire goods, services, finances, and ideas; the movement of people to large cities (often far away) or to towns and small cities within immediate regions; and, a cultural shift among local populations that exhibit increasing affinity with urban agglomerations (Bebbingon 2004; Berdegué, Rosada, and Bebbington 2014; Haggblade *et al.* 2007; Kay 2008, 2015). A *World Development Report* released by the World Bank in 2008 estimated that 77 per cent of the global rural population was living through such transformations.

Oaxaca is one such place where rural people no longer live in relative isola-tion but have broadened their access to public services and markets, to be con-stantly in touch with new ideas, and new social actors. Roads and telecommunication services in rural areas serve to further encourage economic and cultural diversification – enabling people to move around with relative ease and safety, and for goods and services to be traded beyond rural communities and their regions (Berdegué, Rosada, and Bebbington 2014).

What we see in Oaxaca, as people transition from on-farm to off-farm liveli-hoods, is indicative of how remote and rural communities around the world are becoming rural–urban territories, where once sharp distinctions between urban places, people, and societies, and rural ones, become more and more diffused (Tacoli 2006; Woods 2007). Global trends suggest that in places currently char-acterized by low but stable village populations, rural areas will not die or empty out. But people will change how they live, how they interact with their local environments, and may become more interconnected with not only the large cities where family members have migrated to, but also the large towns and small cities in their own regions and state. It is becoming more common, for example, for people to live in rural areas and commute to work or study in a nearby urban centre, or for urban men and women to work in the fields during peak agricultural seasons (Berdegué, Rosada, and Bebbington 2014; Kay 2008; Tacoli 2006). Rural dwellers in places such as Oaxaca shop in nearby towns, and urban merchants rely on those consumers to keep their businesses alive (Tacoli 1998, 2006). In our case study communities, we have seen how edu-cated migrants have returned to the region, often basing themselves in Oaxaca City but becoming regular and active participants and contributors to the village life of their home communities.

Thus, as border enforcement makes it hard for rural people to migrate to the global North, they may turn their attention to urban centres closer to home. The emergence of provincial towns and cities, and their linkages with deep rural areas, is now seen as a critical feature of both rural transformations and of con-temporary rural societies in the global South (Tacoli 2006). These urban places and their rural hinterlands become functionally intertwined as rural–urban ter-ritories. As countries develop, more and more of the rural population lives in these territories (Currie-Alder *et al.* 2014). In Mexico, for example, only 7 per cent of the population live in 554 'deep rural' territories that lack even a small town, but 43 per cent live in 399 rural–urban territories with a small to medium-sized provincial city, which has created functional linkages between urban centres and their rural hinterlands grounded in labour, product, and services markets; public service provision; social networks; and environmental services (Berdegué, Rosada, and Bebbington 2014).

Communities can mitigate those changes

Although important global forces may underpin or drive rural transformations, the way that change unfolds in specific localities is necessarily mediated by localized social structures and institutional frameworks. Human agency provides rural people with an opportunity to influence the nature of the transformation they experience or undergo (Mahoney and Thelen 2011), and shape whether such change is 'brutal' or 'benign' (Wiggins *et al.* 2013). Therefore, to understand the transformations driven by global forces, we must understand community responses to change. We are not seeing rural spaces becoming empty of society, but rather society reorganizing in rural spaces (Berdegué, Rosada, and Bebbington 2014; Timmer and Akkus 2008).

Transformative change in rural areas may pose great challenges to those affected, but change is also associated with opportunity and renewal, and transformation can be expected to open up new development pathways for rural people and communities to explore (IFAD 2016). Indigenous Oaxacans are re-evaluating their lives and structures post-migration, looking to create positive futures for themselves and their communities. This is akin to 'inclusive rural transformation' that IFAD (2016) is promoting for areas undergoing transformative change. What is interesting in the Oaxaca case is that communities are necessarily deviating from IFAD's (2016) preferred path, where agriculture retains 'central importance as transition unfolds'. Small-scale agriculture in rural Mexico has been in decline since the 1980s, with limited, some would say non-existent, government support for farmers (Klooster 2005; Mann 2004). It's a pattern repeated across much of Central America (David Kaimowitz,[3] Director of Natural Resources and Climate Change, Ford Foundation, personal communication). In such cases, communities must find ways to reterritorialize, such as in Oaxaca's Sierra Norte, where communities have responded to a depopulated countryside by diversifying how they use and perceive of their territorial resources (Pazos-Almada and Bray 2018), promoting forestry, ecotourism and land-based activities other than agriculture as members transition into off-farm livelihoods.

It is not an easy shift. Locally, there are concerns as to whether the 'new' activities of ecotourism or conservation can ever replace the foundational contribution of farming to rural livelihoods. Despite migration and engagement with regional, national, and global markets, these communities still self-identify as campesino communities, founded squarely upon ideals of 'working and knowing the land' (Martínez Luna 2013). Nevertheless, the deterritorialization (and, in some cases, reterritorialization) of rural livelihood evident in Oaxaca is strongly suggestive that rural landscapes can persist but will no longer be purely agrarian (Robson *et al.* 2018). This is seen elsewhere, with the changing composition of rural household income demonstrating the shifting importance of farm- and non-farm activities in local economies. For example, rural China went from 17 per cent non-farm income in the early 1980s to 40 per cent in the late 1990s; rural Tanzania, from 11 per cent in 1991 to 46 per cent in 2000; and rural Mexico, from 43 per cent in 1997 to 67 per cent in 2003 (Barrett, Reardon, and Webb 2001; Berdegué, Rosada, and Bebbington 2014; Han 2010). It has been estimated that the shares of non-farm income in total rural household income in the late 1990s was as high as 47 per cent in Latin America, 51 per cent in Asia, and as much as 40 to 45 per cent in Africa (Barrett, Reardon, and Webb 2001).

Such trends point to capitalist development and global change combining to elicit a hybridization in agrarian/rural livelihoods (see Hecht 2014; Woods 2007), and the catalyst for rural economies to be reimagined (Barkin 2013; Davidson-Hunt *et al.* 2016).

Environmental outcomes

The loss of biological diversity in crops is of increasing concern in this context (Boege 2008; Eyzaguirre and Linares 2004; Scherr and McNeely 2008), while the gains associated with forest recovery are an often-mentioned cause of hope for conservationists (Melo *et al.* 2013; Meyfroidt and Lambin 2011; Robson and Berkes 2011). Our findings destabilize that dichotomy. Given the contextual complexity of the role of migration in rural transformation, and considering variations in community responses amid a growing range of non-farm livelihood opportunities, it is not surprising that the environmental outcomes of out-migration in rural areas also vary. What we have seen is that, in many cases, the survival of community means the continuation of farming, although at a reduced scale and extent, and the recovery of forests – which are often managed by the surviving communities for conservation, commercial forestry, ecotourism, and Payment for Environmental Services.

The implications for rural development

Such findings hold important policy implications for the agencies and donors that support local communities in creating sustainable landscapes, maintaining carbon-rich forests, and contributing to biodiversity conservation. The challenge is to help rural communities shape their transformations to remain attractive places to live. According to The Ford Foundation's David Kaimowitz, there have been no clear policy prescriptions, in Mexico or across Central America, to help communities debilitated by migration. He also doubts whether technical or financial support for productive activities and rural sustainable development is the answer – rather, he emphasizes the need to promote the cultural component of Indigenous communities in migrant-sending regions, arguing for policies and programmes directed at multiple aspects of Indigenous identity, from language retention to music, through to village fiestas and other customs. As he notes, 'it is these aspects of community life and identity that feed the process of strong local governance'.

Such development strategies should also promote the feminization of rural livelihood and life. Migration is expected to open up opportunities for women in village governance. This is significant from a scholarly perspective, since we know from international experience that women typically experience fewer territorial governance opportunities than men (e.g. Arora-Jonsson 2013; Colfer *et al.* 2017; Elias *et al.* 2017; Reed 2010). Our Oaxaca work shows some movement

on this front post-migration, but not the level of female integration into municipal and communal decision-making that one might expect following
such extended periods of intense out-migration. A number of our case studies
(Chapters 4 and 6) point to a level of resistance to change, even when the feminization of village governance has been placed on the national agenda. Men
resist women in governance as an insult to tradition, but many women resist
too, because they see it as an unwelcome addition to a workload that is already
excessive and undervalued (Worthen 2015). The need is for inclusion that is
meaningful and provides clear benefits.

Similarly, our work affirms the need for rural development that meets youth
aspirations. Rural communities are challenged to shape their transformations in
such ways that they remain attractive places to live. In many countries, economic growth and development has not reached the most vulnerable or marginalized in rural areas, but remains concentrated in urban areas (United Nations
2017). In cities, for example, access to basic services, to education, to income
opportunities is better and more diversified, or at least that is the perception
held by many eking out a living in rural areas. Despite the problems associated
with cities, urban living constitutes a strong pull-factor on rural populations,
especially youth. This challenge, post-migration and post-transformation, is one
faced by remote and rural communities globally, as collectives adapt to meet
their members' aspirations. Based on the latest censuses, 42 million Indigenous
people were living in Latin America in 2015, representing nearly 8 per cent of
the region's total population (Freire *et al.* 2015). However, although traditional
territories have been one of the main referents of historical continuity, identity,
and self-determination for these groups, 49 per cent of Latin America's Indigenous population now live in urban areas (Freire *et al.* 2015). While over half
remain in rural areas, people will continue to leave if they feel their needs and
desires cannot be met locally.

Because communal ownership in rural Mexico is so extensive, it is local institutions, collective decision-making, and the labour of local people (Klooster
2013; Robson 2010) that most shape how and by whom territories are used and
how benefits are distributed. Currently, these arrangements are dominated by
older, male members. During 'visioning' workshops that Robson organized in
San Juan Evangelista Analco and another Oaxacan Zapotec community, Jalapa
del Valle, in 2017, participating young people (12–27 years of age) spoke about
their future plans, with limited opportunities for meaningful work and a lack of
voice/recognition in village decision-making structures among the stated push
factors. Alienation and loss of young people can deprive communities of critical
energy, talent, and leadership (Aquino Moreschi 2012; Aquino Moreschi and
Contreras-Pastrana 2016), and is being recognized as a particular problem in
places burdened by shortfalls in collective labour (Robson *et al.* 2018; Robson,
Klooster, Hernández-Díaz, field observations).

The problem extends to access to land in such communities, where 'young
people don't have the same rights [as older members] and is a reason why they
leave' (Froylán, programme officer with CONANP). Land, especially good land,

is often accounted for, even in places that have emptied out because of migration (see Chapters 8 and 9), and this can restrict opportunities for young people to kick-start productive livelihoods in their home villages. As Froylán notes, what 'these communities need are new schemes that are inclusive of young people'. This is especially crucial in the current context of small but stabilizing resident populations, and the fact that young people are eschewing wage labour migration for further education. If communities can offer attractive livelihood options to their young people, then more will stay and others may choose to return.

The migratory experience highlights the need for community economies to provide meaningful work for young people, and is a reminder that community futures will be shaped by how many decide to remain in strategic positions that support and benefit from local livelihoods. Exposed to lifestyle ideologies quite different from those that their parents and grandparents experienced, young people will consider both the economic viability of local work and their own aspirations in deciding whether to make a life for themselves elsewhere. In order to encourage more young people to call their home village 'home', it is vital for communities to drive a culture of land-based work that young people see as innovative, entrepreneurial, and creative.

The challenge will be to build or enhance livelihood opportunities and mechanisms of community development in which culture is not used just to achieve economic advancement, but rather as a central aspect in defining the type of development desired and how it is best implemented. Rural communities now transformed or transforming are looking at such paths forward – akin to what scholars have variously called 'ethno-development', 'alter-development', or 'culturally pertinent development', which define development as a process that originates in and is led by communities themselves (Alfred and Corntassel 2005; Corntassel and Bryce 2012; Fenelon and Hall 2008; Hall and Fenelon 2016; Wilson 2012). These models have different – and at times contrasting – views about how to address the balance between cultural continuity and integration, but share a commitment to alternative notions of development that allow rural societies to pursue their own chosen paths of self-improvement, while strengthening their autonomy, reducing their vulnerabilities, and fostering the sustainable management of their environments, resources, and knowledge (Henderson 2017; Van der Ploeg 2009).

Such challenges highlight both the vulnerability and potential of Indigenous communities living in an era of globalized change – where multiple disruptions result from global environmental change, economic and cultural globalization, neoliberal capitalism, and colonial histories (Davidson-Hunt *et al.* 2016). This fits into a broader literature that considers community futures and transitions through the lens of diverse economies (Gibson-Graham 2008; Gibson-Graham and Roelvink 2010). Indigenous scholars have likewise been bringing forward new ideas through concepts such as development with identity (Penados and Chatarpal 2015), intercultural business (Rosado-May *et al.* 2018) or territorial revitalization and nation building (Hall and Fenelon

2016). In rural areas of out-migration, opportunities may come from productive conservation activities such as forestry, conservation management, and Payment for Environmental Services (Pazos-Almada and Bray 2018; Robson and Klooster in press; Zimmerer 2006).

In formulating responses to new and emergent realities, the communities featured in this book are fighting to maintain their place in the world, even as their memberships are stretched across borders. As they consider which pathway to choose, they are working hard to ensure that change comes on their own terms, is rooted in custom, locally valued and emergent from their own daily creativity and resourcefulness – arguably the true definition of community resilience (see Brown 2016).

Final reflections

This book has provided important insights into the nature of change following migration in sending regions, and how this change can impact on community environmental governance – a poorly studied aspect of the migration–environment nexus. Because these are realities that affect local and Indigenous rural communities across Latin America and other global regions, the work holds lessons for places well beyond Oaxaca's and Mexico's borders. It points to the possibilities for community self-governance and survival in the likely future of limited additional migration and steady – but low – populations post-transformation (Berdegué, Rosada, and Bebbington 2014; Timmer and Akkus 2008). It points to the possibilities for 'inclusive rural transformation' (IFAD 2016), whereby local people are not powerless to affect or shape change but may be considered agents in ongoing projects of biological and cultural conservation. It suggests how local perspectives and values will necessarily shift as territorial practice and associated knowledge alters, with rural people challenged to find the political autonomy and human capability to exercise how their views and arrangements fit within this brave new world (Sen 1997, 1999). Finally, it suggests that opportunities exist for communities to survive the rigours of out-migration and shape changes in ways that conserve their surrounding environments, local cultures, and collectivities.

Notes

1 Froylán Martínez was interviewed in Oaxaca City on November 24, 2014. He is Director of the Sierra Juarez and Mixteca programme for the Comisión Nacional de Áreas Naturales Protegidas (CONANP).
2 Following the lead of Berdegué, Rosada, and Bebbington (2014), 'rural' is used here to refer to a society and the space it occupies where farming and other primary (land-based) activities account for a significant proportion of land use, employment, income, and economic output, and where population densities are distinctly lower than those of cities in the same region or country. Indigenous Oaxaca would thus be considered a 'deep rural' area with low population densities, distant from major cities, where almost every household has at least one member employed in a land-based activity.

3 David Kaimowitz was interviewed in Mexico City on September 3, 2014. He is Director of the Natural Resources and Climate Change programme at the Ford Foundation, and a former Director General of the Centre for International Forestry Research (CIFOR).

References

Aquino Moreschi, A., 2012. Cultura, genero, y generaciones en los migrantes'. In: Castro Yerko, Y. (ed.), *La Migración y Sus Efectos en la Cultura*. Mexico City, Mexico: Conaculta.

Aquino Moreschi, A. and I. Contreras-Pastrana. 2016. Comunidad, jóvenes y generación: disputando subjetividades en la Sierra Norte de Oaxaca. *Revista LatinoAmericana de Ciencias Sociales, Niñez y Juventud* 14(1): 463–475.

Aide, T.M., M.L. Clark, H.R. Grau, D. López-Carr, M.A. Levy, D. Redo, M. Bonilla-Moheno, G. Riner, M.J. Andrade-Núñez, and M. Muñiz. 2013. Deforestation and reforestation of Latin America and the Caribbean (2001–2010). *Biotropica* 45(2): 262–271.

Alfred, T. and J. Corntassel. 2005. *Politics of Identity IX. Being Indigenous: Resurgences against Contemporary Colonialism*. Oxford, UK and Malden, MA: Blackwell.

Armitage, D.R., R. de Loë, and R. Plummer. 2012. Environmental governance and its implications for conservation practice. *Conservation Letters* 5: 245–255.

Arora-Jonsson, S. 2013. *Gender, Development and Environmental Governance: Theorizing Connections*. New York: Routledge.

Barkin, D. 2013. La construcción del nuevo mundo del campesino mexicano. In: Padilla, T. (ed.), *El Campesinado y su Persistencia en la Actualidad Mexicana*. Mexico City, Mexico: FCE, Conaculta.

Barrett, C.B., T. Reardon, and P. Webb. 2001. Nonfarm income diversification and household livelihood strategies in rural Africa: concepts, dynamics, and policy implications. *Food Policy* 26(4): 315–331.

Bebbington, A. 2004. Livelihood transitions, place transformations: grounding globalization and modernity. In: Gwynne, R. and C. Kay (eds), *Latin America Transformed: Globalization and Modernity*, pp. 173–192. London, UK: Arnold.

Berdegué, J.A., A.J. Bebbington, and T. Rosada. 2014. The rural transformation. In: B Currie-Alder, R. Kanbur, D.M. Malone, and R. Medhora (eds), *International Development: Ideas, Experience, and Prospects*. Oxford, UK: Oxford University Press.

Berkes, F. 2017. Environmental governance for the Anthropocene? Social-ecological systems, resilience, and collaborative learning. *Sustainability* 9(7): 1232.

Boege, E. 2008. *El patrimonio biocultural de los pueblos indígenas de México: hacia la conservación in situ de la biodiversidad y agro-diversidad en los territorios indígenas*. Mexico City, Mexico: Instituto Nacional de Antropología e Historia, Comisión Nacional para el Desarrollo de los Pueblos Indígenas.

Boillat, S., F.M. Scarpa, J.P. Robson, I. Gasparri, T.M. Aide, A.P. Dutra Aguiar, L.O. Anderson *et al.* 2017. Land system science in Latin America: challenges and perspectives. *Current Opinion in Environmental Sustainability* 26: 37–46.

Brown, K. 2016. *Resilience, Development and Global Change*. London: Routledge.

Cleaver, F., 2017. *Development through Bricolage: Rethinking Institutions for Natural Resource Management*. Abingdon, UK: Routledge.

Colfer, C., M. Elias, B. Basnett, and S. Hummel (eds). 2017. *The Earthscan Reader on Gender and Forests*. London and New York: Routledge.

Corntassel, J. and C. Bryce. 2012. Practicing sustainable self-determination: Indigenous approaches to cultural restoration and revitalization. *Brown Journal of World Affairs* XVIII (II): 151–162.

Currie-Alder, B., R. Kanbur, D.M. Malone, and R. Medhora (eds). 2014. *International Development: Ideas, Experience, and Prospects.* Oxford: Oxford University Press.

Daniels, B. 2007. Emerging commons and tragic institutions. *Environmental Law* pp. 515–571.

Davidson-Hunt, I.J., H. Asselin, F. Berkes, K. Brown, C.J. Idrobo, M.A. Jones, P. McConney, R.M. O'Flaherty, J.P. Robson, and M. Rodriguez. 2016. The use of biodiversity for responding to globalised change: a people in nature approach to support the resilience of rural and remote communities. *People in Nature: Valuing the Diversity of Interrelationships between People and Nature.* Gland, Switzerland: IUCN.

De Koning, J. and Cleaver, F. 2012. Institutional bricolage in community forestry: an agenda for future research. In: Arts, B., S. van Bommel, M. Ros-Tonen, and G. Verschoor (eds), *Forest People Interfaces: Understanding Community Forestry and Biocultural Diversity.* Wageningen, the Netherlands: Wageningen Academic Publishers.

Dietz, G., 2010. Politicization of *comunalidad* and the demand for autonomy. In: Meyer, L. and B. Maldonado (eds), *New World of Indigenous Resistance: Noam Chomsky and Voices from North, South, and Central America.* San Francisco, CA: City Lights Books.

Durand, J., 2013. Nueva fase migratoria. *Papeles de Población* 19(77): 83–113.

Elias, M., S.S. Hummel, B.S. Basnett, and C.J.P. Colfer. 2017. Gender bias affects forests worldwide. *Ethnobiology Letters* 8(1): 31–34.

Eyzaguirre, P.B. and O.F. Linares. 2004. *Home Gardens and Agrobiodiversity.* Washington, DC: Smithsonian Books.

Fenelon, J.V. and T.D. Hall. 2008. Revitalization and Indigenous resistance to globalization and neoliberalism. *American Behavioral Scientist* 51(12): 1867–1901.

Folke, C., T. Hahn, P. Olsson, and J. Norberg. 2005. Adaptive governance of social-ecological systems. *Annual Review of Environmental Resources* 30: 441–473.

Fox, J. and X. Bada, 2008. Migrant organization and hometown impacts in rural Mexico. *Journal of Agrarian Change* 8 (2 and 3): 435–461.

Fox, J. and G. Rivera-Salgado, eds., 2004. *Indigenous Mexican Migrants in the United States.* La Jolla, CA: Center for US–Mexican Studies, UCSD.

Freire, G., O. Schwartz, S. Daniel *et al.* 2015. *Indigenous Latin America in the Twenty-First Century: The First Decade.* Washington, DC: World Bank Group. http://documents. worldbank.org/curated/en/145891467991974540/Indigenous-Latin-America-in-the-twenty-first-century-the-first-decade.

Gavin, M.C., J. McCarter, A. Mead, F. Berkes, J.R. Stepp, D. Peterson, and R. Tang. 2015. Defining biocultural approaches to conservation. *Trends in Ecology & Evolution* 30(3): 140–145.

Gibson-Graham, J.K. 2008. Diverse economies: performative practices for other worlds. *Progress in Human Geography* 32(5): 613–632.

Gibson-Graham, J.K, and G. Roelvink. 2010. An economic ethics for the anthropocene. *Antipode* 41(1): 320–346.

Gorenflo, L.J., S. Romaine, R.A. Mittermeier, and K. Walker-Painemilla. 2012. Co-occurrence of linguistic and biological diversity in biodiversity hotspots and high biodiversity wilderness areas. *Proceedings of the National Academy of Sciences* 109(21): 8032–8037.

Haggblade, S., P.B.R. Hazell, and T. Reardon (eds). 2007. *Transforming the Rural Nonfarm Economy.* Baltimore, MA: Johns Hopkins University Press.

Hall, T.D. and J.V. Fenelon. 2016. *Indigenous Peoples and Globalization*. New York: Routledge.

Han, J. 2010. *Rural Reform and Development in China: Review and Prospect*. Keynote presentation delivered at the International Conference on the Dynamics of Rural Transformation in Emerging Economies, New Delhi, India, April 14–16, 2010. (www.rimisp.org/FCKeditor/UserFiles/File/documentos/docs/sitioindia/documentos/Ppt_Han_Jun.pdf, accessed January 26, 2013).

Hecht, S.B. 2014. Forests lost and found in tropical Latin America: the woodland 'green revolution'. *The Journal of Peasant Studies* 41(5): 877–909.

Hecht, S.B., A.L. Yang, B.S. Basnett, C. Padoch, and N.L. Peluso. 2015. *People in Motion, Forests in Transition: Trends in Migration, Urbanization, and Remittances and their Effects on Tropical Forests*. Vol. 142. Bogor, Indonesia: Centre for International Forestry Research (CIFOR). Indigenous and Northern Affairs Canada (INAC).

Henderson, T.P. 2017. Struggles for autonomy from and within the market of southeast Mexico's small coffee producers. *The Journal of Peasant Studies* (2017): 1–24.

Hirabayashi, L.R. 1993. *Cultural Capital: Mountain Zapotec Migrant Associations in Mexico City*. Tucson, AZ: The University of Arizona Press.

Hunter, L.M., J.K. Luna, and R.M. Norton. 2015. Environmental dimensions of migration. *Annual Review of Sociology* 41: 377–397.

IFAD. 2016. *Rural Development Report 2016: Fostering Inclusive Rural Transformation*. Rome, Italy: International Fund for Agricultural Development.

Jones, R.C. 2009. Migration permanence and village decline in Zacatecas: when you can't go home again. *The Professional Geographer* 61(3): 382–399.

Jones, R.C. 2014. The decline of international migration as an economic force in rural areas: a Mexican case study. *International Migration Review* 48(3): 728–761.

Kay, C. 2008. Reflections on Latin American rural studies in the neoliberal globalization period: a new rurality? *Development and Change* 39(6): 915–943.

Kay, C. 2015. The agrarian question and the neoliberal rural transformation in Latin America. *European Review of Latin American and Caribbean Studies* 100: 73–83.

Klooster, D.J. 2003. Forest transitions in Mexico: institutions and forests in a globalized countryside. *Professional Geography* 55: 227–237.

Klooster, D. 2005. Producing social nature in the Mexican countryside. *Cultural Geographies* 12: 321–344.

Klooster, D. 2013. The impact of transnational migration on commons management among Mexican indigenous communities. *Journal of Latin American Geography* 12(1): 57–86.

Levitt, P. and D. Lamba-Nieves, 2013. Rethinking social remittances and the migration-development nexus from the perspective time. *Migration Letters* 10(1): 11.

Mahoney, J. and K. Thelen. 2011. A theory of gradual institutional change. In: Mahoney, J. and K. Thelen (eds), *Explaining Institutional Change: Ambiguity, Agency, and Power*, pp. 1–37. Cambridge, UK: Cambridge University Press.

Maldonado Alvarado, B., 2011. Comunalidad and the education of Indigenous peoples. In: Maldonado Alvarado, B. (ed.), *Comunidad, Comunalidad y Colonialismo en Oaxaca: La Nueva Educación Comunitaria y su Contexto*. Oaxaca, Mexico: Colegio Superior para la Educación Integral Intercultural de Oaxaca.

Maldonado Alvarado, B. 2013. Comunalidad y responsabilidad autogestiva. *Cuadernos del Sur* 18(34): 21–27.

Mann, C.C. 2004. *Diversity on the Farm: How Traditional Crops around the World Help to Feed Us All, and Why we should Reward the People who Grow Them*. New York: Ford Foundation.

Martínez Luna, J. 2010a. *Eso Que Llaman Comunalidad*. Oaxaca, Mexico: PRODICI.

Martinez Luna, J. 2010b. The fourth principle. In: Meyer, L. and B. Maldonado (eds), *New World of Indigenous Resistance: Noam Chomsky and Voices from North, South, and Central America*. San Francisco, CA: City Lights Books.

Martínez Luna, J. 2013. *Textos Sobre el Camino Andado* (Vol. I). Oaxaca, Mexico: CSEIIO.

Melo, F.P., V. Arroyo-Rodríguez, L. Fahrig, M. Martínez-Ramos, and M. Tabarelli. 2013. On the hope for biodiversity-friendly tropical landscapes. *Trends in Ecology & Evolution* 28(8): 462–468.

Meyfroidt, P. and E.F. Lambin. 2011. Global forest transition: prospects for an end to deforestation. *Annual Review of Environment and Resources* 36: 343–371.

Otero, G. 1999. *Farewell to the Peasantry? Political Class Formation in Rural Mexico*. Boulder, CO: Westview Press.

Pazos-Almada, B. and D.B. Bray. 2018. Community-based land sparing: territorial land-use zoning and forest management in the Sierra Norte of Oaxaca, Mexico. *Land Use Policy* 78: 219–226.

Penados, F. and M. Chatarpal. 2015. Food security and Maya land rights: crafting paths of 'development with identity'. *Research Reports in Belizean History and Anthropology* 3: 104–120.

Reed, M.G. 2010. Guess who's (not) coming for dinner? Expanding the terms of public involvement in sustainable forest management. *Scandinavian Journal of Forest Research Supplement* 9: 45–54.

Robson, J.P., 2010. *The Impact of Rural to Urban Migration on Forest Commons in Oaxaca, Mexico*. Unpublished PhD Thesis. Winnipeg, Canada: University of Manitoba.

Robson, J.P. In press. Indigenous communities, migrant organizations, and the ephemeral nature of translocality. *Latin American Research Review*.

Robson, J.P. and F. Berkes. 2011. Exploring some of the myths of land use change: can rural to urban migration drive declines in biodiversity? *Global Environmental Change* 21(3): 844–854.

Robson, J.P. and D. Klooster. In press. Migration and a new landscape of forest use and conservation. *Environmental Conservation*.

Robson, J.P. and R.E. Wiest. 2014. Transnational migration, customary governance, and the future of community: a case study from Oaxaca, Mexico. *Latin American Perspectives* 41(3): 102–116.

Robson, J.P., D.J. Klooster, H. Worthen, and J. Hernández-Díaz. 2018. Migration and agrarian transformation in Indigenous Mexico. *Journal of Agrarian Change* 18(2): 299–323.

Rosado-May, F.J., V.B. Cuevas-Albarrán, F.J. Moo-Xix, J.H. Chan, and J. Cavazos-Arroyo. 2018. Intercultural business: a culturally sensitive path to achieve sustainable development in Indigenous Maya communities. In: Dhiman, S. and J. Marques (eds), *Handbook of Engaged Sustainability*, pp. 603–629. New York: Springer Books.

RRI. 2017. *Securing Community Land Rights: Priorities and Opportunities to Advance Climate and Sustainable Development Goals*. Available online at: https://rightsandresources.org/en/publication/securing-community-land-rights-rribrief/#.Wk40a1cSCf0.

Rudel, T.K., O.T. Coomes, E. Moran, A. Achard, A. Angelsen, J. Xu, and E. Lambin. 2005. Forest transitions: towards a global understanding of land use change. *Global Environmental Change* 15(1): 23–31.

Scherr, S.J. and J.A. McNeely. 2008. Biodiversity conservation and agricultural sustainability: towards a new paradigm of 'ecoagriculture' landscapes. *Philosophical Transactions of the Royal Society of London B: Biological Sciences* 363(1491): 477–494.

Sen, A.K. 1997. Editorial: human capital and human capability. *World Development* 25(12): 1959–1961.

Sen, A.K. 1999. *Development as Freedom*. New York: Alfred Knopf.

Stephen, L., 2007. *Transborder Lives: Indigenous Oaxacans in Mexico, California, and Oregon*. Durham, NC: Duke University Press.

Stevens, C., R. Winterbottom, J. Springer, and K. Reytar. 2014. *Securing Rights, Combating Climate Change: How Strengthening Community Forest Rights Mitigates Climate Change*. Washington, DC: World Resources Institute. Available at: www.wri.org/sites/default/files/securingrights_executive_summary.pdf.

Tacoli, C. 1998. Rural-urban interactions: a guide to the literature. *Environment and urbanization* 10(1): 147–166.

Tacoli, C. (ed.). 2006. *The Earthscan Reader in Rural-Urban Linkages*. London: Earthscan.

Timmer, C.P. and S. Akkus. 2008. *The Structural Transformation as a Pathway out of Poverty: Analytics, Empirics and Politics* (CGD Working Paper No. 150). Washington, DC: Center for Global Development (CGD).

United Nations. 2017. *World Population Prospects: The 2017 Revision*. Available online at: https://esa.un.org/unpd/wpp/.

Van der Ploeg, J.D. 2009. *The New Peasantries: Struggles for Autonomy and Sustainability in an Era of Empire and Globalization*. Abingdon, UK: Routledge.

Waldinger, R., E. Popkin, and H.A. Magana. 2008. Conflict and contestation in the cross-border community: hometown associations reassessed. *Ethnic and Racial Studies* 31(5): 843–870.

Wiggins, S., J. Farrington, G. Henley, N. Grist, and A. Locke. 2013. *Agricultural Development Policy: A Contemporary Agenda*. Summary of the Background Paper for GIZ.

Wilson, G.A. 2012. Community resilience, globalization, and transitional pathways of decision making. *Geoforum* 43(6): 1218–1231.

Woods, M., 2007. Engaging the global countryside: Globalization, hybridity, and the reconstitution of rural place. *Progress in Human Geography* 31(4): 485–507.

Worthen, H. 2015. Juzgado en favor de la participación de las mujeres: Los tribunales electorales federales y la acción afirmativa para la igualdad de género en Oaxaca. In: Curiel, C., J. Hernández-Díaz, and H. Worthen (eds), *Los dilemas de la política del reconocimiento en México*, pp. 53–115. Oaxaca, Mexico: IISUBAJO/Juan Pablos Editor.

Zimmerer, K.S. (ed.). 2006. *Globalization and New Geographies of Conservation*. Chicago, IL: University of Chicago Press.

Index

Page numbers in bold denote tables, those in *italics* denote figures.